This book belongs to
Md. Muhit Miah
47. Upwell Rd. Luton Beds Lu2.9DZ

The Islamic State

By: Taqiuddin al-Nabhani
Hizb ut-Tahrir

Al-Khilafah Publications

PO Box 1100
London CR4 2ZR

email: info@khilafah.com
website: http://www.khilafah.com

1419 AH / 1998 CE

ISBN 1 899574 00X

AH - After Hijrah
CE - Christian Era

Translation of the Qur'an
It should be perfectly clear that the Qur'an is only authentic in
its original language, Arabic. Since perfect translation of the
Qur'an is impossible, the term "Translation of the Meaning of
the Qur'an (TMQ) has been used throughout the book, as the
result is only crude meaning of the Arabic text.

Qur'anic ayat and the Arabic words have been italicised

Printed and Bound by- De-Luxe Printers,
London NW10 7NR.
website: http://www.de-luxe.com
email: printers@de-luxe.com

Contents

Introduction

The present generation does not recall the Islamic State that implemented Islam, and those who lived during the last years of the Islamic State ('Uthmani Khilafah) against which the West had directed its onslaught, had in fact witnessed the vestiges of a state implementing remnants of Islamic rule. It is extremely difficult for many Muslims to illustrate the structure of the Islamic government. The minds of the Muslims have been consumed by the present day situation, and can only conceptualize the system of government through the depraved democratic regimes foisted upon Muslim countries.

This is not the only unfortunate aspect of a sad situation. An even more difficult task is transforming these minds seduced by Western culture. Western culture was the dagger drawn by the West in the face of the Islamic State, and by which it fatally stabbed her. Then, taking the weapon, dripping with blood, to her sons proudly said to them: I have killed your ailing mother, who deserved to be killed because of her poor guardianship and mismanagement and I have reserved for you the kind of life in which you will relish happiness and prosperity. They then offered to shake the hand of the murderer whose dagger was still stained with the blood of their mother. This, it is claimed, is just what the hyena does to its prey. The prey stands still, stunned and astonished, and does not come back to its senses until it is dealt a hard blow that makes it bleed, or is taken down to the valley to be eaten.

So how could such seduced minds come to realize that the poisonous dagger which killed their mother is the same one that is always threatening their own lives and very existence, unless they remove it from themselves. The concepts which the Muslims carry, such as nationalism, separating the religion from the State and the anti-Islamic notions are the very poison that this Western culture has injected in their veins. The chapter explaining the missionary invasion in this book contains facts and figures clearly showing and in detail the true intentions of the killer and the true motives behind the crime, listing the means and methods used to carry it out. The only reason was to eradicate Islam, and the most effective weapon was this Western culture which the missionaries brandished and incipiently cut into their willing victims.

The Muslims were caught unaware of the potential dangers of such a culture, they began resisting and fighting the physical occupation of their lands while embracing the Western culture, which was the real reason behind the occupation taking root in their lands. The sad irony is that Muslims, while allegedly turning their backs on the foreigner and fighting the occupation, welcomed the West with open arms and drank from its cup of poison until they collapsed, weary, apathetic, and lifeless. One would think of them as casualties of war, while in reality, they were victims of ignorance and misguidance.

What do they actually seek? A state based on other than Islam? Or several states on Muslim land? The West, since becoming the effective ruling authority, has already given them several states; completing therefore its scheme of keeping Islam out of government, dividing the Muslim land and giving the Muslims a trivial and facade of Islamic rule. From time to time, the West creates a new state for the Muslims, and it is more than willing to give them even more as long as they hold on to Western principles and concepts.

The point at hand is not establishing several states, but one single state over the entire Muslim world. And not establishing just any state, nor a state that calls itself Islamic while ruling by other than what Allah (swt) has decreed, nor a state calling itself Islamic and implementing Islamic Laws without carrying Islam via an intellectually based leadership. The crucial point at hand is not the establishment of such pseudo-Islamic states, but of a single state which would resume the Islamic way of life based upon the Islamic *'Aqeedah*, implement Islam within society after this was deeply rooted in the peoples' hearts and minds, and which would carry the Message of Islam to the whole world.

The Islamic State is not a dream, nor is it a figment of the imagination, for it had dominated and influenced history for more than thirteen hundred years. It is a reality, it has always been and always will be. The vital elements of its existence are far greater than can be ignored or fought against by anything or anyone. The enlightened people have adopted it and it is the wish of the *Ummah* which is eager for the return of the glory of Islam. The Islamic State is not a desire that one aims to satisfy, but an obligation that Allah (swt) has decreed for the Muslims and commanded them to fulfill. He (swt) warned of the punishment awaiting those who neglect this duty and promised reward to those who pursue this duty.

How are they to please their Lord if the *'Izzah* in their countries does not belong to Allah (swt), nor to His Messenger (saaw), nor to the believers? How are they to be safe from His punishment if they do not establish a state that would prepare its military might, defend its territory, implement Allah's rules and rule by what Allah (swt) has revealed? Therefore, the Muslims must establish the Islamic State, for Islam would not have an influential existence without it, and their land would not become *Dar al-Islam* unless it is ruled by that which Allah (swt) has revealed.

The Islamic State is by no means an easy endeavor. The pursuit of it should not fuel false hopes to opportunists (with the purpose of acquiring a position in it). The road is embedded with thorns, full of perils, obstacles and hardships, not to mention the non-Islamic culture, shallow thinking and pro-Western regimes which form a formidable obstacle. Those who truly tread the path of the Islamic call to restore the Islamic State, would be aiming to assume the authority in order to resume the Islamic way of life in the Muslim lands, and to convey the Message of Islam to the whole world. That is why they would reject sharing authority with anyone, no matter how great the temptation. They would also reject absolute rule unless they were capable of implementing Islam comprehensively, radically and instantaneously.

Finally, this book about the Islamic State is not meant to narrate its history but to explain how the Messenger of Allah (saaw) established the Islamic State, and to show how the disbelieving colonialists destroyed it. It demonstrates how Muslims should re-establish their State so that the light that guided the world in the darkest of ages returns to enlighten humanity once again.

The Starting Point

When the Messenger of Allah (saaw) was sent, he first invited his wife Khadijah and she believed in him. He (saaw) then invited his cousin 'Ali and he believed in him. He then invited his servant Zayd, and he believed in him. And then he invited his friend Abu Bakr, who also believed in him. He continued to invite people to Islam, some believed and others rejected.

When Abu Bakr embraced Islam, he in turn carried his belief to the people whom he trusted and called towards Allah (swt) and His Messenger (saaw). Abu Bakr was held in high esteem among his people, they enjoyed his company and always consulted him on many issues. He used his influence to persuade 'Uthman ibn 'Affan, together with Zubayr ibn al-'Awwam, 'Abd al-Rahman ibn 'Auf, Sa'd ibn Abi Waqqas and Talhah ibn 'Ubaydullah to embrace Islam. He brought them to the Messenger of Allah (saaw) where they all confirmed their belief and offered prayer. Then, 'Amir ibn al-Jarrah (known as Abu Ubaydah) embraced Islam, and so did 'Abdullah ibn 'Abd al-Asad (known as Abu Salamah) as well as al-Arqam ibn Abi al-Arqam, 'Uthman ibn Maz'un and others. Scores of people subsequently embraced Islam, until it became the topic of discussion amongst the people of Quraysh.

In the beginning, the Messenger of Allah (saaw) would visit people in their homes, telling them that they had been commanded by Allah (swt) to worship Him and to associate none with Him. He (saaw) openly invited people to Islam in Makkah, thus abiding by Allah's command,

"O you enveloped (in garments)! Arise and warn!" [Al-Muddaththir, 74:1-2]

After this, the Messenger of Allah (saaw) would contact people secretly to teach them Islam and gather them on the basis of the *Deen*.

The Sahabah (Companions) used to offer prayers in the hills on the outskirts of Makkah away from the Quraysh. Everytime someone embraced Islam, Allah's Messenger (saaw) would send him or her someone from those who had embraced Islam earlier to teach them the Qur'an. He (saaw) sent Khabbab ibn al-Arrat to teach the Qur'an to Fatimah bint al-Khattab and her husband Sa'id. 'Umar ibn al-Khattab once surprised them while they held their circle, and he embraced Islam then and there. The Messenger of Allah (saaw) realized that this was not enough though, so he set up the house of al-Arqam ibn Abi al-Arqam as the center of his call, a place from which he taught Muslims the Qur'an and perfected their knowledge of Islam, encouraging them to recite the Qur'an and understand it. Everytime someone embraced Islam, Allah's Messenger (saaw) would join him in the house of al-Arqam. He (saaw) pursued this task for three years, teaching this group of Muslims, leading them in prayers, and performing *Tahajjud* at night, motivating their souls, strengthening their belief through prayer and recitation, helping them to improve their way of thinking and to reflect on the verses of the Qur'an and the creation of Allah (swt). He (saaw) taught them how to endure all hardships by submitting to Allah (swt).

The Messenger of Allah (saaw) remained together with his party of Muslims in the house of al-Arqam until Allah (swt) revealed his saying,

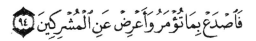

"Therefore, proclaim openly, that which you are commanded, and turn away from "Al-Mushrikun" [Al-Hijr, 15: 94]

Building the Sahabah

At the beginning of his call, the Messenger of Allah (saaw) invited to Islam people whom he felt had the readiness to accept it, regardless of their age, position, race, or origin. He (saaw) never selected people, but rather invited people indiscriminately and then sensed their readiness to accept Islam. Scores of people believed and embraced Islam.

He (saaw) was anxious to educate these new Muslims and perfect their knowledge of the *Deen*, as well as teach them the Qur'an. He (saaw) formed a group from the companions and they carried the *Da'wah* in turn. Their number grew to over forty men and women, who came from all walks of life, though they were mostly young men. There were among them the poor and the rich, the weak and the strong.

This group of Muslims who believed in Allah's Messenger (saaw) and pursued the *Da'wah* were:

1. 'Ali ibn Abi Talib (8 years old)
2. Zubayr ibn al-'Awwam (8 years old)
3. Talhah ibn 'Ubaydullah (11 years old)
4. Al-Arqam ibn Abi al-Arqam (12 years old)
5. 'Abdullah ibn Mas'ud (14 years old)
6. Sa'id ibn Zayd (under twenty)
7. Sa'd ibn Abi Waqqas (17 years old)
8. Sa'ud ibn Rabi'ah (17 years old)
9. Ja'far ibn Abi Talib (18 years old)
10. Suhayb al-Rumi (under twenty)
11. Zayd ibn Harithah (about twenty)
12. 'Uthman ibn 'Affan (about twenty)
13. Tulayb ibn 'Umayr (about twenty)
14. Khabbab ibn al-Arrat (about twenty)

15. 'Amir ibn Fuhayrah (23 years old)
16. Mus'ab ibn 'Umayr (24 years old)
17. Al-Miqdad ibn al-Aswad (24 years old)
18. 'Abdullah ibn Jahsh (25 years old)
19. 'Umar ibn al-Khattab (26 years old)
20. Abu Ubaydah ibn al-Jarrah (27 years old)
21. 'Utbah ibn Ghazwan (27 years old)
22. Abu Hudhayfah ibn 'Utbah (30 years old)
23. Bilal ibn Rabah (about 30 years old)
24. 'Ayyash ibn Rabi'ah (about 30 years old)
25. 'Amir ibn Rabi'ah (about 30)
26. Na'im ibn 'Abdullah (about 30)
27. 'Uthman (30 years old), and
28. 'Abdullah (17 years old), and
29. Qudamah (19 years old), and
30. Al-Saib (about 20, all four being sons
    of Maz'un ibn Habib)
31. Abu Salamah 'Abdullah ibn
    'Abd al-Asad al-Makhzumi (about 30)
32. 'Abd al-Rahman ibn 'Auf (about 30)
33. 'Ammar ibn Yasir (between 30 and 40)
34. Abu Bakr al-Siddiq (37 years old)
35. Hamzah ibn 'Abd al-Muttalib (42 years old)
36. 'Ubaydah ibn al-Harith (50 years old)

A number of women also embraced Islam.

After three years, the Messenger of Allah (saaw) was relieved and reassured when these *Sahabah* matured and when their hearts and minds became filled with nothing but Islamic concepts grounded in the Islamic culture. He (saaw) then became certain that they had acquired a deep understanding of Islam and that their personalities had reached great heights in terms of belief in Allah (swt). Only then were his worries appeased, for this group of Muslims became strong and capable enough to face society, so he (saaw) came out leading his group to confront Quraysh when Allah (swt) ordered him to do so.

The Launching of the Da'wah

The Islamic call was known from the first day the Messenger of Allah (saaw) was sent. People in Makkah had known all along that Muhammad (saaw) was calling for a new *Deen*, and that scores of people had embraced Islam. They also knew that Muhammad (saaw) was gathering his companions and looking after them, and that the Muslims concealed themselves from the rest of the Quraysh while they grouped together and learned about their new *Deen*.

People in Makkah were aware of this new call and of those who believed in it, but they never knew where they met nor who they were. That is why when the Messenger of Allah (saaw) proclaimed his new belief, it did not come as a surprise. What surprised Makkah was the emergence of this new group of Muslims. The Muslims had gained a great deal of strength when Hamzah ibn 'Abd al-Muttalib embraced Islam, followed by 'Umar ibn al-Khattab three days later. Then came the revelation of Allah (swt),

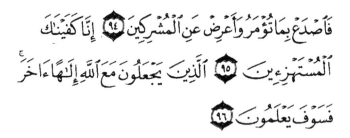

"Therefore, proclaim openly (Allah's Message), that which you are commanded, and turn away from "Al-Mushrikun": Truly! We will suffice you against the scoffers. Who set up along with Allah another god, they will come to know" [Al-Hijr, 15: 94-96]

Allah's Messenger (saaw) duly obeyed Allah's command and presented his group to all of Makkah. He (saaw) went out with his *Sahabah* in two lines, one led by 'Umar and the other by Hamzah. The *Sahabah* walked in a manner that the Quraysh had never witnessed before. He (saaw) then circumambulated the *Ka'bah* with them.

This is the stage when Allah's Messenger (saaw) moved with his *Sahabah* from the secret phase to the open one, from calling and addressing and inviting those whom he felt were ready to answer his call, to addressing all people. The *Da'wah* then took a new turn, the clash between *Iman* and *Kufr* in society began, the interaction between the right concepts and the rotten ones began, setting off therefore the second phase of the *Da'wah*, i.e. the phase of interaction and struggle.

The disbelievers began resisting and fighting the *Da'wah*, inflicting in the process all kinds of harm and injury on the Messenger of Allah (saaw) and his *Sahabah*. This phase was one of the most severest of all. The house of Allah's Messenger (saaw) was stoned and Umm Jamil, wife of Abu Lahab, used to throw impurities outside his home. He (saaw) just ignored or removed them in turn. Abu Jahl once threw a goat's uterus, slaughtered as a sacrifice to the idols, at Allah's Messenger (saaw). He (saaw) bore it all, and would go to his daughter Fatimah's house so that she could clean him up. This only strengthened Allah's Messenger's (saaw) resolve and made him more eager towards the Islamic call.

The Muslims were threatened and hurt, every tribe took it upon itself to torture and persecute its Muslim tribesmen. In one incident, one person left his slave Bilal on the burning sand and placed a heavy rock upon his chest simply because he insisted on Islam. Bilal defiantly uttered the words *'Ahad! 'Ahad!* (the One, the One) and endured all this suffering for the sake of his Lord. One woman died after being subjected to torture, simply because she would not renounce her new belief and return to the faith of her forefathers.

The Muslims endured the suffering, torture, humiliation and deprivation with only one aim in mind, seeking to please Allah (swt).

Hostility Against the Da'wah

When the Messenger (saaw) was sent by Allah, people downplayed him and his Message. The Quraysh ignored him at first thinking that his call would be no more than the talk of monks and sages and that people would eventually return to the faith of their fathers and ancestors.

This is why they did not bother with him. Whenever he passed by them they would say, "Here is the son of 'Abd al-Muttalib who is spoken to from the heavens." After a while however, they realized the threat of his campaign and decided to fight him. At first they simply resorted to degrading and ridiculing his claims of prophecy. They followed this by challenging him to perform miracles as a proof of his Message. They would say: Why does Muhammad not transform al-Safa and al-Marwa into gold? Why does the book revealed to him not descend from the sky already written? Why does Jibreel, whom Muhammad keeps talking about, not appear to them? Why does he not bring life to the dead? Why does he not remove the mountains which surround Makkah? Why does he not dig a source more fresher than *Zamzam*, knowing that his people badly need water? Why does his Allah not forecast the future prices of goods so that they can bid for them?

The smear campaign against Allah's Messenger (saaw) went on for some time. The Quraysh lashed out insults, abuse and sarcasm, but he (saaw) never waned nor deviated from his path and went on inviting people to Islam, ridiculing their idols and demonstrating the idiocy and shallow minds of the people who worshipped them and built their hopes on them.

This became far too much for the Quraysh to bear, and thus they resorted to any means necessary to pressure him (saaw) into renouncing his Message, to no avail. Three of the major methods which the Quraysh used to fight the *Da'wah* were:

1. Torture
2. Internal and external propaganda
3. Boycott.

Torture befell the Messenger of Allah (saaw), despite his family's protection, and his followers. The Quraysh resorted to all types of torture and they became experts at this malignant craft. The family of Al-Yasir were all subjected to horrific types of torture in order to make them abandon their *Deen*, but this only made them more determined and steadfast. Allah's Messenger (saaw) passed by them while they were being tortured and said to them, "Hold on Al-Yasir! Your reward is Jannah. Your destiny is with Allah." Upon this Sumayyah, wife of Yasir said, "I can see it, O Messenger of Allah."

The torture of Allah's Messenger (saaw) and his *Sahabah* went on unabated for some time until the Quraysh realized that it was all in vain, so they resorted to another method in order to fight the *Da'wah*, which consisted of libel and propaganda against Islam and the Muslims within Makkah as well as abroad, such as in Abyssinia. This method was used in all its types and forms, ranging from arguments, debates, mockery and a smear campaign. Libel was used against the Islamic *'Aqeedah* itself, and directly against the Messenger of Allah (saaw). The Quraysh lied about him (saaw) and accused him falsely. They planned and schemed many ways to discredit him.

The Quraysh carefully prepared how best they could discredit Islam especially in the *Hajj* season. They went so far as to confer with al-Walid ibn al-Mughirah in order to formulate ways to libel the Messenger of Allah (saaw). They focused on what they should tell the Arabs coming to Makkah for *Hajj*. Some suggested that they should announce that he was a *Kahin* (fortune-teller). Al-Walid rejected this by pointing out that Muhammad (saaw) was devoid of the unintelligent murmuring and rhymed speech of the *Kahin*. Some claimed that he was a poet, yet they knew poetry in all its forms and metres and so rejected this claim too. Others suggested that he was possessed. Al-Walid also rejected this for Muhammad's behavior was not that of a possessed man. Still others started accusing him of sorcery, al-Walid rejected this idea saying that Muhammad (saaw) did not practice the secret arts performed by sorcerers, such as the well known ritual of blowing on knots.

After a lengthy debate, the Quraysh agreed to accuse him of being a sorcerer possessing the *Sihr al-Bayan* (magic of words). Afterwards, they dispersed among the congregations of pilgrims warning the Arabs against listening to Muhammad (saaw) and depicting him as a magician of speech. They said that his Message separated a man from his brother, or from his father, or from his wife, or from his family. However, this propaganda did not work, and the Message of Islam continued to grip the minds of the people. The Quraysh then approached al-Nadr ibn al-Harith and assigned to him the task of campaigning against the Messenger of Allah (saaw). Whenever he (saaw) held a meeting to which people were invited, reminding them of Allah and His admonishment of bygone generations, al-Nadr ibn al-Harith arose and narrated stories about the kings of Persia and their religion. He proclaimed, "In what respect is Muhammad a better story-teller than I? Does he not expound tales of the past the same as I do?" Quraysh spread such stories and gossip widely. They told people that what Muhammad (saaw) was saying was not from Allah but was instead taught to him by a Christian youth named Jabr. This rumor spread among the people until Allah (swt) replied by revealing the following verse,

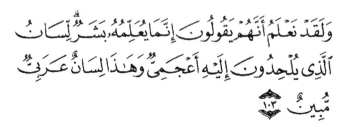

"And indeed We know that they say: "It is only a human being who teaches him (Muhammad)". The tongue of the man they refer to is foreign, while this is a clear Arabic tongue." [An-Nahl, 16:103]

The libel against Islam and the persecution of the Muslims continued in the Arabian Peninsula. When the Quraysh heard that some Muslims, being afraid of forced apostasy, had emigrated to Abyssinia they sent two determined envoys after them to discredit the Muslims in the hope that the Negus would expel them from his kingdom and have them sent back. The two envoys were 'Amr ibn al-'As ibn Wa'il and 'Abdullah ibn Rabi'ah. They reached

Abyssinia and offered presents to the generals of the Negus to help them convince the Negus to extradite the Muslim refugees. They said to them, "Some foolish fellows from our people have taken refuge in the King's country, they have forsaken our *Deen* and not accepted yours, but have brought into being an invented *Deen* which neither we nor you know anything about. Our nobles have sent us to you to return them. So surrender them to us, for their own people have the keenest insight and know most about their faults." They also stipulated that the King should not speak to the Muslims, fearing what they might say to him. The generals met with the Negus and recommended that he surrender the Muslims to their own people.

The Negus summoned the Muslims and demanded to hear what they had to say for themselves. When they came he asked them, "What is this *Deen* for which you have forsaken your people without entering into my *Deen* or any other?" Ja'far ibn Abi Talib answered him by explaining their ignorance before Islam and comparing it to their new position under its guidance. He said, "Thereupon our people attacked us. So when they got the better of us, they treated us unjustly and came between us and our *Deen*, we came to your country, having chosen you above all others, but we hope that we shall not be treated unjustly while we are with you." The Negus said to Ja'far, "Do you have with you anything from what your Messenger brought from Allah to read to me?" Ja'far said, "Yes," and recited *Surah* Maryam from the beginning until where Allah (swt) says,

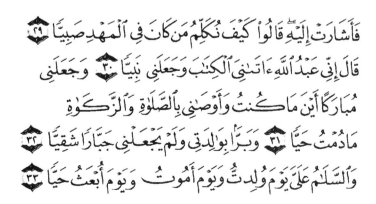

"Then she pointed to him. They said: "How can we talk to one who is a child

in the cradle? He (Jesus) said: Verily! I am a slave of Allah, He has given me the Scripture and made me a prophet; And He has made me blessed wheresoever I be, and has enjoined on me prayer, and Zakat, as long as I live. And dutiful to mother, and made me not arrogant, unblest. And "Salam" (peace) be upon me the day I was born, and the day I die, and the day I shall be raised alive!" [Maryam, 19:29-33]

When the patriarchs heard this they said, "This and what our Lord 'Isa (Jesus) the Messiah brought are from the same source." The Negus said, "Of a truth, this and what Musa brought, come from the same niche. You two may go, for by Allah, I will never give them up and they shall not be betrayed." The two envoys left the Royal Palace and began to think of another way to fulfill their task. The next day 'Amr ibn al-'As went back to the Negus and said to him, "The Muslims say dreadful things about 'Isa, son of Maryam, send for them and ask them about it." He did so and Ja'far replied, "We say about him that which our Prophet brought, saying, he is the slave of Allah and His Messenger, and His spirit, and His word, which He cast into Maryam the blessed virgin." The Negus took a stick from the ground, drew a line in the soil with it and said to Ja'far, "There is nothing more than this line between your *Deen* and ours", and he discharged the two envoys empty-handed.

Ultimately, all the ways and means of propaganda pronounced against the Islamic *Da'wah* failed. The sheer force of truth reflected in what the Messenger of Allah (saaw) was calling for, defeated all rumors, lies and propaganda, and the light of Islam dissipated all attempts at discrediting it. Therefore, Quraysh resorted to a third method, which was the boycott. They agreed to completely isolate the Messenger of Allah (saaw) and his family and they drew up a document in which they decided not to deal with Banu Hashim and Banu 'Abd al-Muttalib, neither to marry their women nor give their own women to them in marriage, neither buy anything from them nor sell anything to them. When they had agreed on these conditions they wrote them in a deed and hung it inside the Ka'bah to remind them of their covenant. They anticipated that this policy of sanctions would bring the desired effect and that it would be more efficient than either propaganda or torture.

The boycott continued for two to three years, all the while the Quraysh were hoping that Banu Hashim and Banu 'Abd al-Muttalib would abandon Muhammad (saaw), that the Muslims would renounce their faith, and that eventually Muhammad (saaw) would be left all alone at their mercy. They hoped the sanctions would either lead to Muhammad (saaw) abandoning his call for Islam, or to the threat that his call posed to the Quraysh and their *Deen* disappearing. However, this technique only strengthened the Messenger of Allah's resolve and made his *Sahabah* more diligent in pursuing the *Da'wah*. The boycott failed to put a halt to the spread of the Message of Islam inside and outside Makkah. News of the boycott reached the Arabs outside Makkah and the call spread among many tribes. Islam was a subject of discussion all over the Arabian Peninsula.

However, the boycott and starvation went on relentlessly and the document which the Quraysh drew up remained enforced. The Messenger's family and the *Sahabah* suffered hunger and deprivation and subsisted on meager provisions which they obtained from sympathizers. Their only respite was during the sacred months, when the Messenger of Allah (saaw) used to go to the *Ka'bah* and invite people to the *Deen* of Allah, telling them of His rewards and warning them about His punishment, then afterwards he had to return to the mountain valley. This earned Allah's Messenger (saaw), his Family and his *Sahabah* the sympathy of the Arabs, some of whom responded to the call and embraced Islam, while others sent food and drink to them secretly. Hisham ibn 'Amr was known to have brought camels laden with food at night and on reaching the mouth of the valley he would release the animal, give it a slap on its side, and send it into the valley to where the Muslims were. They would take the food, slaughter the camel and eat it.

The Muslims were to endure the boycott for about three years, during which life became extremely harsh, until Allah (swt) sent His relief and finally broke the siege. Five young men from Quraysh, Zuhayr ibn Abi Umayyah, Hisham ibn 'Amr, al-Mut'im ibn 'Adi, Abu al-Bakhtari ibn Hisham and Zama'ah ibn al-Aswad gathered together. They talked about the document and its sanctions and they, like many of the Quraysh at that time, expressed their resentment towards it. At length they agreed to resolve the whole issue of the unjust boycott by securing its annulment.

The next day, they went to the *Ka'bah* and Zuhayr went around it seven times. Addressing the crowd who were present, he said, "O people of Makkah, are we to eat and clothe ourselves while Banu Hashim perish, unable to buy or sell? By Allah I will not rest until this damn boycotting document is torn up." Abu Jahl, who was nearby, exclaimed, "You lie, by Allah it shall not be torn up." At this point the other four Zama'ah, Abu al-Bakhtari, al-Mut'im and Hisham, who had dispersed among the crowd, shouted back in support of Zuhayr. Abu Jahl realized that it was a matter which had been arranged beforehand, so he feared the worst and backed off. When al-Mut'im went to tear up the document he discovered that white ants had already eaten it except for the words 'In your name, O Allah'.

The Messenger of Allah (saaw) and his *Sahabah* then proceeded to return to Makkah and the embargo was finally lifted. Thereafter, Allah's Messenger (saaw) continued to pursue his call and the number of Muslims continued to grow steadily, marking the failure of all the methods the Quraysh employed in their attempt to suppress the Message of Islam. The *Kuffar* continued in their attempts to come between the Muslims and their *Deen* and to make Allah's Messenger (saaw) renounce his *Da'wah* which, with Allah's help, became widespread despite all obstacles and hardships.

The Interaction of the Da'wah

The impact that the Islamic call had on Quraysh was only natural, for the Messenger of Allah (saaw) took up the struggle and presented his group to the Quraysh in a conspicuous and challenging manner. It left them with no room to doubt its implications upon them. In addition, the call itself included the struggle against Quraysh and the Makkan society, for it was calling to the Oneness of Allah, to worship Him alone, to abandon the worship of idols and to renounce the decadent system they were living by. Therefore the call was at loggerheads with the Quraysh, and this was inevitable since the Messenger of Allah (saaw) was to discredit their thinking, ridicule their gods, mock their way of life, and deplore their tyrannical practices.

Whenever a verse was revealed to him (saaw), he would attack the Quraysh with it openly. He would recite Allah's words,

$$\text{إِنَّكُمْ وَمَا تَعْبُدُونَ مِن دُونِ اللَّهِ حَصَبُ جَهَنَّمَ}$$

"Certainly! You (disbelievers) and that which you are worshipping now besides Allah, are (but) fuel for Hell!" [Al-Anbiya, 21:98]

He (saaw) strongly attacked the relationship in the society such as *Riba*,

$$\text{وَمَآ ءَاتَيْتُم مِّن رِّبًا لِّيَرْبُوَا۟ فِىٓ أَمْوَٰلِ ٱلنَّاسِ فَلَا يَرْبُوا۟ عِندَ ٱللَّهِ}$$

"And that which you give in usury (to others), in order that it may increase, has no increase with Allah" [Ar-Rum, 30:39]

and attacking cheating in the scales,

17

"Woe to those that deal in fraud those who, when they have to receive by measure, from men, exact full measure. But when they have to measure a weigh to men, give less than due." [Al-Mutaffiffin 83: 1-3]

Quraysh, therefore, confronted him and began fighting him and his *Sahabah*, This they endeavoured to do by means of torture, sanctions and propaganda against him personally and against his *Deen*. In return he (saaw) carried the offensive to them, pursuing his struggle against their erroneous notions and demolishing their corrupt beliefs in order to spread the Message of Islam according to the way decreed by Allah (swt). He (saaw) invited people to Islam openly, without compromising and bargaining, despite all the various types of persecution of Quraysh upon him, and despite being a defenseless figure with no real help, no ally, no material means and no weapons. He (saaw) came conspicuously and challengingly, inviting to the *Deen* of Allah with great resolve and faith, ignoring all the hardships, not allowing weakness to get the better of him, ready to endure the colossal burdens for the sake of the Message. This enabled him to surmount all the obstacles that Quraysh put in his way, which were designed to come between him and the people.

The Messenger of Allah (saaw) succeeded in reaching the people and in conveying the Message to them; in turn they embraced Islam because the truth and the force of reason defeated the falsehood. The light of Islam began shining amongst the Arabs, many idol worshippers embraced Islam, so did many Christians, even the leaders of Quraysh began listening to the Qur'an with yearning hearts.

Al-Tufayl ibn 'Amr al-Dausi came to Makkah when Allah's Messenger (saaw) was there. He was an important nobleman, very intelligent and a poet of some understanding. Quraysh approached him immediately and warned him that this fellow Muhammad (saaw) had done them much harm, that he was a sorcerer and that his talk separated men from their families. They exclaimed that they feared he might have the same effect on him and advised him not to speak to Muhammad (saaw) or listen to a word he said. Al-Tufayl went one day to the Ka'bah and it happened that Allah's Messenger (saaw) was there, he listened to some of his speech and found it beautiful, so he said to himself, "By Allah! Here I am, an intelligent man, a poet, knowing perfectly well the difference between good and evil, so what is to prevent me from listening to what this man is saying? If it is good I shall accept it and if it is bad I shall reject it." He followed the Messenger of Allah (saaw) to his house and told him about himself and what was on his mind. So Allah's Messenger (saaw) invited him to Islam and recited to him the Qur'an. He became a Muslim and declared that it was the truth. Then he went back to his people and proceeded to call them to Islam.

While the Messenger of Allah (saaw) was in Makkah, some twenty Christians traveled to meet him after receiving news about him. They sat and listened to him and accepted and believed in him and declared his truth. This enraged the Quraysh and they later intercepted them as they were leaving Makkah and hurled insults at them saying, "May Allah bring you ruin! What a wretched band you are. Your people at home sent you to bring them information about this man, and as soon as you sat with him, you renounced your religion and believed in what he said." This, however, did not affect them, nor did it affect their belief in Islam, rather it strengthened all the more their belief in Allah (swt). The impact of the Messenger of Allah (saaw) increased, as did people's yearning to listen to the Qur'an. It reached a point whereby his harshest opponents from the Quraysh began wondering whether what he (saaw) was calling for was really true. This led them to listen to the Qur'an in secret.

Abu Sufyan ibn Harb, Abu Jahl 'Amr ibn Hisham and al-Akhnas ibn Shurayq, were each unaware that the other was going to listen to the Messenger of Allah (saaw) as he was praying in his house. Each one was disguised and each chose a place to sit where he could listen. None knew where the other was. Allah's Messenger (saaw) regularly stayed up most of the night reciting the Qur'an. They passed this particular night listening attentively to him, their minds were captured and their hearts affected, until dawn arose when they all quickly dispersed. On the way home they met accidentally, reproaching one another, each one saying to the other, "Don't do it again, for if one of the light-minded fools sees you, it would compromise and weaken your standing, and it would tip the scales in Muhammad's favor." On the second night, each of them felt his legs taking him to the same spot where he had spent the previous night. The three listened once again to Allah's Messenger (saaw) reciting the Book of Allah and, as before, they met at dawn and reproached each other, yet this did not prevent them from attending for a third night. When they realized their weakness towards Muhammad's Message, they took a solemn oath never to return. Nevertheless this incident resulted in an exchange of views concerning what they had heard over the three nights; they were agitated because their actions manifested signs of weakness which none of them, as leader of his tribe, could afford. This, they acknowledged, could be construed as playing into the hands of Muhammad (saaw) and it might encourage the people to accept his Message.

Despite all of the obstacles that the Quraysh laid down, the call succeeded in penetrating Makkah, and the Quraysh became panic stricken fearing the worst, i.e. the spreading of Islam among the Arab tribes. Quraysh, therefore, intensified their hostile campaign against Allah's Messenger (saaw) and his *Sahabah*. The situation eventually became almost unbearable and Allah's Messenger (saaw) went to the city of Ta'if seeking the *Nussrah* (support) and protection of Thaqif in the hope that they might embrace Islam. He approached them on his own, but they spoke to him harshly and treated him very badly. They stirred up their louts and slaves who hurled insults and stones at him until the whole of his body including his feet bled. He (saaw) managed to take refuge in an orchard belonging to Shabeeb and Shayba, sons of Rabi'ah. There he sat thinking about his situation and about the call. He knew that he could not enter Makkah without one of the leaders' protection, neither could he go back to Ta'if after the way he had been treated there, and he could not stay in the orchard for it belonged to two disbelievers. He (saaw) felt very distressed and lifted his arms to the sky lamenting and supplicating to Allah (swt). Painfully and with immense confidence in Allah (swt), he said, "O Allah! To You I complain of my weakness, little resource, and lowliness before man. O Most Merciful! You are the Lord of the weak, and You are my Lord. To whom would You confide in me? To one afar who will misuse me or to an enemy to whom You have given dominance over me? If You are not angry with me, I do not care about anything else. Your favor of well-being on me is sufficient for me. I take refuge in the light of Your countenance by which the darkness is illuminated, and the things of this world and the next are rightly ordered, lest Your anger descend upon me or Your wrath not light upon me but come down on me. It is for You to be satisfied until You are well pleased. There is no power and no might except in You."

Whereupon he returned to Makkah under the protection of al-Mut'im ibn 'Adiy. The Quraysh soon learned of what had happened to the Messenger of Allah (saaw) in Ta'if, and this only made them increase their ill treatment of the Messenger (saaw) and they prohibited people from listening to him. The Makkans deserted him and refrained from listening to his preaching. However, he (saaw) was never disheartened, and went on calling people to the *Deen* of Allah by offering himself to the tribes during the festive seasons, inviting them to Islam, telling them that he was a Prophet sent by Allah (swt) and asking them to believe in him. But Abu Lahab, his hateful uncle, never left his sight. He followed him everywhere telling people not to listen to him, so the people ignored him and paid him no attention.

The Messenger of Allah (saaw) then resorted to visiting the tribes in their dwellings, offering himself to them. He visited the tribes of Kinda, Kalb, Banu Hanifah and Banu 'Aamir ibn Sa'sah. None of them actually responded to his call and they all bitterly opposed him, especially Banu Hanifah. As for Banu 'Aamir, they wanted authority after him in return for giving him allegiance. He (saaw) replied, "Authority is a matter which Allah places where He pleases." Upon hearing this Banu 'Aamir also declined to help.

Therefore, Makkah rejected Islam, as did the people of Ta'if, and the tribes too rejected the Messenger of Allah's call. Those tribes who came to Makkah to conduct business learned of the situation of the Messenger of Allah (saaw) and his isolation, and this only drove them further away from him, thus worsening his isolation. The call for Islam became much more difficult while the hardened Makkan society showed signs of total rejection, disbelief and stubbornness. Expectations for the *Da'wah* in Makkah became very low.

The Two Stages of the Da'wah

The *Da'wah* of the Messenger of Allah (saaw) in Makkah was divided into two stages. The first stage was the stage of teaching, culturing and intellectual and spiritual building. The second stage was the spreading of the Message and the struggle. The first stage was to ensure the correct understanding of new concepts and to incorporate them into personalities and to structure them around these concepts. The second stage was to transfer these concepts into a mobilizing force in the society that drives it to implement them in the different walks of life. Concepts are nothing but a mass of lifeless information unless they are implemented in a society. In order for these concepts to be energized and implemented, they first have to go through the process of being transformed from mere thoughts to becoming a driving force within the society, with people adopting them, realizing, carrying them and struggling to implement them. Eventually, the implementation of these concepts would become inevitable.

This is how the Messenger of Allah (saaw) went about his call in Makkah. In the first stage, he called people to Islam, cultured them with its concepts and taught them its rules. He gathered whoever he could on the basis of the Islamic belief. This was the stage of secretly grouping individuals and orienting them for the *Da'wah*. Allah's Messenger (saaw) relentlessly pursued the call, eager to acculturate all those who embraced Islam. He gathered them in the house of al-Arqam, or sent someone to culture them in circles in their own homes or in the mountain valleys. They did so in secret and gathered in a group. Their belief became stronger, and relations between them closer, and their awareness of the task that they faced daily until they were ready to sacrifice anything in the way of the *Da'wah*. The Message took deep root in their hearts and in their minds, Islam became like the blood in their veins - they became walking examples of Islam. Therefore, the Message could never remain confined within themselves, despite their attempts to keep themselves and the *Da'wah* away from the eyes of Quraysh.

They began talking to people they trusted, and to those in whom they felt a readiness to accept Islam. People, therefore, found out about their Message and felt their presence. At this stage, the call was positioned at the starting point and needed to be launched. This marked the end of the first stage, i.e. the collectivization and acculturation, and the call inevitably moved to the second stage, that of interaction and struggle. It involved expounding Islam and its concepts to the people. Some people responded and accepted, and others rejected and fought it. However, before disbelief and falsehood could be defeated and before *Iman* and righteousness could gain the upper hand, such a clash was inevitable. Yet, no matter how stubborn peoples' minds are, they can never permanently block the path of the right concepts, although they try to avoid them so as to remain unaffected.

Therefore, the stage of interaction commenced, incorporating as it did the struggle between the two disparate streams of thoughts, that of Islam and *Kufr*. It proceeded from the time that the Messenger of Allah (saaw) emerged with his group of *Sahabah*, in a manner never before witnessed by the Arabs, and together they circumumbulated the *Ka'bah* declaring the Message. From that time on, the Messenger of Allah (saaw) publicly invited people to Islam in Makkah, challenging their existing lifestyles.

Qur'anic verses proclaiming the Oneness of Allah (swt) were revealed to the Messenger of Allah (saaw), as were the verses deploring disbelief and idol-worship, and the verses attacking the way people blindly followed their forefathers. These verses were revealed to abhor the corrupt dealings within society, they attacked interest (*Riba*) and corruption and cheating in the scales (*Tatfeef*). In order to address the people, the Messenger of Allah (saaw) talked to them about Islam in groups. He started by gathering together his clan, inviting them for meals. Then he invited them to Islam and asked them to support him, but they rejected him. He gathered the Makkans at al-Safa and talked to them, but this enraged the leaders of the Quraysh, especially Abu Lahab, thus the rift deepened between Allah's Messenger (saaw) and the Quraysh and between him and the other Arabs. Thus, the acculturation of the public was coupled with the concentrated education being delivered in houses, specifically in the house of al-Arqam and in the valleys.

The call moved from inviting individuals who displayed good potential to inviting all people. The public call and acculturation had a visible effect on the Quraysh, for it unleashed from their quarters a great deal of hatred which mounted, as the threat of the call loudened. The Quraysh began taking serious measures to counter and resist the *Da'wah* after realizing that it could no longer ignore Muhammad (saaw) and his Message. Thus, the hostilities intensified against Allah's Messenger (saaw) and his *Sahabah*.

The public approach of the group, however, had a massive effect. It created the public opinion necessary for the growth of the *Da'wah* and this asssisted in its rapid expansion throughout Makkah. Every day that passed saw a growth in the number of Muslims, the poor, the deprived and the oppressed embraced Islam so did the nobles and leaders, and the rich traders whose trading did not distract them from reflecting on what the Messenger of Allah (saaw) was calling for. Those who embraced Islam were the ones whose minds and hearts understood purity, wisdom and truth, and those who raised themselves above stubbornness and haughtiness. They embraced Islam the moment they realized its righteousness and the truthfulness of the one who conveyed the Message. Islam spread in Makkah therein, and men and women embraced it. The collective *Da'wah* played a major role in taking the Message to a wider audience despite the trials and suffering that the Muslims had to endure in the process. The success of the *Da'wah* enraged the leaders of the Quraysh still further, and was like a fire burning through their hearts. The Messenger of Allah (saaw) waged an unrelenting, ***ideological*** campaign against injustice, harshness and oppression that dominated Makkah, and he mocked, attacked and exposed their ill-fated concepts and practices.

This marked the beginning of one of the most severest of stages between the Messenger of Allah (saaw) and his *Sahabah* on one side and the disbelievers of the Quraysh on the other. Although the intermediate phase between the stage of acculturation and the stage of interaction is considered to be the most delicate and sensitive, because it requires a great deal of wisdom, patience and precision, the phase of interaction is actually the most difficult because it requires frankness and defiance without giving any account to results or conditions of the situation at hand. This is so due to the fact that the Muslims would be tested in their *Deen* and *Iman*.

24

The Messenger of Allah (saaw) and his Companions passed through that phase enduring the kind of oppression, torture, persecution and aggression that would weigh down the highest mountain.

Some of them emigrated to Abyssinia, some of them perished under torture and some of them survived the most atrocious types of aggression. They pursued their struggle for a long enough spell to affect the Makkan society with the light of Islam and to begin to dissipate the darkness that disbelief had engendered, and that Makkah had been plunged into. Despite the fact that the Messenger of Allah (saaw) spent three years in the House of al-Arqam, having completed the first stage of the *Da'wah*, he had to struggle against disbelief, even though he had clearly demonstrated his Prophethood through many miracles, for another eight years. All of this transpired without the Quraysh once giving any respite from torturing the Muslims, nor showing any signs of appeasing their harsh stance against Islam. As a result of the interaction between the Muslims and the Quraysh, the impact of the *Da'wah* spread throughout the Peninsula and became a subject on everyone's lips; the pilgrims helped in spreading the news of the call amongst the Arab tribes. However, those Arabs remained mainly spectators and never moved one step towards *Iman*, as their main concern was not to upset the Quraysh. They avoided the Messenger of Allah (saaw) in order not to clash with the Quraysh. This tough situation on Messenger of Allah (saaw) and the *Sahabah* made it evident that moving the *Da'wah* to the third phase in which Islam will be implemented is a must.

However, the signs in Makkah were not indicative towards it being a viable option. Additionally, the increase in hostilities against the Muslims prevented them from fully devoting their time to the call and the people's rejection compounded the situation and made it worse.

The Expansion of the Da'wah

The hostility of the Quraysh towards the Messenger of Allah (saaw) and his *Sahabah* reached a saturation point after the Thaqif tribe in Ta'if unceremoniously chased him away, and when the tribes of Kinda, Kalb, Banu 'Aamir and Banu Hanifah rejected his call to them during the *Hajj* season. The Quraysh managed to increase his (saaw) isolation further, after these setbacks, separating him and his party from any outside support. He (saaw) and his *Sahabah*, however, remained steadfast in their belief in Allah (swt) and never doubted His (swt) promise of victory to them and to Islam.

The Messenger of Allah (saaw) continued inviting people to Islam whenever possible and he approached the tribes and offered himself to them, not worrying in the slightest about the consequences. Some of the louts from the Quraysh attempted to provoke him and hurt him, but he (saaw) never let this affect him nor his hope of a brighter future. Allah (swt) sent him with the Message of Islam and he never doubted that Allah (swt) would help and protect him and secure the establishment of the *Deen*. He (saaw) waited for Allah's relief, while being very troubled about the state of the *Da'wah*.

Fortunately, the Messenger of Allah (saaw) did not have long to wait, for the signs of victory soon came from Yathrib (Madinah) in the shape of a group from al-Khazraj who had come to Makkah during the *Hajj* season where the Messenger of Allah (saaw) met them for the first time and invited them to Islam.

They looked to each other and said, "By Allah this is the very Prophet of whom the Jews warned us about. Do not let them get to him before us." Thereupon they accepted his teaching and embraced Islam. They said to him, "We have left our people (al-Aws and al-Khazraj), for no tribes are so divided by hatred and rancor as they. Perhaps Allah will unite them through you, if so, then no man will be mightier then you."

When they returned to Yathrib (Madinah), they told their people about the Messenger of Allah (saaw) and invited them to accept Islam. They managed to open people's hearts and minds to the new *Deen*. Every household among the Aws and Khazraj began to talk about Muhammad (saaw).

The First Pledge of Al-'Aqabah

In the following year, twelve people from Madinah attended the *Hajj* and met with the Messenger of Allah (saaw) at al-'Aqabah where they gave him the first pledge of al-'Aqabah. They pledged to associate none with Allah, that they should not steal, neither commit fornication nor adultery, nor kill their offspring, and that they should not slander their neighbor, nor disobey the Messenger of Allah (saaw). If they fulfilled this, *Jannah* would be theirs, but if they committed any of those sins, it was for Allah (swt) to punish or forgive as He (swt) pleased. Once they had delivered their pledge and the *Hajj* season was over they returned to Madinah.

The Da'wah in Madinah

When the people of the first pledge of al-'Aqabah returned to Madinah and Islam spread to every single household among the Ansar, they sent a man to the Messenger of Allah (saaw) with a letter asking him to send them someone who would teach them the *Deen* and the Qur'an. The Messenger of Allah (saaw) never used to leave those who embraced Islam without teaching them the rules and nurturing them with the sound Islamic culture which would enable them to understand Islam and realize its essence, for the Islamic culture is vital to every Muslim, and is a means of strengthening the *'Aqeedah* and of understanding the Message of Islam, and thereby guarantees the consistent application of Islam. Those who embraced Islam had sensed this, therefore, they asked for someone to teach them, and the Messenger of Allah (saaw) sent Mus'ab ibn 'Umayr to them.

On arrival, Mus'ab lodged with As'ad ibn Zurarah, he then began visiting people in their homes and camps, calling them to Islam and reciting the Qur'an and consequently a man or two would embrace Islam, until Islam manifested itself and spread to every household of the Ansar, except the households of Khatmah, Wa'il and Waqif who were from (the clan of) Aws-Allah. Mus'ab ibn 'Umayr was teaching them and getting them to recite the Qur'an. Then he wrote to the Messenger of Allah (saaw) asking his permission to gather them. Allah's Messenger (saaw) granted him permission and wrote back, "Wait until the Jews declare their Sabbath, and in the afternoon, approach Allah with two *Rak'at* and then deliver your *Khutbah*." Mus'ab ibn 'Umayr gathered them in the house of Sa'd ibn Khaythamah, they were twelve men and he only slaughtered for them one goat. Mus'ab was the first in the history of Islam to hold *Jum'uah* prayer.

Mus'ab continued to go around Madinah calling people to Islam and teaching them the *Deen*.

One day As'ad ibn Zurarah went out with Mus'ab ibn 'Umayr to the areas of Banu al-Ashhal and of Banu Zafar (Sa'd ibn Mu'adh was incidentally As'ad ibn Zurarah's maternal cousin.) They entered one of the gardens of Banu Zafar by a well called Maraq and sat in it, where some of the men who had accepted Islam had gathered together. Sa'd ibn Mu'adh and Usayd ibn Hudayr were at the time leaders of their clan, the Banu 'Abd al-Ashhal, and both followed the polytheism of their tribe. When they had heard about him, Sa'd said to Usayd, "Go to these fellows who have entered our quarters to make fools of our comrades, drive them out and forbid them to enter our quarters.

If it were not that As'ad ibn Zurarah is related to me as you know I would save you the trouble. He is my aunt's son and I can do nothing to him." So Usayd took his lance and went to them; and when As'ad saw him he said to Mus'ab, "This is the chief of his tribe who is coming to you, so be true to Allah with him." Mus'ab said, "If he will sit down, I will talk to him." He stood over them looking furious and asking what they meant by coming to deceive their weaker comrades. "Leave us if you value your lives." Mus'ab said, "Won't you sit down and listen. If you like what you hear you can accept it, and if you don't like it you can leave it alone." He agreed that was fair, stuck his lance in the ground, and sat down. He explained Islam to him and read the Qur'an. Afterwards they said, according to what has been reported by them, "By Allah, before he spoke we recognized Islam in his face by its peaceful glow." He said, "What a wonderful and beautiful discourse this is! What does one do if he wants to enter this *Deen*?" They told him that he must wash and purify himself and his garments, then bear witness to the Truth and pray two *Rak'at*. He immediately did so and said, "There is a man behind me who if he follows you every one of his people will follow suit. I will send him to you at once. It is Sa'd ibn Mu'adh."

Taking his lance, he went off to Sa'd and his people sitting in a meeting place. When Sa'd saw him coming, he said, "By Allah, Usayd is coming with a different expression from that which he had when he left you." And when he came up he asked what had happened, he said, "I have spoken to the two men and I find no harm in them. I forbade them to go on and they said to me: We will do what you like; and I was told that Banu Harithah had gone out against As'ad to kill him because they knew that he was the son of your aunt so as to make you appear a treacherous protector of your guests."

Sa'd was enraged and got up at once, alarmed at what had been said about the Banu Harithah. He took the lance from his hand saying, "By Allah I see that you have been utterly ineffective." He went out to them and when he saw them sitting comfortably he knew that Usayd had intended that he should listen to them. He stood over them, looking furious. He said to As'ad, "O Abu Umamah, were it not for the relationship between us you would not have treated me thus. Would you behave in our homelands in a way we detest?" As'ad already had said to Mus'ab, "O Mus'ab, by Allah the leader who is followed by his people has come to you. If he follows you, no two of them will remain behind." So Mus'ab said to him, "Won't you sit down and listen. If you like what you hear you can accept it, and if you don't like it you can leave it alone." He agreed that was fair, stuck his lance in the ground, and sat down. He explained Islam to him and read him the Qur'an.

Afterwards they said, according to what has been reported of them, "By Allah, before he spoke we recognized Islam in his face by its peaceful glow." He said, "What a wonderful and beautiful discourse this is! What does one do if he wants to enter this *Deen*?" They told him that he must wash and purify himself and his garments, then bear witness to the truth and pray. He immediately did so. Then he took his lance and went back to his people's meeting place accompanied by Usayd ibn Hudayr. When they saw him coming they said, "We swear by Allah, Sa'd has returned with a different expression from that which he had when he left you." And when he stopped by them he said, "O Banu 'Abd al-Ashhal, how do you rate my authority amongst you?" They replied, "You are our chief, the most active in our interests, the best in judgment and the most fortunate in leadership." He said, "I will not speak to a man or woman among you until you believe in Allah and his Messenger." As a result, every man and woman among the Banu 'Abd al-Ashhal embraced Islam. Mus'ab then returned to the house of As'ad ibn Zurarah and he stayed with him as a guest, and he continued to call the people to Islam until almost every household of the Ansar had Muslim men and women among them. Mus'ab ibn 'Umayr remained in Madinah for one year among the 'Aus and the Khazraj teaching them their *Deen* and witnessing, with great delight, the growing number of the helpers of Allah's authority and of the word of truth.

31

He, may Allah be pleased with him, used to knock on people's doors hoping to contact them and convey the Message of Allah. He used to walk to the fields and contact the farmers to call them to Islam. He also used to confront the leaders and call them to the *Deen* of Allah. He would also perform some deliberate tactics like the one he used with As'ad ibn Zurarah in order to gain access to people and get them to receive the voice of Truth until he managed in one single year to turn the thoughts in Madinah from corrupted idolatry and incorrect emotions to *Tawheed* and *Iman* and Islamic emotions that abhorred *Shirk* and turned away from evil acts such as cheating and fraud and other vices. As a result of Mus'ab's activities and the activities of those who embraced Islam, Madinah had been transformed in one single year from a people who committed *Shirk* to a people who turned to Islam.

The Second Pledge of Al-'Aqabah

The first pledge of al-'Aqabah was a good thing and a blessing. This was so because despite the small number of those who had embraced Islam, the efforts of one companion of the Messenger of Allah (saaw), i.e., Mus'ab ibn 'Umayr were enough to lead them to change Madinah and transform the existing thoughts and emotions within its society, and despite the relatively large number of those who embraced Islam in Makkah, the people at large remained alienated from them, for the groups did not respond to Islam, and society was not affected by the Islamic thoughts and emotions. By contrast, the majority of people in Madinah embraced Islam and Islam made an impact in the collective heart of the Madinan society, and their thoughts and emotions were radically transformed. This clearly demonstrates that when individuals who embrace Islam remain alienated from society and the people at large, an impact within society is not generated, nor within the majority of people no matter how strong the belief of these individuals is. It also demonstrates that if the existing relationships between people were affected by thoughts and emotions they would lead to the desired transformation and change no matter how small the number of the conveyors of the Message are. This also proves that when the society persists in disbelief, as was the case with the Makkan society, it becomes more difficult to transform than a society where such erroneous notions are not dominant, as was the case with the Madinan society, even if such notions were present.

Therefore, the Madinan society was affected by Islam more than the Makkan society. People in Madinah had sensed the falsehood of the thoughts they were carrying and they had been searching for other thoughts and another way of life. By contrast, the Makkan society was satisfied with its state of affairs and anxious to maintain it, especially the heads of disbelief such as Abu Lahab, Abu Jahl and Abu Sufyan. That is why it took Mus'ab ibn 'Umayr only a short time to witness the response to the *Da'wah*, he went on calling people to Islam and acculturating them with its thoughts and rules, he would feel the quick response and witness people's willingness to accept Islam and their enthusiasm to learn and acquire the knowledge of Islam's rules, and this would make him rejoice; he would witness the number of Muslims grow and Islam spread and this would encourage him to multiply his efforts in the *Da'wah*.

When the season of *Hajj* came, he returned to Makkah and reported back to the Messenger of Allah (saaw), giving him an account about the Muslims in Madinah and their growing might, and about Islam and its rapid spread, describing the state of the Madinan society and how people there talked only about Allah's Messenger (saaw), and how Islam occupied center stage. Mus'ab informed the Messenger of Allah (saaw) about the strength of the Muslims and their deterrent might, which made Islam the dominant force in Madinah, he also informed him that some Muslims, whose belief had grown stronger and whose determination to carry the Message and defend the *Deen* of Allah had become greater than ever, would be coming to Makkah that year.

The Messenger of Allah (saaw) was very pleased with the news brought by Mus'ab and began thinking long and hard in the matter and comparing the Makkan society with that of Madinah. He (saaw) spent twelve consecutive years in Makkah calling for the *Deen* of Allah, exhausting all his efforts, devoting all his time and seizing every single opportunity, enduring in the process all types of hardship, suffering and oppression, and despite all that, society in Makkah remained as stubborn as ever and the *Da'wah* never managed to break through, due to the remorseless and frigid hearts and ruthless feelings of the Makkan people whose adamant minds would not break away from the past. The Makkan society was harsh and its openness to the *Da'wah* was absent due to the deeply rooted idolatrous polytheism within the hearts of its people, for Makkah was the main center of *Shirk*. In Madinah, things were different, hardly one year had elapsed since a group of the Khazraj embraced Islam, and the first pledge of al-'Aqabah took place, then came the efforts of Mus'ab ibn 'Umayr the year after, and this was enough to generate an Islamic atmosphere in Madinah and to pave the way for people to embrace Islam at an astonishing rate. The Message of Allah in Makkah had stopped with those who had embraced Islam, with the persecution and oppression inflicted upon them by the Quraysh, but in Madinah, on the other hand, Islam had spread rapidly, with the Muslims there not having to suffer the persecution by the Jews and the disbelievers, and this could only help Islam to become deeply rooted in people's hearts and to pave the way for the Muslims.

Therefore, it became clear to the Messenger of Allah (saaw) that Madinah would become the source of light from which Islam's *'Aqeedah* and system would shine. He (saaw), therefore, thought about emigrating to Madinah and to let his *Sahabah* join their brothers there, to find a sanctuary and safety and rid themselves from the persecution and torture which the Quraysh had been inflicting upon them. This would allow them to concentrate on the *Da'wah* and move towards its practical phase, which is the implementation of Islam and the carrying of its Message with the might and authority of the Islamic State. This was the only reason for the emigration.

It is worth mentioning that the Messenger of Allah (saaw) had never thought about emigrating from Makkah simply because of the obstacles the *Da'wah* was facing, without remaining steadfast and persevering, and without attempting to overcome those obstacles. He (saaw) persevered for ten years in Makkah, always focusing his thoughts on the *Da'wah*. He and his followers endured all types of horror and persecution in the way of the *Da'wah*. The ill-treatment and the resistance by the Quraysh never weakened his resolve and determination, on the contrary, his belief in the Message which he brought from his Lord took him to new heights, and the certainty of Allah's help made him even more steadfast and resolute. Nevertheless, he (saaw) realized after those attempts how hard and stubborn the Makkan society was, how shallow minded people were and how ruthless and misguided they were. This meant that the chances of success were slim, and that pursuing the *Da'wah* there could be a wasted effort, thus it became necessary to move away from such a society and look for another one. He therefore thought about emigrating from Makkah, and that was the only reason for thinking about moving to Madinah, not the hardship nor the persecution.

Indeed the Messenger of Allah (saaw) had ordered his *Sahabah* to emigrate to Abyssinia to escape persecution as it is allowed for the believers to move away from places of affliction if they were persecuted because of their *Deen*, although enduring the torture enhances one's *Iman*, and the oppression increases one's faithfulness and resistance sharpens one's determination. *Iman* pushes believers to belittle all hardships and sacrifice wealth, honor, peace of mind and even their lives. And although belief in Allah (swt) makes the believer ready to give his life willingly in His way, unabated aggression and the continuity of sacrifice would cause the believer to become exhausted. This is so, because his efforts would be diverted towards persevering against and resisting the harm inflicted upon him, rather than towards mobilizing his efforts in the *Da'wah* and broadening his horizons by being allowed to think deeply about the truthfulness of his belief. It was for this reason that the Muslims had no other alternative but to emigrate away from the places where affliction reigned. This was the case when they emigrated to Abyssinia.

However, their later emigration to Madinah was prompted by different reasons. They wanted to move with their Message and bring it to life by implementing it in a society, their new society, and then spread it worldwide. It is only in this context that the Messenger of Allah (saaw) contemplated ordering his *Sahabah* to emigrate to Madinah. But before deciding to join them there, he had to first meet the pilgrims coming from that location and confer with the Muslims among them, in order to assess their readiness to protect the *Da'wah* and to see how far they were prepared to sacrifice themselves in the way of Islam. He (saaw) had to make sure that they were prepared to give him the pledge of war, a pledge of fighting that would form the cornerstone of the Islamic State.

Thus the Messenger of Allah (saaw) waited for the pilgrims. This was the twelfth year of the Message, in 622 CE. The pilgrims were many, among whom were 75 Muslims (73 men and 2 women). One of the women was Nusaybah bint Ka'ab Umm 'Amarah from Banu Mazin ibn al-Najjar and the other was Asma' bint 'Amr ibn 'Adi from Banu Salamah, known also as Umm Mani'.

The Messenger of Allah (saaw) met the Muslim pilgrims secretly and talked to them about a second pledge, which would not be concerned with simply carrying the *Da'wah* and persevering against aggression. It would be a pledge which would go well beyond that, a pledge with far reaching consequences. It was to be a pledge that would entail forming a force capable of defending the Muslims and forming the nucleus that would serve as the cornerstone upon which to build the foundations of a state with the power to protect it, a power that would remove all material obstacles which stood in the way of the Message and its implementation.

The Messenger of Allah (saaw) talked to them about the pledge and felt their readiness, and they in turn agreed to meet him at al-'Aqabah during the days of *Tashreeq*. He (saaw) said to them, "Do not wake anyone, nor wait for anyone who is absent." When a third of the night had passed they went secretly to their appointment with the Messenger of Allah (saaw) at al-'Aqabah, the two women were also with them. They waited for Allah's Messenger (saaw) until he came with his uncle al-'Abbas, who was at that time a disbeliever, albeit he wanted to give his nephew a firm guarantee. He was the first to speak and said, "O people of Khazraj! You know what position Muhammad holds among us. We have protected him from our own people who think as we do about him. He lives in honor and safety among his people, but he decided to turn to you and join you; so if you think you can be faithful to what you have promised him and protect him from his opponents, then assume the burden you have undertaken. But if you think that you will betray and abandon him after he has gone out with you, then leave him now." They replied, "We have heard what you say. Now you speak, O Messenger of Allah, and choose for yourself and your Lord what you wish." The Messenger of Allah (saaw) spoke after reciting the Qur'an and commended Islam and said, "I invite your allegiance on the basis that you protect me as you would your women and children." Al-Bara' took his hand to give the pledge and said, "We give our allegiance O Messenger of Allah, by Allah we are men of war possessing arms which have been passed on from father to son".

While al-Bara' was speaking Abu al-Haytham ibn al-Tayhan interrupted him and said, "O Messenger of Allah, we have ties with other men (meaning the Jews) and if we sever them perhaps when we have done that and Allah will have given you victory, you will return to your people and leave us?" The Messenger of Allah (saaw) smiled and said, "No, your blood is my blood, and what is sacred to you is sacred to me; I am of you and you are of me; I will fight against those who fight against you, and be at peace with those at peace with you." Al-'Abbas ibn 'Ubadah interrupted and said, "O people of Khazraj!

Do you realize to what you are committing yourselves in pledging your support for this man? It means fighting all and sundry. If you think that if you lose your property, and your nobles are killed you will give him up, then do so now, for by Allah it would bring you shame in this world and the next if you did so later. But if you think that you will be loyal to your undertaking even if you lose your possessions and your nobles are killed, then take him, for by Allah it will profit you in this world and the Hereafter." They said that they would accept the Messenger of Allah (saaw) on these conditions and then inquired, "What is in it for us, O Messenger of Allah, in return for our loyalty?" Allah's Messenger (saaw) replied confidently, "*Jannah.*"

They stretched their hands forth, and he (saaw) stretched his hand and they pledged their word by saying, "We pledge ourselves to obey in well and woe, in ease and hardship, and, speak the truth at all times, and that in Allah's service we would fear the censure of none." After they gave the pledge Allah's Messenger (saaw) said, "Bring me twelve leaders who have charge of their people's affairs." They produced nine from al-Khazraj and three from al-Aws. So the Messenger of Allah (saaw) said to these *Nuqaba* (leaders), "You are the guardians of your people just as the disciples of 'Isa, son of Maryam, were responsible to him while I am responsible for my people." They went back to their beds and then back to their caravan and returned to Madinah.

Afterwards, the Messenger of Allah (saaw) ordered the Muslims in Makkah to emigrate to Madinah in small parties, and so they began to migrate either individually or sometimes in small groups. The Quraysh by then had heard of the pledge and they attempted to prevent the Muslims from emigrating. They came between husband and wife in order to stop the migration, but the Muslims continued to leave Makkah for Madinah, while Allah's Messenger (saaw) stayed behind without indicating to anyone whether he would leave or not. There were signs, however, that he (saaw) too would leave. Abu Bakr kept asking Allah's Messenger (saaw) for permission to emigrate until he answered, "Don't be in a hurry, it may be that Allah will give you a companion." Abu Bakr knew then that Allah's Messenger (saaw) wanted to emigrate.

The Quraysh were very concerned about the implications of the emigration of Allah's Messenger (saaw), especially now that the Muslims in Madinah were many and enjoyed the upper hand. Evidently, their position there would be strengthened by the emigration of the Muslims from Makkah. The Quraysh realized that another even more serious potential threat to them was Allah's Messenger (saaw). Should he (saaw) join them there, and with the power that they possessed, it could mean the end of them. They, therefore, thought long and hard about the issue of preventing Allah's Messenger (saaw) from migrating to Madinah. The Quraysh began to fear that once the Muslims had become a force to be reckoned with they would come after them and defend Allah's Messenger (saaw), should he decide to stay in Makkah. With such a dilemma confronting them. They finally decided to resort to killing him (saaw), so as to prevent him from joining the Muslims in Madinah and in order to avoid all future clashes with the people of Madinah, Islam and Muhammad (saaw).

It has been reported in the books of *Seerah* that in the narration of 'Aisha and Abu Umamah ibn Sahm, that when the seventy-three men present at al-'Aqabah left the Messenger of Allah (saaw), having given him the protection and pledging their support, the trials and tribulations of the Muslims in Makkah increased for wanting to leave. The Quraysh harassed them and harmed them, and they complained to Allah's Messenger (saaw) who replied, "I have been shown the homeland to which you will emigrate."

After a few days, he (saaw) emerged very pleased and said, "I have been told that you can emigrate to Yathrib (Madinah), whoever wants to go there can do so." So they began their preparations to vacate the city. Then they left secretly in small groups while the Messenger of Allah (saaw) stayed in Makkah to wait for Allah's permission to emigrate. Abu Bakr kept asking Allah's Messenger (saaw) for permission to emigrate, he (saaw) would say to him, "Don't be in a hurry, it may be that Allah will give you a companion." Abu Bakr hoped that his companion would be Allah's Messenger (saaw) himself.

When the Quraysh learned of the *Sahabah's* emigration, and realized that Allah's Messenger (saaw) had the determination to fight them, they assembled in their council chamber and after a little debate agreed to kill him. Jibreel came to the Messenger of Allah (saaw) and ordered him not to sleep on the bed on which he usually slept. He (saaw) did not sleep in his bed that night and it was then that Allah (swt) permitted him to emigrate.

The presence of the forces of Islam in Madinah, the readiness of the people to receive the Messenger of Allah (saaw), and the establishment of the Islamic State were the only reasons which prompted him (saaw) to emigrate. It would be completely erroneous for anyone to conclude or even to entertain the slightest thought that Muhammad (saaw) emigrated from Makkah out of fear that the Quraysh would kill him. He (saaw) never gave the slightest consideration to the repression and harm that befell him and was more than happy to sacrifice his life in the way of Islam. This is a fact. His (saaw) emigration to Madinah was simply the selfless pursuit of the Islamic *Da'wah* and the necessary establishment of the Islamic State to further that objective. It is clear that the Quraysh had come to the decision to kill him for fear of his emigration to Madinah where he (saaw) would enjoy its protection and power, but the Quraysh, despite their efforts, failed in their bid to dispose of him. The emigration, as the Quraysh feared, proved to be the turning point in the history of the *Da'wah*. It moved from the phase of inviting people to Islam, to the phase of establishing an Islamic society, a state ruling by Islam's authority, inviting for it by means of evidence, proof and persuasion and by the force that would protect it from evil and oppressive forces.

Establishing the Islamic State

The Messenger of Allah (saaw) eventually arrived in Madinah and was greeted by a large number of its people, Muslims, polytheists and Jews alike. They were all eager to witness his awesome presence and he soon came to be surrounded by the Muslims who were all anxious to serve him and to offer him comfort and hospitality. They were ready to sacrifice their lives in the way of the *Da'wah*.

Everyone wanted the Messenger of Allah (saaw) to lodge with him, but he (saaw) left the reins of his she-camel free until it knelt by the storehouse of Sahl and Suhayl, sons of 'Amr. The Messenger of Allah (saaw) subsequently bought it and built a Masjid and his houses around it. The building of the Masjid and the houses turned out to be an easy task, being very modest and cheap to construct. The Masjid consisted of a large courtyard with walls composed of bricks. One part of the ceiling was covered in palm tree branches and the remainder left uncovered. Part of the Masjid served as a shelter to the poor who did not have a home. The Masjid was never lit except during the *Isha* prayer, when torches of hay were used to light it.

The houses of the Messenger of Allah (saaw) were just as simple and modest as the Masjid itself except that they were more lighted. Allah's Messenger (saaw) lodged with Abi Ayub Khalid ibn Zayd al-Ansari while the Masjid and houses were being built and he moved in as soon as they were ready. He (saaw) thought about the new life that he had sought, the way that the *Da'wah* had moved from one stage to another, from the stage of acculturation to the stage of interaction with the non-Islamic society to that of the eventual implementation of the rules of Islam upon people. He (saaw) thought about the new era that took him from calling for Islam and enduring aggression towards the phase of rule, authority and the power that was now able to protect, defend, and propagate the Message of Islam. The Messenger of Allah (saaw) ordered the building of the Masjid from the very first day and it was

41

utilized for *Salah* (prayers), meetings, consultation and a place where he (saaw) looked after the people's affairs and from where he (saaw) judged between them. He (saaw) appointed Abu Bakr and 'Umar as his two assistants, saying, "My two assistants on Earth are Abu Bakr and 'Umar."

The Muslims gathered around the Messenger of Allah (saaw). They would always approach him for guidance and advice in all matters. He (saaw) thus performed the duty of the Head of State, the Judge and the Commander-in-Chief of the army. Therefore, he (saaw) looked after the affairs of the Muslims, settled their disputes and appointed leaders to the State's army divisions, eventually sending them outside Madinah on military campaigns and missions.

Allah's Messenger (saaw) founded the Islamic State from the very first day he arrived in Madinah and began to structure it by forming the society on a solid foundation as well as by gathering the appropriate forces in order to be able to protect the State and convey the Message. With this accomplished, he (saaw) could begin to remove the material obstacles that stood in the way of the spreading of Islam.

Building the Society

Allah (swt) has endowed the human being with the instinct of survival. One of the features of this instinct is for people to gather and live together, and thus the coexistence and interaction of people is a natural human disposition. However, this does not transform them into a society. Instead, they are a group, and they would remain as a group unless they developed relationships that would bind them with a common interest and protected them from common threats. Only if such relationships exist that maintains their common interests they would then become a society. However, these relationships would not result in a homogenous society unless three prerequisites were achieved:

A common outlook towards these relationships achieved through:

1) Unity of thought;

2) Unity in approval and disapproval towards these relationships achieved through unity of emotions;

3) The system addressing their problem is the same.

Therefore, it is essential to study, analyze, and comprehend the thoughts, feelings, and system which characterize a society before forming an opinion about it. For they alone can determine and distinguish one society from another. On this basis, let us shed some light on the society of Madinah once the Messenger of Allah (saaw) had arrived there.

At the time three groups lived in Madinah: the Muslims (Muhajireen and Ansar), who formed the biggest group; the polytheists, from the Aws and Khazraj who did not embrace Islam; and the Jews who themselves were divided into four sections (one inside Madinah called Banu Qaynuqa', and the other three outside Madinah, namely Banu Nadir, Khaybar and Banu

Quraydah). Even before Islam, the Jews formed their own separate society from that of the society in Madinah. This was so because their concepts and emotions were different, as were the ways by which they conducted their affairs. The result of this was that the Jews were never part of the general society of Madinah even though they lived in and around the city. As for the polytheists, they were small in numbers and were overwhelmed by the Islamic atmosphere pervading Madinah. Therefore, their yielding to the Islamic concepts and emotions and to the rules of Islam was inevitable even if they did not embrace Islam. The *Muhajireen* and *Ansar* were united by the Islamic *'Aqeedah*. Islam harmonized their affairs. It rendered their concepts and emotions as the same - organizing their lives and relationships on the basis of Islam was a natural and inevitable outcome.

The Messenger of Allah (saaw) began organizing the relationships of the Muslims on the basis of the Islamic *'Aqeedah*. He (saaw) invited them to form a brotherhood, a brotherhood that would have a visible and lasting effect on their relationships, in their business dealings, and life's affairs. It was with this policy in mind that he (saaw) instituted brotherhood with 'Ali ibn Abi Talib; his uncle Hamzah became the brother to his servant Zayd; and Abu Bakr and Kharijah ibn Zayd became brothers in a similar fashion. He (saaw) then invited the *Muhajireen* and *Ansar* to form a similar brotherhood, so 'Umar ibn al-Khattab and 'Utbah ibn Malik al-Khazraji became brothers to each other, as did Talhah ibn 'Ubaydullah and Abu Ayub al-Ansari, and 'Abd al-Rahman ibn 'Auf and Sa'd ibn al-Rabi'i.

This brotherhood had its material effect as well, for the *Ansar* had shown a great deal of generosity towards their brethren, the emigrants, which served to only strengthen their ties. The *Ansar* offered them money and properties, sharing everything with them. They traded and farmed together. The traders amongst the emigrants turned their hand to commerce, 'Abd al-Rahman ibn 'Auf used to sell butter and cheese, and others who were business minded did likewise. As for those who did not take up trading, they went into farming, like Abu Bakr and 'Ali who worked the lands given to them by the *Ansar*. The Messenger of Allah (saaw) said, "Whoever owns a piece of land should farm it or give it to his brother." So the Muslims worked to earn their living. There was, though, a small group of Muslims who had no money, could find no work and had nowhere to live. They were the needy, being neither emigrants nor *Ansar*. These were Bedouins who came to Madinah and who had embraced Islam. The Messenger of Allah (saaw) took them into his care and housed them in the covered part of the Masjid, where they became known as the Ahl al-Suffah. They lived off the wealthy Muslims whom Allah (swt) had provided for generously. By doing so, Allah's Messenger (saaw) managed to stabilize the Muslims' way of life and determine their relationships with each other on a solid footing. The Messenger of Allah (saaw) thus established the society in Madinah on a strong foundation that stood firmly in the ugly face of disbelief and which was able to resist the conspiracies of the hypocrites and Jews. The Islamic society remained united throughout, and the Messenger of Allah (saaw) became reassured by this unity among the Muslims.

As for the polytheists, they never produced any lasting effect on the structure of the society. At first, they submitted to the Islamic rules and then waned, only to eventually vanish.

The Jews remained always a society apart, different from other societies, even before Islam. When Islam's authority was established in Madinah, differences deepened and the need to establish relations between the Muslims and the Jews on a specific basis became a necessity. So the Messenger of Allah (saaw) determined the Muslims' position towards the other members of the society. In the light of this the Messenger of Allah (saaw) wrote a document concerning the *Muhajireen* and *Ansar* in which he made an agreement with the Jews establishing them in their religion and their property, and in which he stated their reciprocal obligations. He (saaw) began the document as follows, "This is a document from Muhammad the Prophet, governing the relations between the believing Muslims of Quraysh and Yathrib (Madinah), and those who followed them and joined them and fought alongside them. They are one Ummah to the exclusion of all people." He (saaw) then mentioned how the relationship between the believers was to be constituted. He also mentioned the Jews during his talk concerning the relations between the believers, saying, "A believer shall not slay a believer for the sake of a disbeliever, nor shall he aid a disbeliever against a believer. Allah's covenant amongst them is one, the least of them is responsible. Believers are protectors (*Wula'a*) of one to the other to the exclusion of outsiders. To the Jews who follow us belong help and equality. They shall not be wronged nor shall their enemies be aided. The peace of the believers is indivisible. No separate peace shall be made when believers are fighting in the way of Allah. Conditions must be fair to all." The Jews mentioned in this document were the ones who wanted to become citizens of the Islamic State. It was not addressed to the Jewish tribes living on the outskirts of Madinah. Thus, any Jew wanting to become a citizen of the State would enjoy the same rights and receive the same treatment, for he would then be considered a *Dhimmi* (people of the covenant). As for the Jewish tribes mentioned in the document, they were referred to in the latter part of the document and included the Jews of Banu 'Auf and the Jews of Banu al-Najjar and so on.

Their position vis a vis the Islamic State was defined by the document. It was clearly determined that their relationship with the Muslims would be based on the Islamic rule, that it would be subject to the authority of Islam and to safeguarding the interests of the State. Some of the points mentioned in the document were:

1) The close friends of the Jews are as themselves. None of them shall go out except with the permission of Muhammad (saaw).

2) Yathrib shall be a sanctuary for the people of this document.

3) If any dispute or controversy likely to cause trouble should arise, it must be referred to Allah and to the Messenger of Allah.

4) The Quraysh and their helpers shall not be given protection.

The document of Allah's Messenger (saaw) determined the position of the Jewish tribes neighboring Madinah. It imposed on them the condition that they were not to go out of Madinah without his (saaw) permission, i.e. the State's permission. They were forbidden from violating the sanctuary of Madinah by war or by helping in a war. They were also forbidden from help-ing the Quraysh or those who helped the Quraysh and were bound by the conditions of the covenant to refer any dispute arising about the content of the document to the Messenger of Allah (saaw). The Jews agreed to the conditions laid out in the document and all those tribes mentioned in it signed to that effect. They were Banu 'Auf, Banu al-Najjar, Banu al-Harith, Banu Sa'ida, Banu Jushm, Banu al-Aus and Banu Tha'labah. Banu Quraydah, Banu al-Nadir and Banu Qaynuqa' did not sign at the time, but did so at a later date, and they all willingly submitted to the conditions laid down in the document.

By signing this document the Messenger of Allah (saaw) firmly fixed the relationships within the newly born Islamic State. The relationship between the State and the neighboring Jewish tribes was also firmly established on a clear and specific basis. In both instances though, it was Islam that would be the judge and arbiter. It was at this stage that Allah's Messenger (saaw) became reassured knowing that the Islamic society was now properly founded and that he was to a certain degree safe from any immediate acts of betrayal and fighting by the Jews, so he (saaw) began the task of removing the material obstacles that stood in the way of the Message of Islam by preparing for war.

The Preparation for Jihad

When the Messenger of Allah (saaw) was assured that the Islamic society was firmly entrenched, and once he had signed treaties with the neighboring Jewish tribes, he set about preparing the grounds in Madinah for *Jihad*, for it is the duty of the Islamic State to implement Islam in the whole of the land under its rule and to convey the Message of Islam beyond its borders. Conveying the Message of Islam is by no means comparable to missionary work. Instead, it dictates the invitation of the people to Islam, acculturating them with its concepts and rules, and the removal of any material obstacle that stands in the way of the Message through the necessary material requirements.

The Quraysh had always represented a material obstacle barring the Message of Islam. A task force thus had to be prepared to overcome it. Bearing this in mind, and with the objective of spreading Islam outside Madinah, the Messenger of Allah (saaw) began building his army. He (saaw) took several steps by dispatching some expeditions designed to challenge the Quraysh and alarm both the hypocrites and the Jews in Madinah and nearby surroundings. In four months, he (saaw) dispatched three units outside Madinah.

He sent Hamzah to the seashore in the neighborhood of al-'Is at the head of thirty riders from the emigrants, with none of the helpers taking part. Hamzah met Abu Jahl ibn Hisham with three hundred riders on the shore and was about to fight him when Majdi ibn 'Amr al-Juhani intervened between them, causing the people to separate without fighting. The Messenger of Allah (saaw) sent Muhammad ibn 'Ubaydah ibn al-Harith with sixty riders from the *Muhajireen*, there not being a single one of the *Ansar* among them. He encountered Abu Sufyan at the head of more than two hundred riders in the valley of Rabigh. Again, no fighting took place except that Sa'd ibn Abi Waqqas shot an arrow on that day. Allah's Messenger (saaw) also sent Sa'd ibn Abi Waqqas with twenty riders towards Makkah, but they returned without fighting.

These expeditions helped create an atmosphere of war in Madinah, and they also served to frighten the Quraysh, who began to seriously feel the threat coming from Allah's Messenger (saaw). He (saaw) did not stop at that, but went out raiding himself. Twelve months after his arrival in Madinah he (saaw) went forth on a raid looking for the Quraysh and Banu Damrah until he reached Waddan. He (saaw) did not meet the Quraysh that day, and instead Banu Damrah made peace with him. After that the Messenger of Allah (saaw) went raiding at the head of a contingent of two hundred riders from the *Muhajireen* and *Ansar*, until they reached Buwat in the neighborhood of Radwa. They were making for a caravan composed of two thousand five hundred cattle protected by one hundred fighters led by Umayyah ibn Khalaf. But he (saaw) failed to intercept the caravan due to the fact that it had traversed a different route than the one normally used. Three months after returning from the expedition to Buwat, Abu Salmah ibn 'Abd al-Asad was left in charge of Madinah and the Messenger of Allah (saaw) undertook another raid at the head of two hundred plus Muslims until he reached al-'Ushayrah in the valley of Yanbu where he stopped during the month of Jumada al-Ula and resided until some days of Jumada al-Akhirah had passed. This was in the second year of Hijrah. The reason for his camping there was that he (saaw) was waiting for a caravan headed by Abu Sufyan, but once again he missed his target. It was not entirely a wasted effort though, because the Messenger of Allah (saaw) gained from his trip a peace treaty with Bani Mudlaj and their allies from Bani Damrah.

He (saaw) had only been back in Madinah for ten days when Kurz ibn Jabir al-Fahri raided the pasturing camels of Madinah. Allah's Messenger (saaw) went out in search of him, Kurz being one of the allies of the Quraysh. Allah's Messenger (saaw) reached the valley of Safwan in the neighborhood of Badr, but Kurz eluded him. This was the first raid of Badr.

That is how Allah's Messenger (saaw) began defying the Quraysh with his army, by roaming the Peninsula and sending out expeditions. Although no fighting took place, Allah's Messenger (saaw) achieved considerable gains which paved the way for still greater battles, since these raids served as military exercises for the Muslim army and prepared them for war. They also sent shivers down the spines of the Jews and the hypocrites of Madinah and discouraged them from entertaining any thoughts about causing trouble. He (saaw) succeeded in demoralizing the Quraysh by defying them while boosting the morale of the Muslims a great deal. He (saaw) also formed and enforced a blockade on the caravans of the Quraysh on their way to al-Sham by signing treaties with the tribes encamped between Madinah and the Red Sea coast, such as Banu Damrah, Banu Mudlaj and others.

The Jihad Begins

The Messenger of Allah (saaw) settled in Madinah, where he at once began to implement the Islamic rules on the society. It was at this time that the Revelation concerning legislation descended. He (saaw) strengthened the fundamentals of the Islamic State and built the society on the basis of Islam and its systems. He (saaw) created a brotherhood amongst the Muslims and it was then that Islam came to life as a system based on the *Shari'ah*, adopted by a society that took on the task of spreading its Message. The number of Muslims substantially increased and they became a force to be reckoned with, individuals and groups alike embraced Islam every other day, amongst them Jews and others.

Once the Messenger of Allah (saaw) was confident about the status of Islam in Madinah, he began to think about spreading the Message outside to the rest of the Arabian Peninsula. However, he knew that Quraysh formed a formidable obstacle in the way of the *Da'wah*, a material obstacle where the means of intellectual discussion would fall on deaf ears. Therefore, the obstacle would have to be overwhelmed by force.

The Messenger of Allah (saaw) was unable to remove this material obstacle when he was in Makkah because Islam did not have a State capable of generating the required material force necessary to remove that obstacle. However, since the establishment of the Islamic State, the Messenger of Allah (saaw) was able to work to remove such material obstacles by considerable means now at his disposal. With the means to enforce such a policy now available to him, all he (saaw) had to do was to prepare the army and war, and adopting a new policy to spread the *Da'wah*. This is the reason why he (saaw) initiated expeditions and raids, some of which he took part in personally, so as to defy Quraysh with a show of force. The last expedition was that of 'Abdullah ibn Jahsh which served as an introduction to the battle of Badr.

The Messenger of Allah (saaw) sent 'Abdullah ibn Jahsh out with a group of Muhajireen during the month of Rajab in the second year of Hijra. He (saaw) wrote him a letter, and ordered him not to look at it until he had journeyed for two days whereupon he should act on its instructions, but he should not put pressure on any of his companions. When 'Abdullah had traveled for two days he opened the letter and read it, this is what it said, "When you have read this letter of mine, proceed until you reach Nakhlah between Makkah and Ta'if. Lie there for the Quraysh and find out for us what they are up to." He told his companions about the letter and the task assigned to him, he also informed them about Allah's Messenger's instructions not to put any pressure on anyone.

They all agreed to continue and so he proceeded with his companions. They traveled together as a group until Sa'd ibn Abi Waqqas al-Zuhri and 'Utbah ibn Ghazwan became separated when they went to look for the camel they had lost. Eventually they were to fall prisoners to the Quraysh. 'Abdullah ibn Jahsh camped in Nakhlah watching out for the Quraysh and while there one of their caravans carrying merchandise passed by. 'Abdullah and his companions took council among themselves to decide what to do because this was the last day of the sacred month of Rajab and Allah's Messenger (saaw) had not issued any instructions about fighting. They said to each other, "By Allah, if you leave them alone tonight they will get into the sacred area and will be safe from you, and if you kill them, you will kill them in the sacred month." At first they were hesitant and feared to attack them. Then they encouraged each other and decided to fight. One of the Muslims shot the leader of the caravan 'Amr ibn al Hadrami and killed him. The Muslims took two prisoners and escorted the caravan to Madinah.

When they came to the Messenger of Allah (saaw) he said to them, "I did not order you to fight in the sacred month." Then he (saaw) put on hold the issue of the caravan and the two prisoners refusing to take anything from them. That was the conclusion of 'Abdullah ibn Jahsh's expedition whom the Messenger of Allah (saaw) had sent to watch the Quraysh, but instead had led to fighting, killing, and imprisoning some of thier men and taking the caravan as booty during the sacred month. So what would be the Islamic verdict on this action?

This is what concerned Allah's Messenger (saaw) and hence that is the reason why he held the prisoners and the booty in suspense, to wait for the verdict from Allah (swt) on the matter. The Quraysh grabbed the opportunity of using the issue as a source of propaganda against Islam and Muhammad (saaw). They trumpeted among all the Arabs that Muhammad (saaw) and his *Sahabah* had violated the sacred month, shed blood, seized properties and imprisoned people. Arguments arose in Makkah between the Quraysh and the Muslims who had remained there, and in reply the Muslims said that their brothers had attacked the caravan in Sha'ban and not Rajab, but their response was not enough and failed to quell the propaganda launched by the Quraysh against Islam. The Jews picked up on the campaign as well and began disgracing and slandering 'Abdullah ibn Jahsh's action. The propaganda took its toll on the Muslims, meanwhile Allah's Messenger (saaw) kept silent awaiting the Revelation and Allah's verdict on the affair until Allah (swt) revealed in *Surah* al-Baqarah:

يَسْـَٔلُونَكَ عَنِ ٱلشَّهْرِ ٱلْحَرَامِ قِتَالٍ فِيهِ قُلْ قِتَالٌ فِيهِ كَبِيرٌ وَصَدٌّ عَن سَبِيلِ ٱللَّهِ وَكُفْرٌ بِهِۦ وَٱلْمَسْجِدِ ٱلْحَرَامِ وَإِخْرَاجُ أَهْلِهِۦ مِنْهُ أَكْبَرُ عِندَ ٱللَّهِ وَٱلْفِتْنَةُ أَكْبَرُ مِنَ ٱلْقَتْلِ وَلَا يَزَالُونَ يُقَـٰتِلُونَكُمْ حَتَّىٰ يَرُدُّوكُمْ عَن دِينِكُمْ إِنِ ٱسْتَطَـٰعُوا۟

"They ask you concerning fighting in the sacred months. Say, "Fighting therein is a great (transgression) but a greater (transgression) in the sight of Allah is to prevent mankind from following the way of Allah, to disbelieve in Him, to prevent access to Al-Masjid-al-Haram, and to drive out its inhabitants, and 'Al-Fitnah' is worse than killing. And they will never cease fighting you until they turn you back from your religion (Islam) if they can." [Al-Baqarah, 2:217]

When this verse was revealed the Muslims rejoiced and Allah's Messenger (saaw) then proceeded to distribute the booty from the caravan and exchange the two prisoners for Sa'd ibn Abi Waqqas al-Zuhri and 'Utbah ibn

Ghazwan. These verses came as a slap in the face of the Quraysh's propaganda against Islam. The Qur'an answered the Quraysh's question concerning fighting in the sacred month, agreeing that fighting is a sin, but keeping people back from the way of the sacred Masjid and driving its people away from it was far more serious than fighting and killing in the sacred month.

The Quraysh's actions of oppressing the Muslims for their *Deen* by threatening, torturing and persecuting them was far worse than fighting and killing in the sacred month, or any other month for that matter. The Quraysh had relentlessly fought them in an attempt to turn them back from their *Deen*, therefore the Muslims were entitled to fight the Quraysh in the sacred month and nothing could be held against them. It was the Quraysh who were committing the graver offense by standing in the way of the Islamic *Da'wah*, by keeping people back from the way of Allah, by disbelieving in Allah, driving out the people of the sacred Masjid and persecuting the Muslims. They deserved to be fought in any and every month, sacred or otherwise. The fight that 'Abdullah ibn Jahsh initiated against the Quraysh was therefore neither a disgrace to him nor to the Muslims.

Thus, the expedition of 'Abdullah ibn Jahsh was a turning point in the history of Islam. It marked a profound change of policy in the way that the Islamic *Da'wah* was to be conducted. Waqid ibn 'Abdullah al-Tamimi shot the leader of the caravan and killed him. This was the first blood the Muslims shed in the way of Allah (swt). Until the verses of *Jihad* were revealed commanding the Muslims to fight; armed combat during the sacred months had been unauthorized. From that time on though the rules were different. Thus the previous prevention against fighting in the sacred months was abrogated by the specificity of the above mentioned verse.

Life in Madinah

Islam has a specific way of life derived from its concepts concerning life. These are the building blocks of the Islamic culture, which radically differs from all other cultures. It is characterized by three points:

1) It is founded on the Islamic *'Aqeedah*;

2) The criterion of actions in life is based on Allah's commands and prohibitions, i.e. life is based on *Halal* and *Haram* and nothing else (such as benefit or *Maslaha*);

3) The meaning of happiness is to gain Allah's pleasure, i.e. permanent peace of mind cannot be achieved without first gaining Allah's pleasure.

That is the Islamic way of life, the kind of life Muslims look up to and aim to achieve. In order to make the above possible, it is essential to have a State that fully implements Islam and executes its rules without exception. When the Muslims migrated to Madinah, they led a distinguished way of life, with the Islamic *'Aqeedah* as its basis. The verses of the Qur'an concerning the social and penal codes came to be revealed at this time, in addition to the verses concerning other matters of worship which had not been revealed before. *Zakat* (alms) and *Siyam* (fasting) were decreed in the second year of the *Hijrah*. *Adhaan* was decreed and the people of Madinah listened to it being delivered in the sweet voice of Bilal ibn Rabah five times daily. Seventeen months after the arrival of Allah's Messenger (saaw) to Madinah, the *Qiblah* (direction of prayer) was transferred to the *Ka'bah*. The verses of Divine Legislation concerning matters of worship, diet, morals, relationships and penalties were revealed. *Khamr* (intoxicants) and the flesh of swine were forbidden, and the verses concerning the penal and criminal code were also revealed, as were those concerning business transactions, the complete forbidding of

Riba in all its guises and so on. Every time the verses that spoke to the people's affairs in everyday life were revealed to Allah's Messenger (saaw), he explained them and ordered the Muslims to abide by them. He (saaw) looked after the Muslims' affairs by solving their problems and settling their disputes by his sayings, actions and by his silence over what happened right in front of him, for his (saaw) speech, actions and silence are all sources of the *Shari'ah* as Allah (swt) says in *Surah* al-Najm,

"Nor does he speak of (his own) desire. It is only a Revelation that is revealed" [An-Najm, 53:3-4]

Life in Madinah went on following that course with its distinct viewpoint, i.e. the Islamic one. The Islamic society - which is different from any other - was alive and flourishing then, thriving on Islamic concepts and emotions and now that the rules of Islam were being comprehensively implemented, offered solutions and guidelines to all the Muslims. The Messenger of Allah (saaw) was very pleased to see that the *Da'wah* had reached this stage with the Muslims settled in their *Deen*, abiding by its rules individually and collectively without fearing any harm or persecution. They solved their problems according to Allah's rules, always referring new matters that had arisen to the Messenger of Allah (saaw) and never stepping out of line. They applied Allah's rules in every action and from this they achieved happiness and peace of mind. Many of the Muslims shadowed the Messenger of Allah (saaw) in order to learn from him, to memorize the Qur'an and acquire knowledge. Islam grew and spread, and the Muslims became stronger day by day.

Debating the Jews and Christians

The non-Muslims became aware of the strength and power of the Muslims within a short period of time. They realized that their strength was deeply rooted in hearts never short of sacrifice in the way of Islam, hearts that endured all types of pain and persecution, hearts that were always ready to give up life itself for Islam. There they were in Madinah enjoying their *Deen* and implementing its rules, a *Deen* that was reaching new heights each day with the Muslims feeling true contentment and happiness.

The enemies of Islam could not digest this, and signs of revulsion began to outwardly manifest themselves in the neighboring Jews. Their fears grew and they began to rethink and reconsider their position towards Muhammad (saaw) and his *Sahabah* now that the Muslims were becoming unshakable and many people were responding to the call of Islam. The Jews were enraged by those amongst them who converted to Islam. They feared that Islam would infiltrate their ranks and spread among them and so they attacked Islam, its beliefs and rules. Heated argument and a war of nerves ensued between the Muslims and Jews, this was to develop into a much fiercer dispute than the Muslims had to endure with the Quraysh in Makkah.

Conspiracy, hypocrisy and their furtive knowledge of the former Prophets and Messengers were the main weapons used by the Jews in their intellectual war against Muhammad (saaw) and his *Sahabah*. Some of their rabbis pretended to embrace Islam, sat with the Muslims and faked their piety. Soon they were to show signs of doubt and uncertainty by asking Muhammad (saaw) questions in the hope of shaking the conviction of the Muslims in their *'Aqeedah* and the Message of Truth which Islam stood for.

The Jews were joined by a group of the 'Aus and Khazraj who embraced Islam hypocritically in the hope of causing animosity and confusion amongst the Muslims. The argument between the Jews and Muslims turned into physical confrontation at times despite the oath between them.

A vivid example of the Jewish stubbornness and hatred was reflected in Abu Bakr's loss of temper on one occasion, bearing in mind that Abu Bakr was a man noted for his wisdom, patience and calm character. It is reported that Abu Bakr called on a Jew named Finhas to fear Allah and embrace Islam.

Finhas replied, "We are not poor compared to Allah but He humbles Himself to us; we are independent of Him while He needs us. Were He independent of us He would not ask us to lend Him our money as your fellow pretends, prohibiting you to take interest and allowing us to. Had He been independent of us He would not have given us interest." Finhas was referring to Allah's (swt) saying,

$$\text{مَّن ذَا ٱلَّذِى يُقْرِضُ ٱللَّهَ قَرْضًا حَسَنًا فَيُضَٰعِفَهُۥ لَهُۥٓ أَضْعَافًا كَثِيرَةً}$$

"Who is he that will lend to Allah a goodly loan so that He may give it increase manifold?" [Al-Baqarah, 2:245]

Abu Bakr could not control his anger, and was so enraged that he hit Finhas in the face and said, "By whom my destiny rests, were it not for the treaty between us, I would cut off your head, you enemy of Allah!"

The argument between the Muslims and Jews became very heated and went on for quite sometime. Meanwhile, about sixty Christian riders from Najran arrived in Madinah. They must have heard about the animosity between the Jews and Muslims and hoped that the rift would deepen so that Christianity could come to reign and rid itself from both religions, which were both challenging it for supremacy according to their claims. This group of Christians were in touch with the Muslims and the Jews.

Allah's Messenger (saaw) regarded them, together with the Jews, as 'People of the Book' and invited them both to Islam. He (saaw) recited to them Allah's (swt) saying,

قُلْ يَٰٓأَهْلَ ٱلْكِتَٰبِ تَعَالَوْا۟ إِلَىٰ كَلِمَةٍ سَوَآءٍۭ بَيْنَنَا وَبَيْنَكُمْ
أَلَّا نَعْبُدَ إِلَّا ٱللَّهَ وَلَا نُشْرِكَ بِهِۦ شَيْـًٔا وَلَا يَتَّخِذَ بَعْضُنَا
بَعْضًا أَرْبَابًا مِّن دُونِ ٱللَّهِ فَإِن تَوَلَّوْا۟ فَقُولُوا۟ ٱشْهَدُوا۟ بِأَنَّا
مُسْلِمُونَ ﴿٦٤﴾

*"Say (O Muhammad): "O people of the scripture (Jews and Christians) :
Come to a word that is just between us and you, That we worship none but
Allah, and we associate no partners with Him, and that none of us shall take
others as lords besides Allah. Then, if they turn away, say: "Bear witness that
we are Muslims." [Al-Imran, 3:64]*

The Jews and the Christians asked him (saaw) about the Prophets he believed in and he recited to them Allah's saying,

قُولُوٓا۟ ءَامَنَّا بِٱللَّهِ وَمَآ أُنزِلَ إِلَيْنَا وَمَآ أُنزِلَ إِلَىٰٓ إِبْرَٰهِـۧمَ
وَإِسْمَٰعِيلَ وَإِسْحَٰقَ وَيَعْقُوبَ وَٱلْأَسْبَاطِ وَمَآ أُوتِىَ مُوسَىٰ
وَعِيسَىٰ وَمَآ أُوتِىَ ٱلنَّبِيُّونَ مِن رَّبِّهِمْ لَا نُفَرِّقُ بَيْنَ
أَحَدٍ مِّنْهُمْ وَنَحْنُ لَهُۥ مُسْلِمُونَ ﴿١٣٦﴾

*"Say, "We believe in Allah and that which has been sent down to us and that
which has been sent down to Ibrahim, Isma'eel, Isaac, Jacob, and to Al-Asbat
(twelve sons of Jacob), and that which has been given to Moses and Jesus,
and that which has been given to the Prophets from their Lord. We make no
distinction between any of them, and to Him we have submitted (in Islam)"
[Al-Baqarah, 2:136]*

They could find nothing more to say to him. Their hearts would accept
the evidence and the Truth was revealed, but they would not believe out of

fear for their positions, reputation and status, some of them in fact admitted this. It has been narrated that Abu Harithah, an individual from one of the Christian delegations from Najran and one of the most knowledgeable scholars, confessed to a friend that he was convinced by what Muhammad (saaw) had said, and when his friend asked him what prevented him from believing, he replied, "The way these people (the Romans or Byzantines) treated us. They have given us titles, paid us subsidies, and honored us. But they are absolutely opposed to him, and if I were to accept him they would take from us all that you see." This proved that what prevented them from true belief was pig-headedness, stubbornness, selfish and petty personal benefit and interest. Then the Messenger of Allah (saaw) invited the Christians to a mutual invocation of a curse if they opposed him and he read to them Allah's saying,

فَمَنْ حَآجَّكَ فِيهِ مِنۢ بَعْدِ مَا جَآءَكَ مِنَ ٱلْعِلْمِ فَقُلْ تَعَالَوْا۟ نَدْعُ أَبْنَآءَنَا وَأَبْنَآءَكُمْ وَنِسَآءَنَا وَنِسَآءَكُمْ وَأَنفُسَنَا وَأَنفُسَكُمْ ثُمَّ نَبْتَهِلْ فَنَجْعَل لَّعْنَتَ ٱللَّهِ عَلَى ٱلْكَـٰذِبِينَ ٦١

"Then whoever disputes with you concerning him (Jesus) after (all this) knowledge that has come to you, Say: "Come, let us call our sons and your sons, our women and your women, ourselves and yourselves - then we pray and invoke the Curse of Allah upon those who lie." [Al-Imran, 3:61]

They took council among themselves after which they declared that they had decided not to resort to cursing and to leave him (saaw) to his *Deen* while they would return to theirs. In addition to this they asked him to send a man whom he (saaw) could trust to decide between them in certain financial matters in dispute among them. So the Messenger of Allah (saaw) sent Abu 'Ubaydah ibn al-Jarrah to judge between them according to Islam.

The force of the Islamic *Da'wah*, the power of the Islamic belief and the strength of argument emanating as it did from the Truth managed to defeat all the arguments raised by the hypocrites, the Jews and the Christians. Their non-Islamic concepts soon vanished and only Islam remained as the overriding and inherently correct ideology, with people now continuously discussing its rules and inviting others to it. Islam became deeply rooted and its banner engulfed all ideological and ruling matters. However, the hearts of the hypocrites and the Jews remained bent on hatred towards the Muslims, begrudging and despising them all the more. Nevertheless, the authority of Islam in Madinah and the stability and solid foundation of the Islamic society dominated everything. The various expeditions and the show of strength displayed by the Muslims effectively managed to silence all sick minds. The Word of Allah (swt) reigned supreme and the enemies of Islam were forced to remain quiet and to submit to the authority of Islam.

The Battle of Badr

In the second year of the Hijrah, the Messenger of Allah (saaw) set out on the 8th of Ramadhan with three hundred and five of his *Sahabah* mounted on seventy camels. 'Amr ibn Umm Maktum was assigned to lead the prayer while Abu Lubabah was left in charge of Madinah. They rode the camels in turn heading towards a caravan led by Abu Sufyan. As they marched on, they sought news of the caravan until they had reached the valley of Dafran where they settled, and news reached them there that the Quraysh had set out from Makkah to protect their caravan. The whole affair then assumed different proportions for it was no longer the caravan, the question was whether to confront the Quraysh or not. So Allah's Messenger (saaw) consulted the Muslims. Abu Bakr and then 'Umar voiced their opinions, then al-Miqdad ibn 'Amr arose and said, "O Messenger of Allah! Go where Allah tells you, for we are with you. We shall not say as the children of Israel said to Moses 'You and your Lord go and fight and we will stay at home', but you and your Lord go and fight and we will fight with you." The Muslims then went silently, and he (saaw) said, "Give me advice O men!" by which he meant the Ansar who had paid allegiance to him at al-'Aqabah.

They had pledged to protect him as they protected their wives and children, with the stipulation that they were not responsible to fight with him outside Madinah. When the Ansar sensed that he (saaw) meant them, Sa'd ibn Mu'adh who was holding their banner said, "It seems as if you mean us, O Messenger of Allah." He (saaw) said, "Yes." Sa'd said, "We believe in you, we declare your truth, and we witness that what you have brought us is the truth, and we have given you our word and agreement to hear and obey; so go where you wish, we are with you; and by He who sent you, if you were to ask us to cross this sea and you plunged into it, we would plunge into it with you; not a man would stay behind. We do not dislike the idea of meeting our enemy tomorrow. We are experienced in war, capable of fighting. It may well be that Allah will let us show you something which will bring you joy, so take us along with Allah's blessing." The Messenger of Allah (saaw) was delighted with Sa'd's words and said, "Proceed with full confidence, for Allah has promised me one of the two parties, and by Allah, it is as though I can now see the place where they will be killed."

The Messenger of Allah (saaw) and his *Sahabah* journeyed until they had nearly reached Badr. They realized that the Quraysh's troops were nearby and so 'Ali, al-Zubayr ibn 'Awwam, and Sa'd ibn Abi Waqqas with a number of his *Sahabah* were sent to the well at Badr in search of news. They returned with two young men whom they questioned. They disclosed the number of the Quraysh at between nine hundred to a thousand men and that the nobles of the Quraysh were out in force to protect the caravan. The Messenger of Allah (saaw) realized that they were facing a force which was three times the size of his own and that he would be in for a fierce battle. He (saaw) informed the Muslims that Makkah had thrown out the pieces of its liver (or the best of her sons) into the battle and that they should harden their resolve.

The Muslims vowed to stand up to the enemy, they settled by the well of Badr where they built a cistern and filled it with water. Then they stopped up all the other wells so that they would have plenty of water and the enemy would have nothing to drink, at the same time they also built a canopy for the Messenger of Allah (saaw) to reside in. The Quraysh took up their positions and the skirmishes of battle began. Al-Aswad ibn 'Abd al-Asad stepped forward to destroy the cistern that the Muslims had built. Hamzah dealt with him by smiting him and sending his foot flying. He fell on his back with blood streaming from his foot and Hamzah followed him and struck him, killing him near the cistern. Then, 'Utbah ibn Rabi'ah stepped forth between his brother Shayba and his son al-Walid. Hamzah, 'Ali and 'Ubaydah ibn al-Harith stepped forward to meet them. Hamzah quickly dealt Shayba a blow and 'Ali soon disposed of al-Walid. Hamzah and 'Ali turned on 'Utbah who stood firm against 'Ubaydah and they dispatched him, carrying off their injured companion afterwards.

Then the two sides advanced and drew near each other on Friday morning on the 17th of Ramadhan. The Messenger of Allah (saaw) straightened the ranks and incited the Muslims to fight. The Muslims were encouraged by

Allah's Messenger's words and went forward. The fighting broke out fiercely and Qurayshi heads went flying from their bodies, the Muslims becoming stronger in belief all the time chanting 'Ahad! Ahad!' (the One! the One!).

Allah's Messenger (saaw) stood in the middle of the melee, took a handful of pebbles and threw them at the Quraysh saying, "Foul be those faces!" Then he (saaw) ordered his *Sahabah* to charge and they duly obliged until the battle was over and the foe was routed. The Muslims emerged victorious, slaying many warriors and tribal leaders of the Quraysh and capturing many more. The Quraysh fled the battlefield and the Muslims returned to Madinah having achieved a truly great victory.

Dealing with Banu Qaynuqa'

The Jews had held the Muslims in contempt before the battle of Badr. Ever since the Muslim victory their contempt and hatred increased all the more. They began plotting and scheming against the Muslims whenever they had the chance, and cared nothing about breaking the treaty that they had signed with them. The Muslims' response was harsh and firm everytime the Jews stepped out of line. A typical tale of Jewish mischief is reflected in the incident that took place in the market of Banu Qaynuqa'.

A Muslim woman went there and sat at a jeweler's shop with her ornaments. A Jewish man approached her from behind and nailed the back of her dress with a thorn. When she arose her garment came off and the Jews all laughed at her insultingly. She called for help and a nearby Muslim responded and killed the Jew. Following this, the Jews assembled together and killed the Muslim. The family of the Muslim martyr called on the Muslims to punish the Jews, they did so and a fight thus ensued between them.

Allah's Messenger (saaw) had asked the Jews to stop their provocation and mischief, but they showed signs of rebellion and defiance so he went out with the Muslims and surrounded Banu Qaynuqa' from every angle besieging them in their quarters. The Messenger of Allah (saaw) decided after consulting the Muslims to kill them all for their treachery. However, 'Abdullah ibn Ubayy ibn Salul who was on good terms with both Muslims and Jews, went to him (saaw) and pleaded with him saying, "O Muhammad, be lenient with them." Allah's Messenger (saaw) ignored him at first and he repeated the plea, but the Messenger of Allah (saaw) still ignored him.

Then 'Abdullah ibn Ubayy ibn Salul persisted in his pleading, so Allah's Messenger (saaw) decided to grant him his wish as a favor to him provided Banu Qaynuqa' left Madinah. They departed from Madinah heading north until they reached Adhra'at in al-Sham.

Managing the Dissension

The Muslims, outnumbered and badly equipped, entered into warfare against the Quraysh clashing victoriously with them in their first battle, the battle of Badr. The result of this victory shook the Quraysh so violently that they almost lost their senses. The victory of the Muslims over the non-Muslims helped to kill off all the Jewish plots, schemes and civil strife inside Madinah, and as a direct result some Jews were forced to sign a peace treaty and others were expelled from Madinah. The might of the Muslims increased, but the Quraysh never rested and wasted no time in preparing for revenge. In the battle of Uhud, in the next year, the Quraysh managed just that, when the Muslim marksmen guarding the *Mujahideen's* rear disobeyed the instructions of the leader in their haste to gather the spoils of war. The Quraysh were overjoyed, and the Muslims returned to Madinah heartbroken and defeated despite the fact that after the battle they gave chase up to Hamra' al-Asad (about eight miles from Madinah).

The defeat of the Muslims had several repercussions. The authority of the Muslims was deemed to have been undermined, and it triggered sedition by groups within Madinah. Many tribes outside Madinah, who prior to Uhud would never have dared to step out of line, also showed signs of rebellion. The Arabs who lived outside Madinah began to think about challenging Muhammad (saaw), as did the Jews and the hypocrites living within Madinah and they began to provoke the Muslims.

The Messenger of Allah (saaw) was anxious to learn about his enemies' machinations, inside and outside Madinah, in order to counter them. He (saaw) also aimed to restore the standing, prestige and the might of the Muslims by crushing any attempt to belittle or harm them.

One month after the battle of Uhud, news reached the Messenger of Allah (saaw) that Banu Asad wanted to raid Madinah and loot the herds of cattle grazing around the city. So Allah's Messenger (saaw) decided to raid Banu Asad in their stronghold before they could get a chance to raid Madinah. This was to be a preemptive strike. He (saaw) summoned Abu Salmah ibn 'Abd al-Asad and appointed him at the head of an expedition of one hundred and fifty warriors, among whom were a great number of the best Muslim fighters like Abu Ubaydah ibn Jarrah, Sa'd ibn Abi Waqqas, Usaid ibn Hudayr and others. In order to keep their mission a secret and retain the element of surprise, Allah's Messenger (saaw) ordered them to travel by night and hide during the day, taking a different route from that usually taken by travelers. Abu Salmah set off until he reached Banu Asad. He and his men surrounded them at dawn and then raided them while calling his men to *Jihad*. They soon defeated Banu Asad, took their wealth as booty and returned to Madinah victorious and proud, thus re-establishing the Muslims' might and reminding everyone of Islam's grandeur and authority.

News also reached the Messenger of Allah (saaw) that Khalid ibn Sufyan al-Hodhali was encamped in 'Urnah or Nakhlah, gathering and recruiting people to raid Madinah. So he (saaw) summoned 'Abdullah ibn Anees and sent him on an exploratory mission to try and gather news about Khalid's movements. 'Abdullah set off and soon met up with Khalid who asked him, "Who is the man?" He said, "'Abdullah. I am an Arab who heard you were gathering people to fight Muhammad and that is why I am here." Khalid confessed that he was recruiting people to raid Madinah. They walked for a while and chatted, then when the two were isolated from other people, 'Abdullah seized the chance to draw his sword and dealt him a fatal blow. He returned to Madinah and informed the Messenger of Allah (saaw) about his adventure. With the death of Khalid, Banu Lihyan of Hadhayl abandoned their plan to raid Madinah. The Messenger of Allah (saaw) therefore succeeded in neutralizing and removing Khalid's threat, and the threat from many other quarters that loomed over Madinah.

However, these events did not stop some Arabs from continuing to show disdain towards the authority of the Muslims in the wake of the battle of Uhud. A group of people from a tribe neighboring Hadhayl came to Madinah and told the Messenger of Allah (saaw) that they were very keen to learn about Islam and requested that he send to them a group of his *Sahabah* to teach them

Islam and read to them the Qur'an. He (saaw) ordered six of his senior *Sahabah* to accompany them. They set off until they reached the wells of Hadhayl in a place called al-Raji'. The men betrayed the *Sahabah* and summoned the people of Hadhayl against them. The six Muslims were caught by surprise and found themselves surrounded by Hadhayl who charged on them. The Muslims drew their swords and fought until three of them were killed and the other three surrendered and were taken prisoners. Hadhayl took the three prisoners to Makkah to sell them to the Quraysh. On their way to Makkah, one of the prisoners, 'Abdullah ibn Tariq, seized the opportunity to break free and managed to get hold of his sword to fight, but he was soon overpowered and killed. The other two prisoners were eventually sold in Makkah. One of them, Zayd ibn al-Dathnah, was bought by Safwan ibn Umayyah in order to kill him in revenge for his father Umayyah ibn Khalaf. When Zayd was brought to be killed, Abu Sufyan asked him, "I adjure you by Allah, Zayd, don't you wish that Muhammad (saaw) was with us now in your place so that we might cut off his head, and that you were with your family?" Zayd replied, "By Allah, I do not wish that Muhammad now were in my place and that a thorn could hurt him, and that I were sitting with my family." Abu Sufyan was astonished and used to say, "I have never seen a man who is so loved as Muhammad's Companions love him." Zayd was then killed.

Khubayb, the second companion brought to Makkah, was imprisoned until they brought him out to crucify him. He asked them to give him time to make a couple of *Rak'at* and they agreed. He performed his *Salah* in an excellent manner and then turned to the people saying, "Were it not that you would think that I only delayed out of fear of death I would have prolonged my prayer." Then they raised him on the wood and when they had bound him, he looked angrily at them and shouted, "O Allah! Reckon them by number and kill them one by one. Let none of them escape." Those present shuddered from his cry and then they killed him. Allah's Messenger (saaw) was very saddened by the death of the six companions, as were all the Muslims. What made the Muslims even sadder was the manner in which Hadhayl had displayed their contempt and disregard to their companions.

Allah's Messenger (saaw) thought hard about this state of affairs and it was while he was deep in thought that a man called Abu Bara' 'Amir ibn

Malik (the 'Player with the Spears') arrived in Madinah. The Messenger of Allah (saaw) explained Islam to him and invited him to accept it. He would not commit himself, yet he was not far from Islam and never showed any signs of hostility towards the *Deen*. He told Allah's Messenger (saaw), "If you were to send some of your companions to the people of Najd and they invited them to your affair, I have good hopes that they would give you a favorable answer." Allah's Messenger (saaw) feared that his companions would be killed by the people of Najd just like those who had been betrayed by Hadhayl, so he decided against granting Abu Bara' his wish. However, Abu Bara' convinced him that he would go as a surety for them and said, "Let them be sent to invite men to your *Deen*, I will protect them." Abu Bara' was a man of good repute, and his words carried weight, any man protected by him would not fear to be betrayed.

So the Messenger of Allah (saaw) sent al-Mundhir ibn 'Amr with forty of his companions from the best of the Muslims. They set off until they had reached the well of Ma'unah, from there they sent a messenger with a letter from the Messenger of Allah (saaw) to 'Amir ibn Tufayl. When the messenger reached him he rushed him and killed him before he had even looked at the letter, then he called out Banu 'Aamir to fight the Muslims, but they refused to do what he wanted saying that they would not violate the promise of security which Abu Bara' had given the Muslims. Then 'Amir appealed to other tribes and they surrounded the Muslims while they were with their camels. Seeing this, the Muslims drew their swords and fought to the last man. All were killed except two. The Messenger of Allah (saaw) was very saddened by this, as were all the Muslims who were deeply shocked.

The Messenger of Allah (saaw) thought long and hard about how to deal with those Arabs and how to re-establish the Muslims' high standing and dignity. He (saaw) realized, however, that Madinah itself was affected, so he opted to try to deal firstly with the State's internal disturbances. Once he had ensured that stability had returned to Madinah, he would then turn to the Arabs and other external affairs.

The battle of Uhud, together with the events of Raji' and Beer Ma'unah once again undermined the authority and standing of the Muslims in the eyes of the hypocrites and the Jews. They began plotting against the Messenger of Allah (saaw) and they waited for a suitable opportunity to deal him a bad turn. Allah's Messenger (saaw) gradually divulged their intentions until he (saaw) had managed to learn about their conspiracies. Then he (saaw) sent Muhammad ibn Maslamah to them and he said, "The Messenger of Allah sent me to you to tell you to leave his land, for you have breached the oath he made with you by attempting to betray him. You have ten days to leave. Anyone seen here afterwards will have his neck struck!"

Banu Nadir would have left had it not been for 'Abdullah ibn Ubayy prodding them to stay; Huyayy ibn Akhtab also encouraged them to remain in their forts. The ten days expired and Banu Nadir remained in their homes, thus Allah's Messenger (saaw) fought them until they asked him to spare their lives on condition that they retained all the possessions which they could carry on their camels. They finally set off leaving behind all that they owned from their lands, palm trees and armor. The Messenger of Allah (saaw) divided their properties among the Muhajireen to the exclusion of the Ansar, except for two men who were Abu Dujanah and Sahl ibn Hanif who complained of poverty. In expelling Banu Nadir, the Messenger of Allah (saaw) managed to quell the internal unrest and restore the dignity and high status of the Muslims.

Turning once again to the foreign policy, the Messenger of Allah (saaw) went forth to keep his appointment with the Quraysh in a last battle at Badr, but the Quraysh did not meet him there. This was one year after Uhud and Allah's Messenger (saaw) remembered what Abu Sufyan had said, "Today in exchange for the day of Badr; our meeting place is Badr next year." He (saaw) stressed the importance of meeting Abu Sufyan so he (saaw) prepared the Muslims for battle. He (saaw) left 'Abdullah ibn 'Abdullah ibn Salul in charge of Madinah and set off with the Muslims until they reached Badr. There they set up camp waiting for the Quraysh ready to do battle with them. The Quraysh, headed by Abu Sufyan, left Makkah with more than two thousand men, but they soon returned.

The Messenger of Allah (saaw) remained in Badr for eight consecutive days waiting for the Quraysh, but they never turned up. Finally news reached him that the Quraysh had returned to Makkah. So he (saaw) journeyed back with the Muslims to Madinah after realizing handsome profits from their trading at Badr. The Muslims returned victorious despite the fact that no fighting had taken place. Soon after, the Messenger of Allah (saaw) raided Ghatafan in Najd and they fled leaving behind their properties and women, which the Muslims took and returned to Madinah. Then he (saaw) raided Dumat al-Jandal on the border between al-Sham and Hijaz. This was intended as a lesson and a warning to the other tribes who used to attack the caravans. But Dumat al-Jandal never confronted him (saaw), they just fled in terror leaving behind their properties which the Muslims also took returning to Madinah victorious.

These raids, and the measures taken by Allah's Messenger (saaw) at home in Madinah, helped to restore the Islamic State's authority and secured its grandeur in the eyes of the Arabs and Jews. The effects of the defeat at Uhud were thus completely effaced.

The Battle of Al-Ahzab

The raids, taken together with the disciplinary action meted out by the Messenger of Allah (saaw) in the wake of the battle of Uhud, had a great effect in restoring the high standing of the Muslims and in reasserting the authority of the Islamic State.

The Muslims' sphere of influence widened and their authority increased dramatically, reaching new heights. The whole of the Arabian Peninsula became cautioned of the might exercised by the Muslims. Whenever the Arabs got wind of a raid that was about to be launched against them by Allah's Messenger (saaw) they would not contest it but rather run away. This happened in Ghatafan and Dumat al-Jandal. The Quraysh were no longer a match for the Muslims and they could no longer dare to confront them on their own. For example, in the last raid at Badr, the Quraysh backed down and did not even turn up. This helped the Muslims to enjoy some stability and gave them some respite, allowing them to concentrate on life in Madinah. They were able to adopt their living in lieu of the recent changes that had taken place. Now that the *Muhajireen* had gained the booties of Banu Nadir such as their lands, palm trees (date palms), houses and furniture, which had been distributed among them, a considerable change in their fortunes had occurred. However, this did not distract them from pursuing their top priority, which was evidently *Jihad*, for *Jihad* has been decreed till the Day of Reckoning. Nevertheless, their living standards had become better and more stable than before.

Despite the serenity in Madinah, the Messenger of Allah (saaw) always remained on the alert fearing the treachery of the enemy. He was forever keen to gather news about everyone and every development taking place in the Arabian Peninsula. He (saaw) would send people on exploratory and news gathering missions all over the land and beyond. He (saaw) was anxious to learn everything about the movements of the Arabs in order to be ready to deal with any hostilities. This was especially the case at this point, now that the enemies of the Muslims in the Peninsula numbered many, which was the outcome of building an army and a State to be reckoned with, and after expelling the Jews of Banu Qaynuqa' and Banu Nadir, as well as after having dealt the tribes such as Ghatafan, Hadhayl and many others a crushing blow.

In light of the above, the Messenger of Allah (saaw) considered intelligence gathering to be vital. In fact it was through this medium that he received early warnings of the Quraysh, combining together with several other tribes to raid Madinah. He (saaw) was therefore able to make advanced preparations to meet the new threat.

It was the Jews of Banu Nadir who endeavored to incite the Arabs against the Messenger of Allah (saaw) in order to exact their revenge for being expelled from Madinah. A number of them had formed a party against the Messenger of Allah (saaw), among whom were Huyayy ibn Akhtab, Salam ibn Abi al-Huqayq and Kinanah ibn Abi al-Huqayq, and from Banu Wa'il were Haudhah ibn Qays and Abu 'Ammar, and it was this party which approached the Quraysh in Makkah. The Quraysh asked Huyayy about his people and he said, "I left them between Khaybar and Madinah hesitating and waiting for you to march with them against Muhammad and his Companions." They also asked him about Banu Quraydah and he said, "They remained in Madinah to deceive Muhammad. They are waiting for you to raid Madinah to help you from within." At that stage the Quraysh were hesitant, not knowing whether to attack Madinah or not. They considered that there was no dispute between them and Muhammad (saaw) except his (saaw) call to Allah (swt) and Islam. They, therefore, wondered whether Muhammad (saaw) was in the right? To lessen their doubts the Quraysh asked the Jews, "You, O Jews, are the first people to receive scripture and know the nature of our dispute with Muhammad. Is our *Deen* the best or is his ?" The Jews replied, "Certainly your *Deen* is better than his and you have a better claim to be in the right!"

The Jews were monotheistic and they knew very well that the *Deen* of Muhammad (saaw) was the right one, but their burning desire to incite the Arabs against him (saaw) landed them in this despicable blunder. To declare that the worshipping of idols was better than the *Tawheed* was their eternal disgrace and shame, but the Jews did it and are ready to do it over and over again.

Once they were assured that the Quraysh were convinced and that they would gladly respond to their call the Jews went to Ghatafan of Qays Ghaylan, to Banu Murrah and to Banu Fazarah, to Ashja'a, to Salim, to Banu Sa'd, to Asad and to anyone else who held a grudge against the Muslims. In time, a number of Arab tribes allied and went out with the Quraysh heading for Madinah.

The Quraysh marched under the leadership of Abu Sufyan. They numbered about 4,000 warriors, 300 cavalrymen and another 1,500 warriors riding on camels. Banu Fazarah marched under the leadership of 'Uyayna ibn Hisn ibn Hudhayfah with a large number of warriors and 1,000 camels. Ashja'a marched under the leadership of Mis'ar ibn Rakhaylah, and Murrah marched under the leadership of al-Harith ibn 'Auf with 400 warriors. Salim and Bir Ma'una's people marched with about 700 warriors. When these had all gathered they were further reinforced by Banu Sa'd and Banu Asad. Altogether the army totaled about 10,000 men and the coalition force marched under the leadership of Abu Sufyan. When news reached the Messenger of Allah (saaw), he decided to entrench himself inside Madinah. Salman al-Farsi recommended digging a trench around Madinah. The trench was dug and the Messenger of Allah (saaw) worked at it himself encouraging the Muslims on with the hope of reward in Heaven. He (saaw) prodded them to double and redouble their efforts and in this way the trench was completed in six days. In addition, the walls of the houses facing the enemy were fortified, the houses beyond (outside) the trench were then evacuated, and the women and children placed inside the fortified houses within Madinah. The Messenger of Allah (saaw) set off with three thousand Muslims, he had his back to the valley of Sal' and the trench dividing him from the enemy. There he (saaw) encamped, and a red tent was pitched for him.

The Quraysh and their allies set off, hoping to encounter Muhammad (saaw) at Uhud, but it was not to be. The Quraysh then marched on until they reached Madinah and to their surprise they found their way barred by the trench. Clearly the Quraysh and her allies were not familiar with this kind of defensive strategy, they were forced to encamp outside Madinah beyond the trench to consider their next move. Abu Sufyan and those with him soon realized that they were in for a long stay by the trench because they were not able to storm it. This inconclusive situation proved troublesome as it was winter, the winds were fierce and biting cold. Under these conditions the people began to feel demoralized, they wished that they could return home. Huyayy ibn Akhtab was aware of this and so he suggested that Banu Quraydah should be talked into violating the peace treaty, which they had signed with Muslims, and joined the coalition. He told the Quraysh and their allies that if the Quraydah did this the Muslims would lose all links with the outside world and the way would be open to invade Madinah.

The Quraysh and Ghatafan were pleased with the idea and sanctioned Huyayy to approach Ka'ab ibn Asad, the leader of Banu Quraydah. When Ka'ab heard Huyayy coming he shut the door of the fort in his face. However Huyayy persisted until Ka'ab opened the door; he said to him, "Good heavens Ka'ab! I have brought you immortal fame and a great army. I have come with Quraysh with their leaders and chiefs, and Ghatafan with their leaders and chiefs. They have made a firm agreement and promised me that they will not depart until we have made an end of Muhammad and his men." Ka'ab was hesitant and he recalled the Messenger of Allah's (saaw) loyalty and faithfulness. He feared the consequences of what he was letting himself into. But Huyayy kept on wheedling Ka'ab, reminding him of how Muhammad (saaw) had treated the Jews and how strong the Allies were, until at last Ka'ab gave way and accepted what Huyayy had asked of him.

Thus Ka'ab broke his promise and cut loose from the bond that was between him and the Messenger of Allah (saaw). The Quraydah, therefore, joined the Allies without the knowledge of Allah's Messenger (saaw). The news reached the Messenger of Allah (saaw) and his *Sahabah* and this caused them a great deal of concern. They feared the worst, and thus, Allah's Messenger (saaw) sent Sa'd ibn Mu'adh, chief of the 'Aus, and Sa'd ibn 'Ubadah, chief of al-Khazraj, together with 'Abdullah ibn Rawahah and Khawwat ibn Jubayr to go and see whether the report was true or not. He (saaw) asked them to give him a sign which only he could understand so as not to undermine the peoples' morale and that if the Quraydah were still loyal to their agreement they were to speak out openly before the people. So they went forth and found the situation even more deplorable than they had at first heard. When they tried to persuade the Quraydah not to dishonor their agreement, Ka'ab demanded that they allow their brothers Banu Nadir to return back to their homes. Sa'd ibn Mu'adh, who happened to be an ally of the Quraydah, attempted to persuade them to stick to their agreement. They spoke disparagingly of the Messenger of Allah (saaw) saying, "Who is the Messenger of Allah? We have no agreement or undertaking with Muhammad." The envoys returned and briefed Allah's Messenger (saaw) of their findings. The situation was obviously extremely serious and fear was everywhere.

The Allies prepared for combat. The Quraydah meanwhile asked the Allies to allow them ten days in order to prepare for battle while they, the Allies, would fight the Muslims fiercely during that time. They formed three divisions to fight the Messenger of Allah (saaw), the division of Ibn al A'war al-Silmi closed in on Madinah from the valley, the division of 'Uyayna ibn Hisn moved in from the side, and Abu Sufyan came before the trench. Panic gripped the Muslims and they became terrified. The Allies' strength was apparent, and their morale very high, they went for the trench and a few of them managed to storm it. Some Qurayshi horsemen amongst whom were 'Amr ibn 'Abdu Wudd, 'Ikrimah ibn Abi Jahl and Dirar ibn al-Khattab made for a narrow part of the ditch and beat their horses so that they dashed through it and carried them into the swampy ground between the trench and Sal'.

'Ali ibn Abi Talib with some Muslims came out to hold the gap through which they had forced a passage. Now 'Amr ibn Abdu Wudd went forth when his contingent had come to a halt and challenged anyone to fight him. 'Ali accepted the challenge and said to him, "I call on you to dismount." 'Amr replied, "O son of my brother, I do not want to kill you." 'Ali said, "But I want to kill you." So they fought and 'Ali killed him. The remaining horsemen fled bursting headlong in flight across the trench. This upset, however, did not affect the Allies' morale it actually enraged them and made them all the more determined to terrorize the Muslims. In the meantime the zealots of Banu Quraydah began to leave their forts and enter Madinah, this was with the aim of terrorizing nearby houses. Torment, anxiety and terror intensified within the Muslims' quarters, but the Messenger of Allah (saaw) was always confident that Allah (swt) would grant him victory.

Relief came through Nu'aym ibn Mas'ud. He had already embraced Islam though his own people did not know it and he came to the Messenger of Allah (saaw). Nu'aym proposed to the Messenger of Allah (saaw) a way in which he could jeopardize the coalition. So Nu'aym went to Banu Quraydah, with whom he had been a close friend in the days of *Jahilliyah*, and reminded them of his affection and the special ties that existed between them." Nu'aym told Banu Quraydah what their fate would be if Ghatafan and the Quraysh were to leave them to face Muhammad (saaw) alone. He emphasized that the Quraysh and Ghatafan might not bear waiting for a long time because they were not inhabitants of that area. He told them that if they were left to face Muhammad on their own they would not be able to do so.

Finally, he suggested to them not to fight alongside the Allies until they had taken hostages from their chiefs who would remain in their hands as security in order to have Ghatafan and the Quraysh stay. Only then should they fight Muhammad (saaw) with their allies until they made an end of him. The Quraydah thought that this was excellent advice. Nu'aym then went to Quraysh and told them that the Jews of Quraydah had regretted their action in opposing Muhammad (saaw) and are working to overcome their shortcoming. He stated that they were prepared to make it up with him by handing over some chiefs of the two tribes, Quraysh and Ghatafan, so that he could cut their heads off. He said to them, "So if the Jews demand hostages, do not send them a single man." Then he went to Ghatafan and told them the same story that he had told Quraysh.

The Arabs' suspicion of the Jews grew and Abu Sufyan sent for Ka'ab informing him that they had been besieging Muhammad (saaw) for a long time and that they should make ready for battle the next day. Ka'ab replied that it was the Sabbath, a day on which they did nothing, no fighting and no work. Abu Sufyan was enraged and he came to believe what Nu'aym had told him. He sent an envoy back to the Quraydah to tell them to make another Sabbath instead of this one for it was essential to fight Muhammad the next day. The envoy also told the Quraydah that if Quraysh and Ghatafan went out to fight alone, their coalition would be broken so they would end up fighting Muhammad alone. When the Quraydah heard Abu Sufyan's comments they asserted their stand that they would not violate the Sabbath, and mentioned the hostages whom they should hold as security. When Abu Sufyan heard this he had no doubt left concerning what Nu'aym had told him. He began to think of a new strategy and he conferred with Ghatafan only to find out that they too had second thoughts about fighting Muhammad (saaw).

That night, Allah (swt) sent a bitter wind and a thunderous storm which overthrew their tents and upset their cooking pots. They were stricken with panic and thought that the Muslims would seize the chance to direct their onslaught against them, so Tulayha arose and shouted, "Muhammad has come after you, so run for your lives". Abu Sufyan said, "O Quraysh! Be off, for I am going." So they grabbed hurriedly whatever they could carry and fled. Ghatafan and the rest of the Allies did the same. In the morning they were all gone.

When the Messenger of Allah (saaw) saw this, he (saaw) and the Muslims left the trench and returned to Madinah. Allah (swt) had spared the Muslims from fighting. Now that Allah's Messenger (saaw) ridded himself of the Quraysh he decided to deal with Banu Quraydah once and for all. It was they who had broken their agreement and had conspired with the allies to exterminate the Muslims, therefore Allah's Messenger (saaw) ordered the *Mu'adhin* (caller to the prayer) to inform to the people that whoever was obedient should not perform the afternoon prayer until he had reached the location where Banu Quraydah was. Allah's Messenger (saaw) sent 'Ali forward with his banner and the Muslims hastened to it full of joy and zeal until they reached Banu Quraydah whereupon they besieged them for twenty-five nights. The Jews told the Messenger of Allah (saaw) that they wanted to negotiate with him. After much negotiation they settled for the arbitration of Sa'd ibn Mu'adh and he gave judgment that, "The men should be killed, the property divided and the women and children taken as *Sabi*." The judgment was implemented, and thus the entity of the tribe ceased to exist and Madinah was rid of them once and for all.

The defeat of the Allies marked the end of any serious attempt by the Quraysh to confront the Messenger of Allah (saaw) and the annihilation of Banu Quraydah meant that all three Jewish tribes, which had originally lived around Madinah and who had agreements with Allah's Messenger (saaw) (which each broke in the course of time), were not there any more. This meant that the supremacy of Allah's Messenger (saaw) and the Muslims over Madinah was absolute and as a result, the Arabs were just as alarmed of the Muslims as ever.

The Treaty of Al-Hudaybiyah

Six years had elapsed since the emigration of Allah's Messenger (saaw) from Makkah. By now he (saaw) had become reassured about his army and the general state of the Islamic society in Madinah. The Islamic State had become a major force of contention for all the Arabs. But inspite of this, the Messenger of Allah (saaw) was continually thinking of new moves which would enable him to strengthen the Islamic Message, which in turn would lead to the weakening of his enemies.

News had already reached Allah's Messenger (saaw) that the people of Khaybar and Makkah were conspiring to raid the Muslims. Muhammad (saaw) designed a plan with the aim of appeasing the people of Makkah. It was hoped that this would result in them leaving the way clear for the Messenger of Allah (saaw) to pursue his *Da'wah* within the Arabian Peninsula as well as to isolate the Jews of Khaybar from their allies, the Quraysh. To achieve this, the plan called for a peaceful visit to the Sacred House of Allah. He (saaw) knew that his plan would be easy to fulfill because the Arabs would not fight during the sacred months. He (saaw) also knew that the Quraysh was divided and had become fearful of the Muslims, therefore they would have to think twice before attempting any rash move against him. So he (saaw) decided to go to the Sacred House as a pilgrim, if the Quraysh were to prevent him then he would use this as a powerful propaganda tool against them and this would serve to further promote the Message of Islam in the eyes of the general public.

With the above in mind, the Messenger of Allah (saaw) announced that he was to go on the *Hajj* in the sacred month of Dhul al-Qa'dah and he sent to the other Arab tribes enjoining them to take part in the pilgrimage to the Sacred House peacefully. The purpose of this last move was to signal to the Arabs that he (saaw) was coming out as a pilgrim and not as a raider. He (saaw) had asked the non-Muslim Arabs to join him although they were not of his *Deen* simply because he wanted to emphasize that he did not want to fight.

The Messenger of Allah (saaw) left Madinah with 1,400 men and seventy camels leading them on his she-camel, Quswa'. He (saaw) was in *Ihram* for the purpose of clarifying to the people that he did not intend to fight and that he simply wished to visit the Sacred House of Allah. Six or seven miles after leaving Madinah, Allah's Messenger (saaw) and the Muslims reached a place called Dhil Halifah, and there they donned the pilgrim garb. Then they marched towards Makkah. The Quraysh heard that the Muslims had come for *Hajj* and not to fight, but they feared that it was a ploy that Muhammad (saaw) was using to enter Makkah. This possibility was never far from their minds and they decided to prevent Muhammad (saaw) from entering the city.

The Quraysh, therefore, appointed Khalid ibn al-Walid and 'Ikrimah ibn Abi Jahl at the head of a great army that included a cavalry of two hundred. The army of the mushrikeen set off from Makkah towards the pilgrims in order to prevent them from going there. They encamped at Dhi Tuwa to await the coming of the pilgrims. Information about the movements of the Quraysh reached the Messenger of Allah (saaw) and when he entered the village of 'Usfan he met a man from Banu Ka'ab and asked him about them; he replied, "There are the Quraysh who have heard of your coming and have come out with their milch-camels and have put on leopard skins, and have encamped in Dhi Tuwa swearing that you will never enter Makkah in defiance of them. This man Khalid ibn al-Walid is with their cavalry which they have sent in advance to Kura' al-Ghamim." Kura' al-Ghamim was about eight miles from Usfan where the Muslims were encamped.

When Allah's Messenger (saaw) heard this he said, "Woe to Quraysh, war has devoured them! What harm would they have suffered if they had left me and the rest of the Arabs to go our own way? If they should kill me that is what they desire, and if Allah should provide me with victory over them they would enter Islam in flocks. If they do not do that, they will fight while they have the strength, so what are the Quraysh thinking of? By Allah, I will not cease to fight for the mission with which Allah has entrusted me until He make it victorious or I perish."

The Messenger of Allah (saaw) reflected on the plan that he had designed and he thought hard about the situation. He had already decided on a peaceful strategy and had not prepared for battle, but the Quraysh had sent an army to fight him though he did not want to fight. Would he go back, or change his plan and fight? He knew very well that the Muslims had enough *Iman* to face their enemy and engage in a battle with the Quraysh if they were left with no choice but to fight.

However, Allah's Messenger (saaw) had not come out for war and he had decided not to fight. He had instead come out to accomplish the *Hajj* and had only peace in mind. He (saaw) thought that if he was prevented from fulfilling the *Hajj*, which is expected, he wanted it to be peacefully; not aggressive prevention nor a *Hajj* performed under hostile circumstances. The peaceful plan which Allah's Messenger (saaw) had masterminded was designed to create public opinion within Makkah and amongst the Quraysh about the glory and nobleness of the Message of Islam, and to contrast it with the misguidance, arrogance and aggression of the Quraysh. This public opinion was crucial and it had to be built if the Islamic *Da'wah* was to have the right grounds to prosper and spread. Public opinion was one of the most important contributory factors which would help to spread the *Da'wah* and enable it to emerge victorious. Allah's Messenger (saaw) was in danger of slipping in his chance to gain the public opinion on his side if he was to fight, therefore he decided not to change his original plan and to continue on in peace.

The Messenger of Allah (saaw) thought long and hard about his next move. His shrewdness and statesmanship were far better than any person. He decided to go with his peace plan, lest he miss the opportunity that presented itself and lest his plan backfires. Under which circumstances the Quraysh would be gifted with an excuse to launch a smear campaign amongst the Arabs against him, resulting in shifting the public opinion in their favor. Allah's Messenger (saaw) then called on the Muslims, "Who will take us out by a way in which we shall not meet them?" A man volunteered to do so and he took them by a rugged rocky tract between passes which was very hard on them until they managed to emerge from it into a valley below Makkah in a place called al-Hudaybiyah. There they camped. When the armies of Khalid and 'Ikrimah saw them they became scared and galloped back to defend Makkah. The Muslims' daring move sent shivers down the disbelievers' spines. They could not believe that the Muslims had managed to out maneuver them and turn up at their doorstep unchecked. The disbelievers stationed themselves in Makkah while Allah's Messenger (saaw) and his army stationed themselves in al-Hudaybiyah. The two camps faced each other and each thought about what action to take against the other. Some Muslims predicted that the Quraysh would never allow them to perform the *Hajj* and that they were preparing for war. They thought that there was no other way for them but to fight the Quraysh, crush them and then perform the *Hajj*. In so doing, they maintained that this would see off the Quraysh once and for all.

The Quraysh, meanwhile, flirted with the idea of fighting the Muslims till it threw them away, even if this meant perishing itself, but this idea soon evaporated for they knew that the Muslims were formidable opponents. Thus, the Quraysh opted to wait for the Muslims to make the first move.

In order to achieve what he (saaw) had really come for, the Messenger of Allah (saaw) firmly adhered to his original plan ever since his *Ihram* status in Madinah. He (saaw) simply remained stationed in Hudaybiyah, waiting to see what the Quraysh would do next. He (saaw) knew that the Quraysh were scared of him and that they would soon send out envoys to negotiate with him about his coming on *Hajj*, so he (saaw) patiently awaited their representatives. The Quraysh first sent Budayl ibn Warqa' with some men of Khuza'ah to ask Allah's Messenger (saaw) what he had come for, and after a short exchange of words they were convinced that the Muslims had not come out to fight but to visit the Sacred House and venerate the sacred precincts.

The envoys returned to inform the Quraysh and persuade them of this, but the Quraysh accused them of being biased towards Muhammad (saaw) and did not trust them. The Quraysh sent out another delegation and it too returned shortly with the same findings. Then the Quraysh sent to Allah's Messenger (saaw) al-Hulays, chief of al-Ahbash (Abyssinians) to negotiate. Quraysh was counting on al-Hulays to stop Muhammad (saaw), they actually meant to incite him against the Muslims. The Quraysh hoped that once he had failed in his negotiations with Muhammad (saaw) his hatred towards Muhammad (saaw) would increase and he would become more determined to defend Makkah. However, when the Messenger of Allah (saaw) heard that al-Hulays was coming he (saaw) ordered the sacrificial animals to be let loose to meet him so as to demonstrate to him and make him realize that what the Muslims intended was *Hajj* and not war.

Al-Hulays saw the animals going past him from the side of the valley and as people about to perform *'Umrah*, through observing their camp site engulfed in an atmosphere of worship, and that they did not appear to be equipped for fighting, he came to be greatly impressed. He was certain that these people really had come to worship and not to fight and so he went back to the Quraysh even before meeting Allah's Messenger (saaw) and he informed them of what he had seen. He demanded that the Quraysh allow the Muslims to perform the *Hajj*, and became furious threatening to withdraw his troops if the Quraysh attempted to come between Muhammad (saaw) and the *Ka'bah*. The Quraysh, however, managed to calm him by changing their tone to a conciliatory one, and they asked him for extra time in the hope of obtaining more acceptable terms. He did so and the Quraysh then sent 'Urwa ibn Mas'ud al-Thaqafi after reassuring Thaqafi that they trusted his judgment. He went to Allah's Messenger (saaw) and tried in vain to convince him to go back.

Eventually, he had to concede that the Messenger of Allah (saaw) was in the right. So he returned to the Quraysh and said to them, "O people of Quraysh! I have been to Chosroes in his kingdom, Caesar in his kingdom, and the Negus in his kingdom, but never have I seen a king among a people like Muhammad among his *Sahabah*; whenever he performed his ablutions they performed ablutions the same way he did. If a hair of his head fell they ran to pick it up. They will never abandon him for any reason, so makeup your mind."

This only served to increase the Quraysh's hostility and stubbornness and further negotiation and debate went on to no avail. The Messenger of Allah (saaw) thought about sending a delegation himself, presuming that maybe the Quraysh's envoys were too scared to approach him. He (saaw) thought that his representative might be able to persuade them and so he sent to them an envoy, but they hamstrung the camel that he was riding on and tried to kill him. Fortunately, the al-Ahbash troops protected him. The Quraysh's animosity grew by the day and they sent their louts out at night to throw stones at the Muslims' camp. This angered the Muslims and caused them in turn to want to fight the Quraysh, but the Messenger of Allah (saaw) managed to calm them down. Next, the Quraysh sent fifty men with orders to surround the Messenger of Allah's camp and beat them, but they were caught and brought before the Messenger of Allah (saaw) who forgave them and let them go their own way.

This last development had a profound effect on the people of Makkah and it proved without a shadow of a doubt that Muhammad (saaw) had been truthful all along. It demonstrated to them that he had genuinely come to perform the *Hajj* and not to indulge in warfare. With this move he (saaw) thus managed to motivate public opinion in Makkah in his favor. Now if he was to enter the city and the Quraysh attempted to prevent him the people of Makkah and the Arabs would back him all the way and support him against them. The Quraysh, therefore, ceased their provocative activities and began to seriously contemplate peace. The Messenger of Allah (saaw) decided to send another envoy to negotiate with the Quraysh and he asked 'Umar ibn al-Khattab to go, but 'Umar told him, "O Messenger of Allah, I fear for my life with the Quraysh, there is no more of Banu 'Adi ibn Ka'ab in Makkah to protect me and the Quraysh know of my enmity and my rough treatment of them. However, I recommend a man more prized there than myself, 'Uthman ibn 'Affan."

The Messenger of Allah (saaw) then summoned 'Uthman and sent him to Abu Sufyan. So 'Uthman went off and conveyed the Messenger of Allah's (saaw) message to them. They said to him, "If you want to go around the Sacred House, go around it." He said, "I cannot do so until the Messenger of Allah (saaw) does so." 'Uthman then initiated peace negotiations with the Quraysh, but they continued to reject the idea. The negotiations were extensive and proved difficult at times, however, the Quraysh's position began to shift from a categorical refusal to an attempt to reach a compromise which would satisfy both parties. They searched together for a way out, they took to 'Uthman's style and felt at ease with him, and so it was that they ultimately endeavored to work to secure an end to the crisis and thereby terminate their state of war with Muhammad (saaw).

When 'Uthman extended his stay and was nowhere to be seen in Makkah, a rumor broke out in the Muslim camp that the Quraysh had killed him. The Muslims were incensed by the news and they all reached for their swords ready to do battle with the Quraysh. At this point, the Messenger of Allah (saaw) found it necessary to review his whole plan now that the Quraysh had apparently betrayed 'Uthman in the sacred month, despite being an envoy. Because of this, he (saaw) said, "We shall not leave until we fight the enemy." He (saaw) summoned his *Sahabah* and stood under a tree where he sought an undertaking (pledge), and it was there that they all pledged to him that they would fight until death. Once the pledge had been given, Allah's Messenger (saaw) clapped his hand against the other as a pledge on behalf of 'Uthman, as if he had been with them. The pledge became known as the Bay'at al-Ridwan regarding which Allah (swt) said,

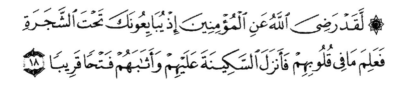

"*Indeed, Allah was pleased with the Believers when they gave their Ba'yah (pledge) to you under the tree, He knew what was in their hearts, and He sent down "As-Sakinah" (Calmness and tranquillity) upon them, and He rewarded them with a near Victory*" [Al-Fath, 48:18]

Once the *Ba'yah* had been given, and while the Muslims were preparing for battle, news reached the camp that 'Uthman had not been killed. Soon after 'Uthman returned and briefed the Messenger of Allah (saaw) about what the Quraysh had said. Peaceful negotiations then resumed between Allah's Messenger (saaw) and the Quraysh. The Quraysh then sent Suhayl ibn 'Amr to negotiate with the Messenger of Allah (saaw) over the issue of the armistice to be signed between the two camps, and as well over the broader issues concerning the performance of the *Hajj* and *'Umrah*. In the case of the latter the condition was that the Messenger of Allah (saaw) should only be allowed back the following year.

The Messenger of Allah (saaw) agreed to conduct peace negotiations on these terms because they secured for him what he had really come for in the first place. It would not matter therefore whether he visited the Sacred House this year or the next. What he (saaw) truly wanted was to isolate Khaybar from the Quraysh and to remove all the obstacles that stood between him and the Arabs which hindered his *Da'wah* and conveyance of the Message of Islam. That is why he wanted to sign a treaty with the Quraysh and hold a truce which would put a halt to their war. As for the *Hajj* and *'Umrah*, he could always perform that next year.

Allah's Messenger (saaw) entered into long and delicate negotiations with Suhayl ibn 'Amr about the truce and its conditions. The negotiations proved to be hard at times and were threatened with collapse had it not been for the shrewdness of the Messenger of Allah (saaw). The Muslims followed the developments closely and thought that the negotiations were about the *'Umrah*, whereas the Messenger of Allah (saaw) was all along aiming at securing a truce. Therefore, the Muslims were irritated, but Allah's Messenger (saaw) thought this to be a blessing, for he conducted the negotiation the way he wanted, regardless of the details and short term benefits. A deal was struck between the two sides once certain specific conditions had been laid down.

These conditions triggered the anger of the Muslims and they tried to persuade the Messenger of Allah (saaw) to reject them and resort instead to war. 'Umar jumped up and went to Abu Bakr saying, "Why should we agree to what is demeaning to our *Deen*?" 'Umar tried to force Abu Bakr to go with him to persuade the Messenger of Allah (saaw) not to accept the terms. Abu Bakr, however, tried to dissuade him from pursuing such an initiative, but to no avail. 'Umar ended up going to Allah's Messenger (saaw) on his own. He spoke to him (saaw) and expressed his anger and exasperation. However, that did not diminish Allah's Messenger's determination and perseverance, reminding 'Umar, "I am Allah's slave and His Messenger. I shall not go against His commandment and He will not make me the loser."

In drawing up the treaty, the Messenger of Allah (saaw) summoned 'Ali ibn Abi Talib and told him to write, "In the name of Allah, *ar-Rahman, ar-Raheem*." Suhayl said, "Hold it! I do not recognize *ar-Rahman, ar-Raheem*, but write 'In your name, O my Lord'." The Messenger of Allah (saaw) told 'Ali to write the latter and he did so. Then he (saaw) said, "Write 'This is what Muhammad the Messenger of Allah has agreed with Suhayl ibn 'Amr'." Suhayl said, "Hold it! If I witnessed that you were Allah's Messenger I would not have fought you. Write your own name and the name of you father." The Messenger of Allah (saaw) said, "Write 'This is what Muhammad ibn 'Abdullah has agreed with Suhayl ibn 'Amr'." After these opening lines the treaty between the two sides was written comprising the following terms:

1) To lay aside from war and refrain from hostilities during the period of the truce.

2) If anyone from the Quraysh embraced Islam and came to Muhammad (saaw) without the permission of his guardian, he would return him to them, and if anyone from those with Muhammad came to the Quraysh, they need not return him to Muhammad.

3) Whosoever wished from amongst the Arabs to enter into an alliance with Muhammad could do so, and he who wished to enter into an alliance with the Quraysh could do so.

4) The Muslims and Muhammad's Companions had to retreat from Makkah that year and return the following year when they would be free to enter Makkah and stay there three nights. They would be allowed to carry swords in their sheaths and nothing more.

5) The treaty was for a limited period of time, ten years from the date of its ratification.

The Messenger of Allah (saaw) and Suhayl signed the treaty amidst agitation and anger of the Muslim army. Suhayl returned to Makkah leaving the Messenger of Allah (saaw) disturbed and exasperated by the reaction of the Muslims. The Messenger of Allah (saaw) felt awkward and depressed about the stand of the Muslims, their eagerness and zeal to fight, and he went to his wife Umm Salamah who was accompanying him and confessed to her his anguish. She said to him, "O Messenger of Allah, verily the Muslims will not disobey you, they only are zealous about their *Deen* and their *Iman* in Allah and your Message, shave your head and slaughter your animals and you will find that the Muslims will follow suit, then march with them back to Madinah."

The Messenger of Allah (saaw) came out and shaved his head, marking the *'Umrah* after which he felt calm and satisfied. When the Muslims saw him in that state they rushed to slaughter the animals and shave their heads. Then Allah's Messenger (saaw) returned with the Muslims to Madinah. When they were half way back, *Sura* al-Fat'h was revealed. Allah's Messenger (saaw) recited it in its entirety and it was then that everyone realized that the treaty of Hudaybiyah was indeed a clear victory for the Muslims.

As soon as the Muslims had arrived in Madinah, the Messenger of Allah (saaw) began drawing up plans to deal with Khaybar and spread the Message of Islam beyond the Arabian Peninsula while strengthening Islam within it. He (saaw) wanted to take advantage of his truce with the Quraysh to concentrate on abolishing a few pockets of resistance and to establish foreign ties. The treaty enabled him (saaw) to achieve this. The Messenger of Allah (saaw) managed to carry out the plan that he had so shrewdly pieced together under the pretext of performing the *Hajj*. Despite all the various difficulties and obstacles, he (saaw) managed to achieve all of the political goals he had set out to achieve. Thus, without a shadow of a doubt, the treaty of Hudaybiyah was a great victory. Some of its achievements were:

1) The Messenger of Allah (saaw) managed to create public opinion for the Message of Islam among the Arabs in general and among the Quraysh in particular. This enhanced the respect of the Muslims and diminished that of Quraysh.

2) The belief and trust of the Muslims in Allah's Messenger (saaw) was demonstrated. It proved that the *Iman* of the Muslims was unshakable, their courage and readiness to sacrifice themselves were second to none.

3) The Muslims learned that political maneuvers were an effective means to promote the Islamic *Da'wah*.

4) The Muslims who remained in Makkah among the disbelievers

formed a pocket within the enemy's stronghold.

5) The Hudaybiyah treaty demonstrated that the method in politics is derived from the same thought (source), truthfulness and faithfulness. However, the means must be coupled with shrewdness, and this can be achieved by concealing the means and the real aims from the enemy.

The Battle of Khaybar

The Messenger of Allah (saaw) remained in Madinah for fifteen nights after returning from al-Hudaybiyah, he then ordered the Muslims to prepare for a raid on Khaybar provided that only those who had been with him at al-Hudaybiyah take part.

Before marching to al-Hudaybiyah, news was received that the Jews of Khaybar were secretly conspiring with the Quraysh to raid Madinah in an effort to exterminate the Muslims. Being aware of this, Allah's Messenger (saaw) opted for a peace plan with the Quraysh in order to secure a truce with them so that he could concentrate his efforts towards taking care of Khaybar. As soon as he (saaw) had concluded his peace treaty, which isolated the Jews of Khaybar from the Quraysh, he turned to Jews of Khaybar and ordered the Muslims to prepare the army just days after his return from al-Hudaybiyah.

The Messenger of Allah (saaw) marched at the head of 1,600 Muslims accompanied by 100 riders and all were assured of Allah's support. They reached Khaybar after a march of three days and took the people of Khaybar by surprise. Although the Muslims spent the night just outside their forts. In the morning, the peasants of Khaybar came out with their spades and baskets and when they saw the army of the Muslims they turned and fled crying, "Muhammad with his force." The Messenger of Allah (saaw) said, "Allahu Akbar! Khaybar is destroyed. When we arrive at a people's area it is a bad morning for those who have been warned."

The Jews were expecting Allah's Messenger (saaw) to attack them, for when they heard about the treaty of Hudaybiyah they considered it to be a let down by their allies, the Quraysh. In response to the new dangerous situation some of them suggested forming an alliance with the Jews of Wadi al-Qura and Tayma' in order to raid Madinah. They would then be without the need to rely on the pockets of Arab tribes, especially now that the Quraysh had signed a treaty with the Messenger of Allah (saaw). Others actually flirted with the idea of entering into a pact with the Messenger of Allah (saaw) in the hope that this would efface the Muslims' hatred towards them. They used to remind each other of this ever since they felt the danger nearing. They were aware that the Messenger of Allah (saaw) had divulged their conspiracy with the Quraysh and that he (saaw) was about to raid them, but they were caught by surprise before they could enact their plans and instead had to call on Ghatafan to help them. They attempted to fortify their positions and resist the attack, but the Muslim army was swift and their defensive lines crumbled.

Eventually, they became desperate and sought peace with the Messenger of Allah (saaw) provided he spared their lives. The Messenger of Allah (saaw) agreed and he allowed them to remain in their homes. Since their land and their vineyards became his under the law of conquest, he allowed them to work and live there provided they gave him half of their crops and fruits annually. They agreed to his (saaw) terms. Allah's Messenger (saaw) then returned to Madinah and stayed there until he left for the *'Umrah* of *Qada'*.

By his abolition of Khaybar's political authority and by making them submit to the authority of the Muslims, the Messenger of Allah (saaw) neutralized the perilous northern path to al-Sham, as he had done likewise in the south after the Hudaybiyah treaty. This action paved the way for the Message of Islam to be spread within the Arabian Peninsula as well as abroad.

Delegates to the Neighboring Countries

Once the Messenger of Allah (saaw) had found his mind at ease about the status of the Message within the whole of Hijaz, he (saaw) initiated his *Da'wah* of relentlessly spreading Islam beyond Hijaz, for Islam is a universal *Deen* and he (saaw) was sent to the whole of mankind. Allah (swt) says in *Surah* al-Anbiya',

وَمَآ أَرْسَلْنَٰكَ إِلَّا رَحْمَةً لِّلْعَٰلَمِينَ ۝

"And We have sent you not but as a Mercy for the 'Alamin." [Al-Anbiya, 21:107]

Allah (swt) also says in *Surah* Saba',

وَمَآ أَرْسَلْنَٰكَ إِلَّا كَآفَّةً لِّلنَّاسِ بَشِيرًا وَنَذِيرًا

"And We have not sent you except as a giver of glad tidings and a warner to all mankind." [Saba', 34:28]

Allah (swt) says in *Surah* al-Taubah,

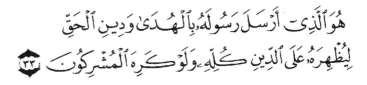

هُوَ ٱلَّذِىٓ أَرْسَلَ رَسُولَهُۥ بِٱلْهُدَىٰ وَدِينِ ٱلْحَقِّ لِيُظْهِرَهُۥ عَلَى ٱلدِّينِ كُلِّهِۦ وَلَوْ كَرِهَ ٱلْمُشْرِكُونَ ۝

"It is He Who has sent His Messenger with Guidance and the Deen of Truth (Islam), to make it superior over all religions even though the Mushrikun hate it." [At-Tauba, 9:33]

93

The Messenger of Allah (saaw) initiated contact abroad once he had secured and strengthened the State and the Islamic *Da'wah* at home. He (saaw) began by sending envoys abroad. He (saaw) considered the scope of foreign policy to cover any part of the Peninsula which was not under his rule. Once the whole of Hijaz had fallen under his (saaw)'s rule, foreign policy came to be defined as the dealings with any land outside the Hijaz, such as the Persian and Roman empires. Now that he (saaw) had signed the treaty of Hudaybiyah and the authority of Khaybar had been eliminated, the entire Hijaz came under his rule, for the Quraysh no longer had the force to stand in his way. The Messenger of Allah (saaw) therefore sent his envoys abroad. However, he (saaw) did not do so until he (saaw) had ensured that his authority at home was strong enough to support his foreign policy.

The Messenger of Allah (saaw) told his *Sahabah* one day after returning from Khaybar, "O people! Verily Allah has sent me as a mercy to all mankind, so do not differ about me like the *Hawaryyun* differed about 'Isa, son of Maryam." The *Sahabah* asked, "And how did the *Hawaryyun* differ O Messenger of Allah?" He (saaw) said, "He invited them to what I invited you, as for the one who was sent to a near place he accepted, while the one who was sent to a far place he disliked and slowed down."

And he (saaw) mentioned to them that he would send envoys to Heraclius (the Emperor of Rome), Chosroes (the Emperor of Persia), al-Muqawqis (the King of Egypt), al-Harith al-Ghassani (the King of al-Hirah), al-Harith al-Himyari (the King of Yemen) and to al-Najashi (the King of Abyssinia), inviting them to Islam. The *Sahabah* of Allah's Messenger (saaw) responded positively and they made a silver seal for him with the words "Muhammad the Messenger of Allah" engraved on it. He (saaw) then sent his envoys with the messages he had written, inviting these rulers to Islam. His message to Heraclius was assigned to Dahiah ibn Khaleefah al-Kalbi; the one to Chosroes was assigned to 'Abdullah ibn Hudhayfah al-Sahmi; that of al-Najashi to 'Umar ibn Umayyah al-Damri; that of al-Muqawqis to Hatib ibn Abi Balta'a; that of the King of 'Uman to 'Amr Ibn al-'As al-Sahmi; that of the King of al-Yamamah to Sulait ibn 'Amr; that of the King of Bahrain to al-'Ala' ibn al-Hadhrami; that of al-Harith al-Ghassani, King of Tukhum al-Sham to Shuja' ibn Wahab al-Asadi; and the message to al-Harith al-Himyari was assigned to al-Muhajir ibn Umayyah al-Makhzumy.

The envoys simultaneously set off, each one to where Allah's Messenger (saaw) had sent them. They delivered their messages and most of those leaders whom Allah's Messenger (saaw) had addressed replied somewhat favorably, while some replied in the negative and very rudely. As for the Arab rulers, the Kings of Yemen and 'Uman replied rudely; the King of Bahrain responded positively and embraced Islam; the King of Yamamah replied that he was ready to embrace Islam if he were to be appointed ruler, so Allah's Messenger (saaw) condemned him. As for the non-Arab rulers, Chosroes, the Persian monarch, was enraged and tore up the message when it was read to him. He wrote to Badhan, his governor in Yemen, asking him for the head of that man in Hijaz.

When Allah's Messenger (saaw) heard this he said, "May Allah tear up his kingdom." However, when the message of Chosroes reached his governor Badhan in Yemen, he inquired about Islam and soon declared his acceptance of it. He remained Muhammad's governor over Yemen, although he was not actually al-Harith al-Himyari, King of Yemen. As for al-Muqawqis, the Leader of the Copts, he answered favorably and sent a present to the Messenger of Allah (saaw). Al-Najashi also answered favorably, and it was said that he embraced Islam. As for Heraclius, he did not actually pay any attention to the message, neither did he contemplate sending an army nor did he say anything. When al-Harith al-Ghassani sought permission to head an army to punish this preacher (Muhammad (saaw), he did not reply to him, but summoned him to al-Quds (Jerusalem).

As a result of these messages, the Arabs began entering the *Deen* of Allah in multitudes, their congregations hurried to the Messenger of Allah (saaw) proclaiming their Islam. For the non-Arabs, Allah's Messenger (saaw) prepared a task force and declared Jihad against them.

The Battle of Mu'tah

As soon as the envoys returned, the Messenger of Allah (saaw) prepared the army and declared *Jihad* outside the Arabian Peninsula. He (saaw) began monitoring the news about the Romans and the Persians, and since he had frontiers with the Romans he was constantly gathering intelligence about them. He (saaw) anticipated that the Message of Islam was about to spread rapidly once it had reached beyond the Arabian Peninsula. Therefore, he was sure that al-Sham (greater Syria today) would be the breakthrough. Ever since Badhan, the governor of Chosroes in Yemen, had embraced Islam, he (saaw) was assured against any imminent danger emanating from there and began to think about sending troops to al-Sham to fight the Romans. So in the month of Jumada al-Ula, in the 7th year of the Hijrah, i.e. just a few months after the treaty of Hudaybiyah, he (saaw) gathered an elite force of three thousand warriors and appointed Zayd ibn Harithah as their commander. He (saaw) said to them, "If Zayd gets hurt, Ja'far should take charge and if Ja'far gets hurt, 'Abdullah ibn Ruwahah should take charge."

The army set off, and Khalid ibn al-Walid (who had embraced Islam after the treaty of Hudaybiyah) was among them. The Messenger of Allah (saaw) marched with them to the outskirts of Madinah, he (saaw) instructed them not to harm any women, those with a handicap, or children, or to cut any trees or destroy buildings. Then he (saaw) and the rest of the Muslims prayed for them saying, "May Allah be with you, protect you and return you to us safe and well."

The army marched on and its leaders drew up their war plan, deciding that it should be a quick and decisive assault. They decided to take the people of al-Sham by surprise, just as Allah's Messenger (saaw) always did in his raids. The army commanders agreed on this plan and set off to accomplish it. However, when they reached Mu'an (north of Arabia) they learned that Sharhabeel al-Ghassani, Heraclius' governor of al-Sham had gathered an army of 100,000 fighters to confront them. The news came as a shock to them and they encamped at Mu'an for two nights thinking what to do now that they were faced with such a formidable army. The most favored option was for them to write to the Messenger of Allah (saaw) informing him about the enemy's numbers, and if he (saaw) sent reinforcements well and good, otherwise they would await his orders.

'Abdullah ibn Ruwahah encouraged the men saying, "O men! By Allah, what you dislike is that which you have come out for: viz. martyrdom. We are not fighting the enemy with numbers or strength or multitude, but we are fighting them with this *Deen* with which Allah (swt) has honored us. So come on! Both prospects are fine: victory or martyrdom." The men were roused by these words and their *Iman* strengthened. They, therefore, went forward until they reached the village of Masharif. When the enemy approached the Muslims withdrew to a village called Mu'tah. There, the battle between them and the Romans began.

It was one of the fiercest battles ever, death and blood baths loomed. The battle was between three thousand Muslims who were ready for martyrdom, and two hundred thousand disbelievers (an extra 100,000 men were sent to reinforce the Roman army) gathered to destroy the Muslim force. The fighting was fierce and Zayd ibn Harithah fought holding the Messenger of Allah's banner, he went forward unabated deep into the heart of the enemy's forces, not fearing for one moment the consequences. He fought bravely knowing that it was martyrdom in the way of Allah, his courage was phenomenal, his heroism unmatched, until he died of the wounds caused by the enemy's spears that ripped his body. Then Ja'far ibn Abi Talib took over the banner; he was a handsome young man 33 years of age. He too fought hard, defying death until the enemy surrounded his roan (horse), so he jumped off and hamstrung her and went forward into the heart of the enemy striking them with his sword until a Roman struck him and cut him in half, killing him. 'Abdullah ibn Ruwahah took the banner and advanced with it riding his horse. He had to put pressure on himself as he felt reluctant to go forward. He then proceeded and fought until he too was killed. Then Thabit ibn Arqam took over the banner and said, "O Muslims! Do rally around one man." So they rallied to Khalid ibn al-Walid. He took the banner and gathered the Muslims around him and organized them trying all the while to keep the enemy at bay. He managed to restrict the fighting to a few skirmishes until night had fallen.

During the night, Khalid ibn al-Walid drew up a shrewd withdrawal plan having realized the magnitude of the enemy's army compared to the meager numbers of his. And following his carefully drawn up plan, Khalid ordered a section of the army to create some uproar and noise at the rear to let the enemy into thinking that reinforcement had arrived. When they did so, the enemy became frightened and refrained from attacking the Muslims, they were even elated when Khalid did not attack them. Then Khalid withdrew and took his troops back to Madinah, not victorious, nor defeated, but having achieved quite a considerable feat.

The commanders of this battle and its warriors had known all along that death was beckoning to them, yet they fought heroically and were killed. Islam commands the Muslim to fight in the way of Allah, kill and be killed, and it is this type of fighting that is regarded as the soundest investment, for it is *Jihad* in the way of Allah. He (swt) says in *Surah* al-Taubah,

$$\text{﴿ إِنَّ ٱللَّهَ ٱشْتَرَىٰ مِنَ ٱلْمُؤْمِنِينَ أَنفُسَهُمْ وَأَمْوَٰلَهُم بِأَنَّ لَهُمُ ٱلْجَنَّةَ يُقَٰتِلُونَ فِى سَبِيلِ ٱللَّهِ فَيَقْتُلُونَ وَيُقْتَلُونَ وَعْدًا عَلَيْهِ حَقًّا فِى ٱلتَّوْرَىٰةِ وَٱلْإِنجِيلِ وَٱلْقُرْءَانِ وَمَنْ أَوْفَىٰ بِعَهْدِهِۦ مِنَ ٱللَّهِ فَٱسْتَبْشِرُوا بِبَيْعِكُمُ ٱلَّذِى بَايَعْتُم بِهِۦ وَذَٰلِكَ هُوَ ٱلْفَوْزُ ٱلْعَظِيمُ ﴾}$$

"Verily, Allah has purchased of the believers their lives and their properties; for the price that theirs shall be the Paradise. They fight in Allah's Cause, so they kill (others) and are killed. It is a promise in truth which is binding on Him in the Torah and the Gospel and the Qur'an. And who is Truer to his Covenant than Allah? Then rejoice in the bargain which you have concluded. And that is the supreme success." [At-Tauba, 9:111]

That is the reason why those heroes fought despite the certain death that faced them. The Muslim fights if there is no other way left but to fight and regardless of whether death is certain or not. In *Jihad*, matters are not measured by the number of the enemy and its weaponry, nor by its multitude, but by the result it achieves no matter how high the sacrifice is, regardless of the outcome.

The Muslims' war with the Romans in Mu'tah was absolutely crucial, the commanders had no choice but to engage the enemy in battle, despite the fact that death was beckoning. Thus, it is that the Muslim should never fear death, nor should he consider anything else but to fight in the way of Allah (swt). The Messenger of Allah (saaw) had known all along that sending his troops to the Roman state to fight them along their frontiers was dangerous, but it was necessary to scare the life out of them and to demonstrate how the believers fight and how their courage and their belief were unmatched despite their paltry numbers. The risk was worth taking for it paved the way for further *Jihad* by the Muslims in order to spread Islam and implement it in the lands that they would conquer. The risk and the adventure was successful for it turned out to be an introduction to the battle of Tabuk and it landed a heavy blow against the Romans who shivered at the prospect of facing the Muslims again until Al-Sham was conquered.

Liberation of Makkah

As soon as the treaty of Hudaybiyah was signed between the Messenger of Allah (saaw) and the Quraysh, the tribe of Khuza'ah came under the protection of Allah's Messenger (saaw) and Banu Bakr sided with the Quraysh. Relations between the Quraysh and the Messenger of Allah (saaw) remained peaceful and both sides resumed their business. The Quraysh expanded their trade in order to make up for what they had lost during the wars against the Muslims. Allah's Messenger (saaw) pursued his task of conveying the Message of Islam to the whole of mankind while simultaneously strengthening the position of the Islamic State over the Arabian Peninsula and providing safety and security within the State itself.

The Messenger of Allah (saaw) defeated the Jewish fortifications at Khaybar and then he (saaw) sent his envoys to the kings of various states and established foreign contacts. He (saaw) expanded the authority of the Islamic State to the point where it engulfed the whole of the Arabian Peninsula. Then exactly one year after al-Hudaybiyah the Messenger of Allah (saaw) called on the people to prepare for the 'Umra ul Qada (making up the Umrah missed at Hudaybiyah) having been excluded from performing it the previous year. A convoy of two thousand men marched from Madinah and, in accordance with the Hudaybiyah agreement, none of the men carried more than the single sword in its sheath as prescribed by it.

However, the Messenger of Allah (saaw) feared betrayal by the Quraysh and he prepared an army of a hundred riders appointing Muhammad ibn Maslamah at its head, with instructions to lead the convoy, but not to trespass the sanctity of Makkah, which they duly obeyed. The Muslims went on to perform the fulfilled 'Umrah and they returned to Madinah without incident. After their return to Madinah the people of Makkah began embracing Islam. Khalid ibn al-Walid, 'Amr ibn al-'As and the guardian of the Ka'bah, 'Uthman ibn Talhah embraced Islam, followed by a large number of people from Makkah. The Muslims grew stronger by the day, whereas fear and weakness crept into the Quraysh's ranks.

When the Muslims returned from the battle of Mu'tah, having suffered a large number of casualties, the Quraysh deemed that the Muslims were finished, so they motivated the tribe of Banu Bakr against Khuza'ah and supplied them with weapons. Banu Bakr attacked Khuza'ah killing some of their men and the remaining Khuza'ah fled to Makkah for refuge. 'Amru ibn Salim al-Khuza'i then hurried to Madinah and told the Messenger of Allah (saaw) what had happened and implored his help. The Messenger of Allah (saaw) replied, "May you be helped, O 'Amru ibn Salim."

Upon this the Messenger of Allah (saaw) decided that this breach of the treaty by the Quraysh could not be ignored nor could it be corrected except by the conquest of Makkah. The Quraysh became afraid of the consequences of breaking the treaty, so they sent Abu Sufyan to Madinah with the aim of strengthening the treaty by asking for an extension. However, Abu Sufyan did not go directly to meet Allah's Messenger (saaw) and instead went to the home of his daughter Umm Habibah, wife of the Messenger of Allah (saaw). As he moved to sit on the Messenger of Allah's bed she folded it up so that he could not sit on it. When her father asked her whether she had folded it because he was too good for it or whether it was too good for him, she replied, "It is the Messenger of Allah's bed and you are a filthy polytheist so I do not want you to sit on it." Abu Sufyan replied, "By Allah since you left me you have turned bad." He then left in a rage.

Later Abu Sufyan managed to talk to the Messenger of Allah (saaw) and to ask for the extension to the treaty which he so badly desired, but he did not receive any reply as he was ignored completely. Next he went to Abu Bakr and pleaded with him to speak to the Messenger of Allah (saaw) on his behalf. Abu Bakr refused to do so. Then he approached 'Umar ibn al-Khattab who rebuked him harshly saying, "Should I intercede for you with the Messenger of Allah? By Allah if I had only an ant I would fight you with it." Finally he went to see 'Ali ibn Abi Talib who was with Fatimah and he appealed to him to intercede with the Messenger of Allah (saaw). 'Ali answered that if the

Messenger of Allah (saaw) had determined a thing then it was useless for anyone to try to talk him out of it. Turning to Fatimah he asked her to let her son Hasan be a protector between men. She said, "None could give protection against the Messenger of Allah." At this point Abu Sufyan became desperate and he rode off shortly back to Makkah where he told his people about his experience in Madinah. Meanwhile, the Messenger of Allah (saaw) urged his people to prepare for battle and he marched with them towards Makkah. He (saaw) was hoping to take the Quraysh by surprise in order to force them to surrender and thus avoid bloodshed.

The Muslim army set off from Madinah to conquer Makkah numbering ten thousand. They eventually reached Marr al-Dahran, which was about five kilometers from Makkah, without the knowledge of the Quraysh. Although, the Quraysh expected an invasion and their leaders were still debating how they should counter it. During this time, the ever vigilant Abu Sufyan came out to assess the danger that was looming over Makkah when he was met by al-'Abbas, who had by then accepted Islam. He was riding the Messenger of Allah's white mule on an errand to warn the Quraysh to seek protection or face annihilation from the Muslims, since the Quraysh were not in a position to stand in the Messenger of Allah's way. Al-'Abbas said to Abu Sufyan, "This is the Messenger of Allah and his army and I fear for you and the Quraysh if he should enter Makkah by force." Abu Sufyan asked, "What is there to do?" Al-'Abbas asked him to ride behind him and together they would go to meet the Messenger of Allah (saaw) and seek his protection. As they proceeded through the Muslim encampment, they passed by 'Umar's fire. 'Umar recognized the Messenger's mule and also spotted his implacable enemy Abu Sufyan.

Realizing that al-'Abbas wanted to seek protection for Abu Sufyan, 'Umar dashed to the tent where the Messenger of Allah (saaw) was in order to ask him to cut off Abu Sufyan's head. However, al-'Abbas galloped his mule there ahead of 'Umar exclaiming as he entered, "O Messenger of Allah, I have offered him my protection." A serious argument between 'Umar and al-'Abbas arose, whereupon the Messenger of Allah (saaw) said to al-'Abbas, "Take him away to your quarters and bring him back in the morning." The next day Abu Sufyan was brought to the Messenger of Allah (saaw) whereupon he embraced Islam.

Al-'Abbas said to the Messenger of Allah (saaw), "O Messenger of Allah! Abu Sufyan is a man who likes to have some cause for pride, could you not do something for him?" Upon hearing this Allah's Messenger (saaw) proclaimed that, "He who enters Abu Sufyan's house is safe, and he who locks his door is safe, and he who enters the Masjid is safe." Allah's Messenger (saaw) then ordered that Abu Sufyan be detained in the narrow part of the valley where the mountain projected so that the whole Muslim army would pass by him and he would see them. Afterwards, he hurried back to his people shouting at the top of his voice, "This is Muhammad who has come to you with a force you cannot resist. He who enters Abu Sufyan's house is safe, and he who locks his door is safe, and he who enters the Masjid is safe." On hearing this the Quraysh aborted their resistance. Then the Messenger of Allah (saaw) marched and entered Makkah, while remaining on the alert. He (saaw) had instructed his commanders to split into four divisions and not to fight or shed any blood unless they were forced to do so. The army entered Makkah meeting no resistance except the division of Khalid ibn al-Walid, who quickly dealt with it.

The Messenger of Allah (saaw) dismounted at the top of Makkah where he stopped for awhile before marching towards the *Ka'bah*, which he circumambulated seven times. He (saaw) then summoned 'Uthman ibn Talhah and he opened the *Ka'bah*. People gathered around him, and he (saaw) addressed them by reciting the verse,

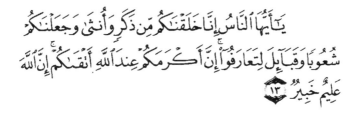

"O mankind, We created you from male and female, and made you into peoples and tribes, that you may know one another. Verily, the most honourable of you in the sight of Allah is that who has "At-Taqwa". Verily, Allah is All knowing. All-Aware." [Al-Hujurat, 49:13]

Then the Messenger of Allah (saaw) asked, "O Quraysh, what do you

think I am about to do with you ?" They replied, "Good! You are a noble brother, son of a noble brother." He (saaw) said, "Go your own way for you are free." Inside the Ka'bah, the Messenger of Allah (saaw) ordered the pictures of angels and prophets which were decorating its walls to be torn down. He (saaw) also found a dove made out of wood which he broke in his hands and then threw it away. Lastly, Allah's Messenger (saaw) pointed to the multitude of idols present with a stick in his hand and he recited the verse,

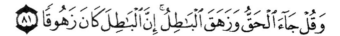

"And say: Truth has come and Batil has vanished. Surely! Batil is ever bound to vanish." *[Al-Isra, 17:81]*

All the idols collapsed onto their backs one after the other, then they were burned, broken up and disposed of. Now the sacred house was finally purified.

The Messenger of Allah (saaw) remained in Makkah for fifteen days, during which time he (saaw) organized its affairs and taught the people Islam.

Thus was Makkah completely liberated and as a result the main obstacle standing in the way of the Islamic campaign had finally been overcome. The great victory was achieved with only a few pockets of resistance, such as Hunayn and the city of Ta'if, remaining in the Arabian Peninsula. These were not expected to prove difficult to remove.

The Battle of Hunayn

When the tribe of Hawazin heard how the Muslims had liberated Makkah, they feared that they might be raided and their quarters stormed by the
Muslims. Therefore, they set about countering the Muslim threat by preparing
themselves for battle. Malik ibn 'Auf al-Nadri assembled Hawazin and Thaqif
together and marched with them until they reached the valley of Autas.

The news of the impending armies of Hawazin and Thaqif reached the
Muslims fifteen days after the conquest of Makkah and they prepared themselves to meet them. Malik did not encamp in the valley of Autas. Instead, he
moved his troops up into the hills of Hunayn in the most inaccessible part of
the valley, where he organized them carefully in strategic positions. He instructed his men to attack the Muslims, once they had entered the valley so as
to cause confusion among them which would lead to them breaking ranks.
The plan was carefully worked out, while he waited there for the arrival of the
Muslims.

After a few days the Muslims appeared. The Messenger of Allah (saaw)
had marched with two thousand Makkans and another ten thousand men from
the army which had entered Makkah. This formidable force marched towards
the battlefield and reached Hunayn in the evening, where they rested until just
before dawn. Then they moved on into the valley during the twilight. The
Messenger of Allah (saaw) was riding his white mule at the rear of the army as
they entered the valley when the enemy squadrons attacked, following the
order of his commander. They showered the Muslims with spears, and amidst
the darkness the Muslims were stunned by the sudden surprise attack. As the
spears hit them from every direction, the Muslims broke and fled in terror,
none heeding the other. They passed by the Messenger of Allah (saaw) without stopping and continued running en masse. Only al-'Abbas and the Messenger of Allah (saaw) were left on the battlefield. As for the rest of the army,
they were as good as defeated and fleeing for their lives. The Messenger of

Allah (saaw) stood where he was, surrounded by a small group of the *Ansar*, *Muhajireen* and his family, and he called to the people, "Where are you going O people?" But the people were unable to hear his call, they just continued running without turning back fearing death all the while. Hawazin and Thaqif chased them and killed them wherever they reached them.

At that moment the Messenger of Allah (saaw) experienced one of the most critical situations in his life. His reaction to the hopeless turn of events was outstanding. With his army in full flight, his *Sahabah* as well as the new Muslims having deserted him, there he stood steadfast calling them all back to him. Some of those who had only recently embraced Islam openly disclosed their enmity and hatred on that day. They expressed their malicious joy at the defeat of the Muslims. Kalda ibn Hanbal said, "Surely sorcery is vain today." Shaybah ibn 'Uthman ibn Talhah said, "Today I will get my revenge on Muhammad." Abu Sufyan said, "Their flight will not stop before they get to the sea."

The prospect of utter defeat prompted those who had embraced Islam during the liberation of Makkah and who had come out supposedly to fight alongside the Messenger of Allah (saaw) to divulge their true nature and intentions. The situation that the Messenger of Allah (saaw) faced was very dark indeed. Instead of retreating (in view of the overwhelming odds), the Messenger of Allah (saaw) remained on the battlefield where he (saaw) proceeded to move forward towards the enemy riding his white mule. His uncle al-'Abbas ibn 'Abd al-Muttalib remained with him as did Abu Sufyan Ibn al-Harith ibn 'Abd al-Muttalib (not to be confused with Abu Sufyan ibn Harb Abu Mu'awiyah), who was holding the nose band of his mount preventing it from moving any further under the dangerous conditions. Al-'Abbas cried out loudly, "O *Ansar* who hosted and protected, O *Muhajireen* who gave your pledge under the tree! Muhammad is verily alive so come on."

Al-'Abbas repeated his cry which echoed around the valley. The defeated Muslims heard him and they remembered the Messenger of Allah (saaw) and their duty of *Jihad*. They realized just what their defeat would entail and just what the consequences would be if they were to be defeated and crushed by the polytheists. They understood that it could mean the end of the *Deen* which they had vowed to protect with their lives. They responded to the call and began to gather around the Messenger of Allah (saaw). They rejoined the battle with great zeal and courage until their numbers began to swell and the battle became fiercer. As this was happening the Messenger of Allah (saaw) became more and more reassured until he took up a handful of pebbles and threw them towards the enemy saying, "Today the faces have turned ugly."

Then the Muslims launched a counter offensive against Hawazin and Thaqif without any fear for their lives. The heavy fighting soon forced the polytheists to realize that they were in danger of being exterminated and they had no choice but to run for their lives. They fled leaving behind them their property and women which the Muslims took as booty.

The Muslims continued to give chase, imprisoning many polytheists on the way. They pursued them even further up the valley and killed many of them. Their commander, Malik ibn 'Auf fled to Ta'if where he sought protection. Allah (swt) helped the Muslims gain a great victory that day, and the following verses were revealed in conjunction with the events:

لَقَدْ نَصَرَكُمُ ٱللَّهُ فِى مَوَاطِنَ ﴿٢٤﴾ كَثِيرَةٍ وَيَوْمَ حُنَيْنٍ إِذْ أَعْجَبَتْكُمْ كَثْرَتُكُمْ فَلَمْ تُغْنِ عَنكُمْ شَيْئًا وَضَاقَتْ عَلَيْكُمُ ٱلْأَرْضُ بِمَا رَحُبَتْ ثُمَّ وَلَّيْتُم مُّدْبِرِينَ ﴿٢٥﴾ ثُمَّ أَنزَلَ ٱللَّهُ سَكِينَتَهُ عَلَىٰ رَسُولِهِ وَعَلَى ٱلْمُؤْمِنِينَ وَأَنزَلَ جُنُودًا لَّمْ تَرَوْهَا وَعَذَّبَ ٱلَّذِينَ كَفَرُوا وَذَٰلِكَ جَزَآءُ ٱلْكَافِرِينَ ﴿٢٦﴾ ثُمَّ يَتُوبُ ٱللَّهُ مِنۢ بَعْدِ ذَٰلِكَ عَلَىٰ مَن يَشَآءُ وَٱللَّهُ غَفُورٌ رَّحِيمٌ ﴿٢٧﴾

"Truly Allah has given you victory in many battlefields, and on the day of Hunayn when you rejoiced at you great number but it availed you naught and the earth, vast as it is, was constraitened for you, then you turned back in flight. Then Allah did send down His Sakinah (calmness, tranquillity) on the Messenger and the believers, and sent down forces (angels) which you saw not, and punished the disbelievers. Such is the recompense of disbelievers. Then after that, Allah will accept the repentance of whom He will. And Allah is Oft-Forgiving, Most Merciful." [At-Tauba, 9:25-27]

The booty that passed into the hands of the Muslims after defeating the enemy proved to be enormous. They counted what amounted to twenty thousand camels, forty thousand sheep and four thousand silver shields. Many disbelievers were killed. A large number, amounting to six thousand, were imprisoned and taken to Wadi al-Ji'ranah. As for the Muslim martyrs they were not counted, however. They also numbered many. Some of the books of Seerah narrate that two entire Muslim tribes were exterminated.

The Messenger of Allah (saaw) left the spoils and the prisoners in al-Ji'ranah and besieged Ta'if where Malik ibn 'Auf had gained sanctuary after his defeat. Ta'if belonged to the tribe of Thaqif. It was built like a fortress and its people were experts in the art of siege warfare. They were also extremely wealthy and had plenty of provisions. Thaqif were experts at archery and they showered a group of Muslims, as they attempted to advance on the city, killing them. It proved very difficult for the Muslims to storm the fort and they instead camped out of shooting range waiting to see what the Messenger of Allah (saaw) would do. The Messenger of Allah (saaw) sought the help of Banu Daus to bombard Ta'if with the catapult and they arrived four days after the siege had begun with their armaments. Now the Muslims attacked with the catapult and they sent out tanks to creep forward and make contact with the city walls in an attempt to burn down the wall of Ta'if. As they approached, however, they were showered with hot pieces of metal which burnt the tanks forcing the Muslim operators inside to flee. Thaqif seized the opportunity to shower the retreating Muslims with arrows, killing many of them. The Muslims failed to storm Ta'if directly so they resorted to cutting down and burning the vineyards in an attempt to force Thaqif to surrender. This Thaqif did not do and time finally ran out for the Muslim besiegers.

The sacred months began and it was the first of Dhul al-Qa'dah when the Messenger of Allah (saaw) together with the Muslims withdrew from Ta'if heading for Makkah. They stopped in al-Ji'ranah where their spoils and prisoners had been left. Amongst many other settlements concluded at this time the Messenger of Allah (saaw) promised to return to Malik ibn 'Auf his family and his assets if he would embrace Islam. When Malik ibn 'Auf heard this news he promptly appeared before the Messenger of Allah (saaw) and declared his Islam to him. Incredibly, the Messenger of Allah (saaw) after having just fought for his life against Malik gave him what he had promised together with an additional one hundred camels.

Eventually, the people feared that their share of the spoils would diminish if Allah's Messenger (saaw) continued to give out the spoils to whoever came to him from Hawazin. They asked that the spoils be divided so that each could get his share. They murmured amongst themselves about these concessions and their murmuring reached the ears of the Messenger of Allah (saaw). He (saaw) publicly removed a hair from the hump of a nearby camel and holding it aloft in his fingers said, "O People! By Allah I have nothing but a fifth of your booty even to this hair, and the fifth I will return to you; so whoever took anything in dishonesty, even a needle, it will be a shame and a flame and an utter ignominy on him and his family on the Day of Resurrection." The Messenger of Allah (saaw) took a fifth of the share for himself and split the rest among his *Sahabah*. From his share he (saaw) gave to those whose hearts were to be won over, those in the past who had been his arch enemies. He (saaw) gave Abu Sufyan, his son Mu'awiyah, al-Harith ibn al-Harith, al-Harith ibn al-Hisham, Suhayl ibn 'Amr, Huwaytib ibn 'Abd al-'Uzza and the leaders of the tribes one hundred camels each on top of their share of the booty. He (saaw) gave others, in addition to their share, fifty camels each.

In distributing the booty, the Messenger of Allah (saaw) showed a great deal of generosity and forgiveness. He (saaw) also exhibited supreme shrewdness and political awareness. However, some of the Muslims did not realize the motives behind these maneuvers. The Ansar, who had been given nothing from the spoils, began to whisper among themselves about these actions of the Messenger of Allah (saaw). Unfortunately, they took the matter to the heart. One of them summed up the collective feelings of the others with the words, "By Allah, the Messenger of Allah has met his own people." Sa'd ibn 'Ubadah went to the Messenger of Allah (saaw) and told him what had happened. He (saaw) asked, "Where do you stand in this matter Sa'd ?" In reply Sa'd said, "I stand with my people." Allah's Messenger (saaw) said to him, "Then gather your people to this enclosure." When all concerned were assembled the Messenger of Allah (saaw) addressed them so, "What is this I hear of you? Do you think ill of me in your hearts? Did I not come to you when you were erring and Allah guided you? Poor and Allah made you rich? Enemies and Allah softened your hearts?" They answered, "Yes indeed, Allah and His Messenger are most kind and generous." He (saaw) continued, "Why don't you answer me O people of *Ansar*?" They said, "How shall we answer you O Messenger of Allah? Kindness and generosity belong to Allah and His Messenger." He (saaw) said, "Had you by Allah so wished you could have said - and you would have spoken the truth and have been believed - you came to us discredited and we believed you; deserted and we helped you; a fugitive and we took you in; poor and we comforted you. Are you disturbed in mind because of the good things of this life by which I win over a people that they may become Muslims while I entrust you to your Islam? Are you not satisfied that men should take away flocks and herds while you take back with you the Messenger of Allah? By him in whose hand is the soul of Muhammad, but for the migration, I should be one of the *Ansar* myself. If all men went one way and the *Ansar* another I should take the way of the *Ansar*, O Allah, send Your mercy on the *Ansar*, their sons and their sons' sons." The people wept until the tears ran down their beards and they said, "We are satisfied with the Messenger of Allah as our lot and portion."

The Messenger of Allah (saaw) returned to Makkah from al-Ji'ranah in order to perform the 'Umrah together with the army. Afterwards he (saaw) appointed 'Utab ibn Usayd as *Wali* (governor) of Makkah and assigned the task of teaching the people Islam to Mu'adh ibn Jabal. The Messenger of Allah (saaw) returned to Madinah with the *Ansar* and the *Muhajireen*.

The Battle of Tabuk

News reached the Messenger of Allah (saaw) that the Romans were pre-paring to raid the North of the Arabian Peninsula in order to wipe out the memory of the spectacular tactical withdrawal which the Muslim army had staged in the battle of Mu'tah. This time he (saaw) decided to face the foreign threat himself, so he (saaw) drew up a plan designed to finally kill off any ambitions that the Roman leaders held about interfering in the affairs of the Muslims or any thoughts that they may have entertained about raiding their lands.

It was the end of the summer, the heat was intense and there was a drought in effect. The distance between Madinah and al-Sham was long and hard and it was not the season for traveling. Therefore, the journey would require en-durance. The Messenger of Allah (saaw), taking these factors into account, uncharacteristically disclosed the destination to his men in order for them to make adequate preparations. In his other military encounters the Messenger of Allah (saaw) always kept his aims a secret, misleading the enemy by adopt-ing a strategy of deceptive maneuvers.

However, on this occasion, in view of the extenuating circumstances, the Messenger of Allah (saaw) declared his intention to fight the Romans along-side their borders from the first day. He (saaw) sent for all the tribes asking them to prepare for war so that as many *Mujahideen* as possible could be gathered. He (saaw) ordered the wealthy Muslims to spend from what Allah (swt) had generously provided them with in order to arm, if possible, the Muslim army to the teeth. The Messenger of Allah (saaw) also began inciting and exhorting people to join in the *Jihad*. In reply the Muslim response varied. Those who had embraced Islam with their hearts full of guidance and light hurried to the call of Allah's Messenger (saaw) with great zeal and courage. Some of them were poor, not even possessing a mule to ride on, and others were rich, they brought all their possessions and handed them to the Messenger of Allah (saaw). It was these who volunteered wholeheartedly to fight in the way of Allah (swt), longing all the while for martyrdom. But those who had embraced Islam for no other reason than out of fear or personal gain - fear of the Muslims or anticipation of gaining a share of the booty - those were lukewarm in their response and they were the ones who began finding excuses. They whispered among themselves about the raid that was to take place in this far off land that cooked in the burning heat. These were the hypocrites. They said to each other, "Do not fight in this heat." Allah (swt) revealed the following concerning their predicament,

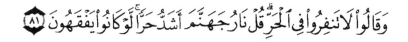

"And they said: "March not forth in the heat." Say: "The Fire of Hell is more intense in heat, if only they could understand" [At-Tauba, 9:81]

The Messenger of Allah (saaw) said to Jadd ibn Qays, "Would you like to fight the Banu Asfar, Jadd?" Jadd replied, "Will you allow me to stay behind and not tempt me, for everyone knows that I am strongly addicted to women and I am afraid that if I see the Roman women I shall not be able to control myself?" On hearing this the Messenger of Allah (saaw) turned away from him. It was about him that Allah (swt) revealed the following verse,

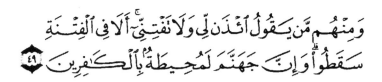

"And among them is he who says: "Grant me leave (to be exempted from Jihad) and put me not into trial" Surely, they have fallen into trial. And verily, Hell is surrounding the disbelievers." [At-Tauba, 9:49]

The hypocrites did not stop there, they began inciting people not to join in the *Jihad* and so the Messenger of Allah (saaw) decided to deal with them harshly and teach them a lesson. When news reached him that some of the hypocrites were meeting in the house of Suwaylim the Jew, where they were plotting and introducing doubt into the peoples' minds by urging them to stay behind and not fight, he (saaw) sent Talhah ibn 'Ubaydullah to them along with a group of his (saaw) *Sahabah* and they burned the house down. Everyone fled the scene and one of them broke his leg while escaping from the building. This served as a warning to others and none of the hypocrites dared to repeat such sedition again.

The firmness and forcefulness with which the Messenger of Allah (saaw) went about preparing the army produced a deep effect on the public and a very large number of troops were gathered. In all, about thirty thousand people answered the call to *Jihad*. The army was named the army of 'al-'Usrah (crisis or hardship) because it was asked to face a formidable Byzantine force in the summer heat far away from Madinah. The army also required massive financing. The assembled army was led in prayer by Abu Bakr, while the Messenger of Allah (saaw) sorted out his unfinished business in Madinah and issued his instructions during his absence. These were that Muhammad ibn Maslamah would be in charge of Madinah and 'Ali would remain behind to look after the wives of Allah's Messenger. The Messenger of Allah (saaw) then rejoined the army and took command. Thereupon, the order went out to move forward. They proceeded to advance en masse in a spectacular display of strength and might which was witnessed by the people remaining in Madinah. Women climbed onto the rooftops to see off this massive force of *Mujahideen*.

The army moved relentlessly towards al-Sham, not entertaining any second thoughts, unperturbed by the heat, thirst or famine. Some of those who lagged behind were moved by this display of strength and courage and so they soon joined the force and marched towards Tabuk where the Roman armies were encamped ready to raid the Muslims. However, when the Romans heard about the size and strength of the Muslim army, the recollection of Mu'tah flashed before their eyes. They recalled the bravery and resolve of the Muslims despite their inferior weapons and lack of numbers. The fact that this time the Messenger of Allah (saaw) was at the head of the Muslim army sent shivers down their spines. They were simply terrified and this led to them rushing back into the interior of al-Sham and the safety of their fortresses.

After their withdrawal from Tabuk the Roman positions on the border of al-Sham became deserted. When the Messenger of Allah (saaw) heard this he moved unmolested into Tabuk, occupied it without a fight and encamped there. He (saaw) chose not to chase the Romans, but contented himself with the occupation of Tabuk and control of the nearby border regions. The Muslim force remained in Tabuk for about a month dealing with those remaining forces who wished to fight or resist them. He (saaw) sent messages to the leaders and governors who were under Roman control in the area. He (saaw) wrote to Yuhanna ibn Ru'mah governor of Aylah, the people al-Jarba' and of Adhrah telling them to submit or face invasion and they yielded to him and obeyed. They made peace with the Messenger of Allah (saaw) and paid the *Jizyah*. Having completely fulfilled his objective the Messenger of Allah (saaw) then returned to Madinah.

In his absence, the hypocrites took advantage of the situation to spread rumors and cause division among the believers. They strengthened their seditious operations within the society by building a "masjid" in Thu Awan, a town about an hour journey (during daylight hours) from Madinah. The "masjid" was used to shelter the hypocrites who tried to distort the words of Allah and who attempted to cause division in society by spreading poisonous tales. The owners of the "masjid" had approached the Messenger of Allah (saaw) as he was preparing for the expedition to Tabuk asking him to come and pray there. He (saaw) asked them to wait until he returned from his trip. On returning the Messenger of Allah (saaw) heard of their mischievous deeds and the truth about the "masjid" was revealed to him. The "masjid" was ordered to be destroyed and it was categorically burned down. The hypocrites were dealt with very harshly indeed. In light of their experience they became terrified and never again thought to indulge in such ventures.

The Tabuk expedition marked the completion of the Muslims' authority over the whole of the Arabian Peninsula. The word of Allah spread all over the land and Allah's Messenger (saaw) secured his (saaw) dominance and established his (saaw) authority without anyone remaining to challenge him. After this time, the congregations of Arab tribes came to him in crowds pledging their obedience and declaring their Islam.

Dominating the Peninsula

The raid on Tabuk enabled the Messenger of Allah (saaw) to secure the frontiers of the State which led the enemies to take the State seriously. It also set the example for all of his (saaw) successors to emulate in order to carry the Message of Islam to the outside world.

As soon as Allah's Messenger (saaw) returned from the raid on Tabuk the whole of the south of the Peninsula from Yemen, Hadramaut and 'Oman came and declared their Islam to him. They submitted to the rule and authority of the Islamic State.

In the ninth year of *Hijrah*, the delegates anxiously went to the Messenger of Allah (saaw) to declare their Islam and that of their people. This marked the total dominance of the Islamic State over the Arabian Peninsula. The only internal threat which remained were the polytheists who had been allowed to continue worshipping their idols and performing the pilgrimage to the Sacred House of Allah due to the agreement that the Messenger of Allah (saaw) had made with them. The agreement stated that the people were not to be forbidden from visiting the Sacred House, nor were they to be harmed during the sacred months.

However, this state of affairs could not be allowed to last, for how could it be that the Sacred House would be able to play host to people of contradictory beliefs, one despising the other? How would it be possible for two conflicting beliefs to come together around the House of Allah when one of those beliefs had led to the destruction of the others' idols? More seriously still, could the adherents of the opposing faith be left to their own devices while the rest of society had submitted to the authority of the Islamic State and the oneness of Allah (swt)? Clearly, polytheism had become an anachronism and a danger to the unity of society and thus it had to be eradicated. Concerning the polytheists, Allah (swt) revealed the *Surah* of al-Taubah to the Messenger of Allah (saaw) after the raid on Tabuk and once the *Hajj* led by Abu Bakr was underway. The Messenger of Allah (saaw) summoned 'Ali ibn Abi Talib and asked him to join Abu Bakr in Makkah where he was instructed to address the people with the new revelation. 'Ali went there and met with the people. Then he, with Abu Hurayrah next to him, arose and recited from the Qur'an,

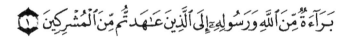

"Freedom from all obligations (is declared) from Allah and His Messenger to those of the "Mushrikun", with whom you made a treaty." [At-Tauba, 9:1]

until he reached the point where Allah (swt) says,

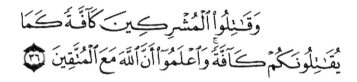

"And fight against the Mushrikun collectively, as they fight against you collectively. But know that Allah is with those who are Al-Muttaqun." [At-Tauba, 9:36]

When 'Ali finished reciting these verses he paused for awhile and then shouted, "O people, verily no disbeliever will enter paradise, no polytheist will go on pilgrimage after this year and nobody should circumambulate the House naked. Afterwards there will be no covenant except for those who had an agreement with the Messenger of Allah (saaw) for a period, he can have it for that specified period." 'Ali declared these four orders and then he gave the people four months in which to return to their homes. Never again after that year did any polytheist go on the pilgrimage nor did anyone ever circumambulate the Sacred House naked.

The Word of Allah had now engulfed the whole of the Arabian Peninsula through the agency of the newly established Islamic State which was, and remained, based on the Islamic *'Aqeedah* as revealed by the Creator, Allah (swt). With the revelation of *Surah Bara'ah* (*Taubah*), the last *Surah*, the abolition of polytheism in the Arabian Peninsula and the founding and establishment of the Islamic State was complete. All thoughts contradictory to Islam were eradicated, and all authorities other than the Islamic State were wiped away. The grounds for carrying the Message of Islam to the rest of mankind were thus firmly laid.

The Structure of the Islamic State

The Messenger of Allah (saaw) ruled over both Muslims and non-Muslims and he (saaw) managed their affairs from the first day he (saaw) set foot in Madinah. Once the Islamic State was founded, he (saaw) set about forming an Islamic society in which the welfare of the people was properly catered for. Acting in his capacity as a statesman he (saaw) signed treaties with the Jews, with Banu Dhamrah and Banu Madlaj. He (saaw) then later signed treaties with the Quraysh and with the people of Aylah, al-Jarba' and Uzrah. He (saaw) also agreed that no one would be prevented from performing the pilgrimage to the House nor should have any fear in the sacred month. As commander of the armed forces, the Messenger of Allah (saaw) planned and executed many military campaigns. He (saaw) sent Hamzah ibn 'Abd al-Muttalib, Muhammad ibn 'Ubaydah ibn al-Harith and Sa'd ibn Abi Waqqas in raids against Quraysh. He (saaw) invested Zayd ibn Harithah, Ja'far ibn Abi Talib and 'Abdullah ibn Rawahah with the authority to fight the Romans, as he did likewise with Khalid ibn al-Walid when he (saaw) sent him to lead the fight against Dumat al-Jandal. He (saaw) led the army himself in numerous actions where fierce battles were fought.

Additionally, Rasulillah (saaw) appointed a *Wali* (governor) in every province and an *'Amil* (Sub-Governer) in every area. For example, he (saaw) appointed 'Utab ibn Usayd as *Wali* over Makkah shortly after its liberation and once Badhan ibn Sasan embraced Islam, he was appointed *Wali* of Yemen. Mu'adh ibn Jabal al-Khazraji was appointed as *Wali* over al-Janad and Khalid ibn Sa'id ibn al-'As was appointed *'Amil* over San'a. Allah's Messenger (saaw) also appointed Zayd ibn Lubayd ibn Tha'labah al-Ansari as the *Wali* of Hadramaut, Abu Musa al-Ash'ari as the *Wali* of Zabeed and Aden, and 'Amr ibn al-'As as the *Wali* of 'Oman. At home, Abu Dujanah was appointed the *'Amil* of Madinah. The Messenger of Allah (saaw) would select those who were best suited for the job at hand. Those who could fill the hearts of those they governed with *Iman*. He (saaw) would ask them about the methods they would employ when they governed. It has been narrated that Allah's Messenger (saaw) asked Mu'adh ibn Jabal al-Khazraji before sending him to Yemen, "What would you rule by?" In reply he said, "By the book of Allah." He (saaw) said, "What if you did not find the verdict in there?" He said, "I would rule by the Sunnah of Allah's Messenger." Then he (saaw) said, "And what if you did not find the verdict in there?" Mu'adh answered, "I would exert my own *Ijtihad.*" Upon this the Messenger of Allah (saaw) said, "Praise be to Allah for guiding the Messenger of Allah's Messenger to what Allah and His Messenger love." It was also reported that when Allah's Messenger (saaw) appointed Abban ibn Sa'id as *Wali* of Bahrain he said, "Be nice to the people of 'Abd Qays and be generous to them."

The Messenger of Allah (saaw) would appoint the most exemplary Muslims as governors. In most instances, he (saaw) would assign the task of collecting the funds to the *Wali* as well as ordering them to bring to the people the glad tidings of the arrival of Islam, acculturating them with the Qur'an and making them understand the *Deen.* He (saaw) would instruct the *Wali* to be gentle and lenient in the face of truthfulness and firm in dealing with rebellion and injustice, and to prohibit people from referring to the tribes and clans if there was agitation amongst them, so that their reference was to Allah (swt) alone without any other associate.

The Messenger of Allah (saaw) would instruct his governors to take the fifth of the booty, to collect what had been prescribed on the Muslims as *Sadaqah* and to tell the Jews and Christians, who had embraced Islam willingly, that they had become believers enjoying the same rights and obliged to fulfill the same duties as any other Muslim. The *Wali* was instructed to prevent any abuse of the Christians and Jews whatsoever. The Messenger of Allah (saaw) told Mu'adh before sending him to Yemen, "You will go to people who are People of the Book. Let your first task be to invite them to worship Allah. If they believed in Allah, inform them that He has imposed on them *Zakat,* taken from the wealthy among them and given to the needy. If they obeyed, do take it from them and look after their money; and fear Allah with the plea of the oppressed for there is no screen between it and Allah."

The Messenger of Allah (saaw) used to send 'Abdullah ibn Ruwahah to the Jews of Khaybar to assess their crops and fruits and collect their dues. They complained to the Messenger of Allah (saaw) about his appraisal and they once tried to bribe him by offering some of their ornaments to him. They said, "Take this and go easy with your assessment." 'Abdullah replied, "O Jewish people! You are to me the most despised creatures of Allah, however, this does not make me treat you unjustly. What you offered me as bribery is forbidden and we do not take it." They commented, "By this, the Heavens and the Earth were created."

The Messenger of Allah (saaw) would check on the governors and administrators and monitor their work. He (saaw) would listen to reports about them. He removed al-'Ala' ibn al-Hadrami, the *'Amil* of Bahrain, because a delegation of 'Abd Qays complained about him. He (saaw) would check the administrators' collections and assess their revenues and expenditures. In one instance he (saaw) appointed one man to collect the *Zakat* and when the man returned he said, "This is for you and this has been given to me as a present." Upon hearing this, Allah's Messenger (saaw) said, "What is it with the man? We appoint him to work on what Allah has entrusted in us, and he says this is for you and this is a present given to me? Won't he stay in his parents home and see if he gets any presents? If we appoint someone to do a job and pay him for it, anything he takes besides that would be ill gained."

The Messenger of Allah (saaw) appointed judges to settle the people's disputes. He (saaw) appointed 'Ali as judge over Yemen and 'Abdullah ibn Nawfal as judge over Madinah. He (saaw) also appointed Mu'adh ibn Jabal and Abu Musa al-Ash'ari as judges in Yemen as well. He (saaw) inquired from them, "What would you judge by?" They replied, "If we do not find the judgment in the Book nor in the *Sunnah* we shall use *Qiyas* and extract a judgment." He (saaw) approved of that method. The Messenger of Allah (saaw) did not content himself solely with appointing judges. He (saaw) also established tribunals (*Madhalim*) to deal with complaints concerning judges and *Wulaa'* alike. He (saaw) appointed Rashid ibn 'Abdullah as an *Amir* of the judiciary and the tribunals of complaints, with powers to supervise the cases brought before such tribunals.

The Messenger of Allah (saaw) managed all aspects of the people's affairs. He appointed registrars, who functioned as the heads of departments of State. 'Ali ibn Abi Talib was the writer of treaties, al-Harith ibn 'Auf was in charge of the Messenger's seal, Mu'ayqeeb ibn Abi Fatimah was secretary of the booties, Hudhayfah ibn al-Yaman was in charge of appraising the crops and fruits throughout Hijaz, Zubayr ibn al-'Awwam was secretary of *Sadaqah*, al-Mughira ibn Shu'bah was given the task of writing all the loan agreements and transactions, and Sharkhabeel ibn Hasanah was employed as the writer of messages which were sent to various kings. He (saaw) would appoint for every department a secretary or director regardless of the number of departments. In these matters, he (saaw) consulted his *Companions* extensively, especially those who showed a large degree of understanding and deep thinking and who possessed great devotion to Islam. There were seven such companions from the Ansar and seven from the Muhajireen. Some of these were Hamzah, Abu Bakr, Ja'far, 'Umar, 'Ali, ibn Mas'ud, Salman, 'Ammar, Hudhayfah, Abu Dharr, al-Muqdad and Bilal. He (saaw) also consulted others as well, but the above mentioned companions were those whom he (saaw) consulted most. In all they comprised the *Majlis al-Ummah* (Assembly of the *Ummah*).

The Messenger of Allah (saaw) levied taxes upon Muslims and non-Muslims on land and on some properties, fruits and livestock. These consisted of the *Zakat*, the *'Ushr* (1/10 of specific crops), the *Fay'i* (war booty), the *Kharaj* (land tax) and the *Jizyah* (paid by the non Muslim covenanted citizens of the State). The *Anfal* and the booties belonged to the State treasury. The *Zakat* was distributed among the eight categories of people entitled to it, as mentioned in the Qur'an, and nobody else. The *Zakat* fund was never siphoned off to pay for government expenditures, as those were covered by the *Fay'i*, *Kharaj*, *Jizyah* and spoils of war. These were sufficient to cover the State's expenditure and finance the war effort. The State was never short of money.

This is how the Messenger of Allah (saaw) founded the system and structure of the Islamic State. He set up everything himself and completed it during his (saaw) lifetime. He (saaw) was the head of State, he (saaw) had assistants, governors, judges, an army, secretaries and a council of *Shura*. This type of structure must be followed and adopted when implementing the Islamic State. Information concerning all these details of the structure of the Islamic State has been transmitted from generation to generation via *Tawatur* (collective and assured testimony). The Messenger of Allah (saaw) held the post of head of State from the very first day he (saaw) arrived in Madinah, until his (saaw) death. Abu Bakr and 'Umar were his two assistants. The *Sahabah* agreed after his death on the obligation of appointing a *Khaleefah* to follow him as the head of State only, and not in the Message, nor as a Prophet, for he (saaw) was verily the seal of Prophets.

Therefore, he (saaw) established a complete system of government during his lifetime. He (saaw) left behind him the type of rule and the governmental structure known by and evident to everyone.

The Jewish Attitude Towards the Islamic State

The Jews did not amount to a serious challenge in front of the Islamic State. What presented major challenges to his (saaw) authority were the Arabs in general and the Quraysh in particular. Therefore, he (saaw) signed treaties with the Jews stipulating that they would submit to his authority and that they would not enter into an alliance with any of his (saaw) enemies. However, as the Jews watched the Islamic State grow stronger by the day and the authority of the Muslims expand, they began defaming and slandering the Muslims. They became further alarmed after the sweeping victory of the Muslims over the Quraysh in the Battle of Badr, increasing their libeling of the Muslims and began to plotting against the Messenger of Allah (saaw).

News reached the Messenger of Allah (saaw) and the Muslims about the mischief that the Jews were up to. This led to animosity and hatred between the Muslims and the Jews and subsequently both camps began to lie in wait for each other. The arrogance of the Jews continued to increase. Abu 'Afak, one of Banu 'Umar ibn 'Auf, would recite poems insulting Muhammad (saaw) and the Muslims; 'Asma' bint Marwan would defame Islam and ridicule Allah's Messenger (saaw); Ka'ab ibn al-Ashraf would intercept Muslim women and use abusive language on them, and would also travel to Makkah to recite incendiary poems against the Messenger of Allah (saaw). The Muslims could bear it no longer and they killed them in the hope that this would deter the Jews. Despite this, the Jews intensified their campaign of hatred and abuse.

The Messenger of Allah (saaw) warned them of the consequences if they did not refrain from insulting and harming the Muslims, but the Jews did not take his (saaw) warning seriously and they arrogantly repulsed him with the following rebuke, "O Muhammad! You seem to think that we are your people. Do not deceive yourself because you encountered a people with no knowledge of war and got the better of them, for by Allah if we fight you, you will find that we are the real men."

At that point the Messenger of Allah (saaw) was left with no recourse but to fight the Jews of Madinah. The Muslims went to Banu Qaynuqa' and besieged them in their quarters for fifteen days, not allowing anyone in or out, preventing anyone from taking them any food. The Jews had no choice but to submit to the authority and rule of Muhammad (saaw). He (saaw) allowed them in his (saaw) mercy to evacuate Madinah with their possessions. This they did and they went out of the city until they reached Wadi al-Qura where they remained for awhile. Then they traveled further north until they reached Adhra'at on the frontiers of al-Sham. With their expulsion, the backbone of the Jews was broken and those who remained submitted to the Muslims for fear of reprisal. When they had regained their strength they resorted to their habits of old. Their hatred flared up once again after the defeat of the Muslims in the battle of Uhud. They began plotting against the Messenger of Allah (saaw) and they eventually conspired to kill him.

The Messenger of Allah (saaw) sensed their true intentions so he (saaw) decided to take the initiative in order to be aware of their scheme. One day he (saaw) together with ten of his (saaw) *Sahabah*, among whom were Abu Bakr, 'Umar and 'Ali, went to Banu Nadir on business. The Jews pronounced their insincere joy and goodwill towards Allah's Messenger (saaw), however, he (saaw) soon felt that they were plotting something. One of the Jews was seen going to one side, another was spotted entering the house from where the Messenger of Allah (saaw) was sitting. Fearing their treachery he (saaw) arose from his position and left at once implying he (saaw) would return, pausing only to ask his (saaw) *Sahabah* to wait until he (saaw) returned.

The Jews did not know what to do and they became confused as they tried to establish a conciliatory atmosphere with the Muslims. The *Sahabah* waited for a while, and then decided to go outside and look for Allah's Messenger (saaw). They found him (saaw) in the Masjid in Madinah and were informed of the treachery of the Jews by the Prophet (saaw). Thereby, the Prophet (saaw) sent Muhammad ibn Maslamah back to Banu Nadir with orders for them to leave the country. Banu Nadir were given ten days to comply with these instructions, then he (saaw) besieged them until they too gave up hope and departed. Some of them stopped at Khaybar and others went on until they reached Adhra'at in al-Sham.

Madinah was, therefore, free from the Jewish mischief and only one major Jewish tribe, Banu Quraydah, remained there. Since they did not violate their treaty, Allah's Messenger (saaw) did not interfere with them.

This state of affairs persisted only temporarily. Because Banu Quraydah had witnessed what had happened to Banu Qaynuqa' and Banu Nadir, and, fearing the might of the Muslims, they maintained a low profile. However, they too soon changed their spots when they listened to Huyayy ibn Akhtab and were persuaded to side with the *Ahzab* (allies) who had come to exterminate the Muslims during the Battle of the Trench (*Khandaq*). They violated their treaty when they prepared to join in on the extermination of the Muslims. Once again they showed the worst malice and treachery for a covenant. As soon as the Messenger of Allah (saaw) had rid himself of the threat of the Allies, he (saaw) turned on Banu Quraydah and besieged them for twenty-five nights. The Jews would not leave their forts and they became sore pressed. Allah (swt) cast terror into their hearts.

Eventually, they sent to the Messenger of Allah (saaw) saying, "Send us Abu Lubabah that we may consult him." Abu Lubabah was from the tribe of Aus, their previous allies. When they saw him they arose to meet him. The women and children came to him weeping in his face and he felt sorry for them. They said, "O Abu Lubabah, do you think that we should submit to Muhammad's judgment ?" He replied, "Yes," and pointed with his hand to his throat, signifying slaughter if they did not comply. Then he left them. Ka'ab ibn Asad made a few suggestions which they refused and he said to them, "You have no other choice but to submit to Muhammad's judgment." The Jews sent word to the Messenger of Allah (saaw) that they wished to be allowed to leave for Adhra'at without their possessions. He (saaw) refused insisting that they submit to the judgment.

In the light of this they asked their former allies the Aus to intercede on their behalf. The Aws came to the Messenger of Allah (saaw) and he said to them, "Will you be satisfied, O Aus, if one of your own number pronounces judgment on them?" They replied, "Yes." Whereupon he (saaw) said, "Tell them to choose whoever they wish."

The Jews chose Sa'd ibn Mu'adh. Sa'd took an oath from both parties that they would accept his judgment. Having done so, Sa'd ordered Banu Quraydah to come out and lay down their weapons, which they did. Then he pronounced the judgment that the men should be killed, their property divided and their women and children taken as captives. When the Messenger of Allah (saaw) heard this he exclaimed, "By Him in Whose hand is the soul of Muhammad, Allah and the Muslims approved of your judgment and on my turn I shall execute it." Then the Messenger of Allah (saaw) went to the market in Madinah and ordered trenches to be dug there. The Jews were sent for in batches, their necks were struck and their bodies buried there. He (saaw) divided the possessions of the Jews, their women and their children among the Muslims, and took a fifth for himself. He (saaw) saved some of the booty and gave it to Sa'd ibn Zayd al-Ansari to go to Najd and buy horses and weapons to strengthen the Muslim army and increase its arsenal.

Thus, Banu Quraydah were exterminated. However, other Jewish tribes were still lurking nearby. The most strong of these were those of Khaybar and they declined to enter into a treaty with the Messenger of Allah (saaw). The Jews of Khaybar had conspired with the Quraysh against the Muslims before the treaty of al-Hudaybiyah. Their presence remained a constant threat to the Islamic State. As soon as the Messenger of Allah (saaw) had concluded the treaty of al-Hudaybiyah, he (saaw) ordered his army to prepare for the conquest of Khaybar. The Muslims set off with 1,700 *Mujahideen*, 100 of whom were mounted, confident of Allah's victory. They went to Khaybar and stood outside the fortresses ready to storm them. Inside, the Jews conferred amongst themselves, Salam ibn Mashkam suggested that they shelter their families and their property in the forts of al-Watih and al-Salalim and store their ammunition in the fort of Na'im. The Jewish fighters then dug themselves inside the fort of Natat with Salam ibn Mashkam there egging them on.

The two sides first clashed near the fort of Natat and a fierce battle ensued. It was reported that fifty Muslim fighters were injured that day. On the Jewish side, Salam ibn Mashkam was killed and al-Harith ibn Abi Zaynab had to take command. He ventured boldly out of the fort of Na'im to chal-lenge the Muslims, but the Khazraj forced him back inside.

The Muslims intensified their siege of Khaybar and the Jews resisted with all their force. The days went by and the Messenger of Allah (saaw) sent Abu Bakr to storm the fort of Na'im. He fought hard and returned empty handed. The next day, he (saaw) sent 'Umar and he too returned without any gain. Finally, the Messenger of Allah (saaw) called 'Ali and said to him, "Take this banner and go with it until Allah gives victory to you." 'Ali went off with it and when he neared the fort some people came out and fought with him. A Jew struck him so that his shield fell from his hand, 'Ali grabbed hold of a door by the fort and used it as a shield. He kept it in his hand until he had stormed the fort. Then he used the door as a makeshift bridge which the rest of the Muslims used to enter the stronghold.

Once the fortress of Na'im was captured the Muslims turned on the other forts and proceeded to storm them one after the other until they reached the last two forts of al-Watih and al-Salalim. By this stage the Jews despaired and capitulated. They sought peace provided that the Messenger of Allah (saaw) spared their lives. Allah's Messenger (saaw) agreed and he allowed them to remain in their land, which became the property of the Muslims after its con-quest, on condition that they handed over half their fruits and crops in ex-change for their labor. Khaybar then yielded. The Jews of Fadak heard of Khaybar's collapse and they feared for their lives, so they sought peace in exchange for half of their assets. The Messenger of Allah (saaw) prepared to return to Madinah via Wadi al-Qura. On his (saaw) way the Jews of Tayma' accepted to pay the *Jizyah* without a fight.

This marked the end of any Jewish authority within the Arabian Penin-sula. Thus, the Messenger of Allah (saaw) achieved stability at home by spread-ing his (saaw) authority all over the Peninsula.

The Continuity of the Islamic State

Once the Messenger of Allah (saaw) died, the Sahabah unanimously agreed on giving the *Bay'ah* to the *Khaleefah* to replace him (saaw) as the head of State. The Muslims continued appointing the *Khulafah* until the year 1342 Hijri, i.e. 1924 CE. They also called this man *Amir al-Mu'mineen* or just simply the *Imam*.

No Muslim becomes a *Khaleefah* without the *Ba'yah* and the Islamic State followed that rule until the last days of its reign. The application of the *Ba'yah* varied. In some cases, the *Khaleefah* was given the *Ba'yah* directly. Some *Khulafah* recommended another person other than their relatives. Some passed it on to their sons or other members of their family. And others recommended more than one person from his family. However, this recommendation was not enough to make them the *Khaleefah*, they had to receive the *Ba'yah* before taking office. No *Khaleefah* has ever been appointed without a *Ba'yah*. The giving of the *Ba'yah* also varied. It was taken from *Ahl al-Hall wal 'Aqd* (prominent and distinguished figures - linguistically the people who loosen and bind); it was also taken from the people; and in some cases it was taken from *Sheikh* al-Islam (the leading scholar). There were certain instances where the taking of the *Ba'yah* was abused. However, it was still a valid *Ba'yah* and not simply a succession to the post of *Khaleefah*, head of the *Khilafah*.

Each *Khaleefah* would appoint his assistants who were in some periods of history called *Wazirs*, (assistants). The *Khaleefah* would appoint the governors, the Chief Justice, the Army Commanders and the Heads of the State Department. This was how the structure of the State was constituted at all times. The structure never changed until the colonial disbelieving powers destroyed the 'Uthmani State and divided the Islamic world into many statelets.

Many internal events took place within the Islamic State throughout its history. This was generally not caused by alien factors, but instead due to a misunderstanding of Islam for the prevailing circumstances at the time. Those who later interpreted the situation attempted to change the status quo according to their own understanding. Each one of them attempted to exert an opinion to redress the existing state of affairs at the time. However, these different opinions were still considered Islamic[1].

Therefore, such differences were connected with the *Khaleefah* himself as a person, and not with the post of *Khaleefah*. For example, differences were about who should be *Khaleefah* and not about the ruling structure. Differences were restricted to some details and consequently, had nothing to do with the basics nor with the outlines. The Muslims never differed about the Book (Qur'an) and *Sunnah*. The differences arose out of their understanding of the Qur'an and *Sunnah*. Similarly, the Muslims never differed about the appointment of the *Khaleefah*, but on who should fill the position. They never differed about the obligation of implementing Islam comprehensively, nor about carrying it to the whole world. All of the *Khulafah* ruled on that basis, implementing Allah's rules and inviting people to the *Deen* of Allah. Some of them actually maladministered the rules of Islam due to misunderstanding them, and some of them maladministered the rules deliberately. However, they all implemented Islam and nothing else. They all held their relations with other countries, peoples and nations on the basis of Islam and for the sake of carrying the Message to the whole world.

Therefore, internal differences never affected the expansion of the Islamic conquests and the spreading of Islam. The Islamic State went on conquering other countries with the aim of spreading Islam, from its inception until the 11th century Hijri (17th century CE). It conquered Persia, India, Caucasia (in Russia) until it reached the frontiers of China, Russia and the Caspian sea to the East. The Islamic State conquered al-Sham to the North; Egypt, North Africa and Andalus (Spain) to the West; as well as conquering

---

1 Translator - There is a difference between an Islamic opinion and the Islamic opinion. The Islamic opinion means that the opinion is the only opinion for the issue. An example of the Islamic opinion is that the structure of the Ummah has to be united without any separation such as borders. However, an Islamic opinion means an opinion amongst many others derived from Islamic sources. An example of an Islamic opinion are the requirements for the post of Khalifah.

the Anadhoul (Turkey), the Balkans, Southern and Eastern Europe until they reached the Black Sea, together with al-Qaram (Crimean Peninsula) and the South of the Ukraine. The armies of the Islamic State reached the very gates of Vienna. It never stopped conquering other countries nor did it relent from conveying the Message of Islam until weakness crept in and the misinterpretation of Islam became apparent. It then rapidly deteriorated to the point where it began adopting rules and legislation from other systems alien to Islam, thinking that they did not contravene the *Shari'ah*, and finally it was destroyed.

The progress and prosperity of the Islamic State was commensurate to its intellectual strength, its creative ability and its *Ijtihad* and *Qiyas* (analogical reasoning for extracting a rule from the Islamic texts). In the first century, its conquests expanded the State vastly and *Ijtihad* reached new dimensions as the State faced new problems in the conquered lands. The application of the *Shari'ah* laws concerning new issues which arose in Persia, Iraq, al-Sham, Egypt, Spain, India and other countries encouraged the inhabitants to embrace Islam. This state of affairs confirmed the validity of *Ijtihad* which was performed and the creativity of the Muslims. This continued until the 5th century Hijri, and then the creativity and *Ijtihad* waned resulting in the deterioration of the State's structure.

During this time, the crusades occurred and they preoccupied the Muslims for a time until they emerged victorious. Following this, the Mamluks came and ruled over the Islamic State, and they paid little attention to the intellectual aspects, so the intellectual abyss expanded and the political thinking stultified. The subsequent invasion of the Tatars resulted in the loss of a great number of books thrown into the Tigris river and the destruction of this considerable intellectual heritage only served to rub salt into the wounds. The intellectual ailment which these factors engendered contributed to the stagnation of *Ijtihad*. The search for new verdicts concerning new issues that arose was restricted to the issuing of *Fatawa* and the twisting and misinterpretation of the texts.

As a result, the intellectual and political level of the State spiraled downward. Then came the 'Uthmanis and they assumed power. They concentrated on military might and conquered Istanbul (Constantinople) and the Balkans and they stormed Europe in a spectacular manner, making them the leading state. However, this did not lift the intellectual level. The military might was not backed up by an intellectual revival and this resulted in the military power of the State evaporating by the day until it completely vanished. In any case though, it did carry the Message of Islam and it managed to spread Islam successfully, for the people of the conquered lands embraced Islam and they accounted for millions who are Muslim to this day.

Two factors contributed to give some *Khulafah* and governors the ability to run the affairs in a manner which impaired the unity and might of the State. Those factors are:

1) The existence of many different opinions (in understanding the *Hukm Sharii* in some issues), and

2) The reluctance of the *Khaleefah* to adopt some specific rules related to the political system though adoption occurred in other areas such as economics.

However, this factor did not affect or endanger its existence. As an example, the rule of the governors was general and they were given wide mandatory powers enabling them to deputize on behalf of the *Khaleefah* over many issues. This developed in some governors a sense of supremacy, becoming almost independent and autonomous. They simply contented themselves with giving the bay'ah to the *Khaleefah* and praying for him at *Jum'uah*, as well as issuing currency bearing his name, and other trivial issues. The authority remained firmly within their grasp and this turned those *Wilayat* (regions) into semi-independent statelets; for example, Hamdaniyeen and the Saljuqs and others. However, this wide mandatory power given to the *Wali* was not by itself the cause of the State disintegrating into statelets.

As an example, the governership of 'Amr ibn al-'As over Egypt had wide mandatory power, as was that of Mu'awiyah ibn Abi Sufyan's over al-Sham and these governors never separated themselves from the *Khilafah*. However, when the *Khulafah* weakened and accepted the status quo from the *Wulaa'*, this trend took root and each *Wilayah* acted like a state of its own even though they remained part of a single State and under one system of government. Despite all of this the State still remained intact, a single unity, where the *Khaleefah* always appointed and removed *Wulaa'*. No matter how powerful a *Wali* became, he never dared to disassociate officially from the rule of the *Khaleefah*. The Islamic State was never at any time a confederation of *Wilayat*, even at the height of the independence enjoyed by the *Wulaa'*. It always remained one State with one *Khaleefah* who was the only body with mandatory powers engulfing the whole State, including the small villages.

As for the issue concerning the *Khilafah* in Spain and the birth of the Fatimid State in Egypt, these are different from the issues of the governors. In the case of Spain, the governors actually took over the *Wilayah* and declared independence, but the *Wali* there was never given *Ba'yah* as a *Khaleefah* for all Muslims. However, later he carried the title of *Khaleefah* of the people of that *Wilayah*, but not over all the Muslims. The *Khaleefah* of the Muslims remained one and the ruling belonged to him. The *Wilayah* of Spain in that situation was regarded as a *Wilayah* which was not under the authority of the *Khaleefah*. This was also the case for Iran during the 'Uthmani rule, as there was no *Khaleefah* there, but Iran was a *Wilayah* outside the rule of the *Khaleefah*. As for the Fatimids in Egypt, it was established by the Ismailis, which is a non-Islamic sect.

Therefore, their action cannot be considered a legitimate one and their state cannot be considered Islamic one. Their presence along with the presence of the Abbasid *Khilafah* cannot be considered a presence of multiple *Khilafah* since the Fatimids was not a legitimate *Khilafah*. It was a coup attempt orchestrated by this sect to change the Islamic State to one that is controlled by their false understanding. Therefore, the Islamic State remained one unit without division, it was never divided into states, although there were some attempts to capture the rule based on specific understanding. These attempts failed and the State remained One.

The Islamic State remained one and undivided, it was not a group of states, what took place was a host of attempts to seize power with a desire to implement a certain Islamic understanding of ruling. These attempts eventually came to an end and the *Khilafah* reverted to a single entity. The proof of the unity of the Islamic State despite the existence of numerous ruling situations can easily be demonstrated by considering that the Muslim could travel at that time from one *Wilayah* to another. From East to West, wherever Islam reigned, without being asked about his origins and without being restricted, for the Islamic domain was one single land.

This is how the Islamic State has always united Muslims under one jurisdiction and remained as such. It remained strong and prosperous until the colonial disbelieving forces destroyed it as a State in 1924 when they abolished the *Khilafah* at the hands of Mustafa Kamal.

The Domestic Policy of the Islamic State

The domestic policy of the Islamic State is to execute the rules of Islam internally. The Islamic State would implement these rules in the land which were under its jurisdiction. It organized and supervised relationships and transactions, implemented the hudud, carried out punishments, enforced high morals, ensured the performance of the Islamic rituals and acts of worship, as well as looking after the citizens' affairs according to the rules of Islam. Islam has determined the method by which its rules are to be implemented on the people who submit to its authority, whether Muslims or otherwise. The Islamic State implemented the rules of Islam following this specific method. Since, the method is by itself a *Hukm Sharii*, as well as the rules concerning the issues. Islam came to address all people, for Allah (swt) addressed all mankind with Islam as human beings and nothing else. Allah (swt) says,

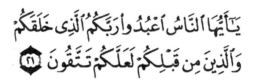

"O Mankind! Worship your Lord (Allah), Who created you and those who were before you so that you may become Al-Muttaqun (the pious)." [Al-Baqarah, 2:21]

He (swt) also says,

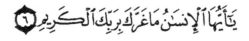

"O man! What has made you careless concerning your Lord, the Most Generous?" [Al-Infitar, 82:6]

134

The scholars of *Usul ul-Fiqh* (foundation of jurisprudence) considered the *Shari'yah* as being addressed to every human mind capable of understanding, be it Muslim or not. Imam al-Ghazali said in his book *Al-Mustasfa fi al-Usul*,

> "Verily the governed must be a responsible person in a legal capacity, the condition being that he is sane and able to understand the address of the Legislator. What qualifies the person to be liable to observe the rules is his human nature which enables him to accommodate the mental capability by which he receives and understands the commandments of Allah."

Therefore, all humans have been addressed by Islam. This address has taken the form of an invitation and an obligation, the first one being intended to invite people to embrace Islam and the latter intending to oblige people to adhere to its rules; this is regarding people in general. As for those whom the Islamic State rules over, Islam considers these as a group of humans who abide by that rule, regardless of their sect, race or creed. All that is required from them is simply allegiance to the State and the ruling system.

Ethnic minorities do not exist as all people are viewed from a humanistic point of view and are citizens of the Islamic State so long as they fulfill the duties of citizenship. Every person holding the citizenship of the State enjoys the full rights decreed for him by the *Shari'ah*, whether he is Muslim or not. Anyone not holding that citizenship is deprived of these rights, even if he were Muslim. For instance, if a Muslim man had a Christian mother who held the Islamic citizenship and a father who did not, then his mother would qualify to receive sustenance from him and his father would not. If the mother claimed it from him the judge would rule in her favor because she would be classified as a citizen of the Islamic State, whereas if the father attempted to do likewise the judge would reject his claim because he would not be classified as one of its citizens. Therefore, the *Shari'ah* considers those ruled by Islam as citizens and made the citizenship something which they all hold in common and which qualifies them to enjoy the rights of guardianship and welfare decreed by Islam by living in the Islamic State as citizens.

This is regarding their position from a ruling and guardianship point of view. As for the application of the Islamic laws, this is considered from a legal point of view and not from a religious point of view. This is so, because the *Shari'ah* texts should be viewed from a legal aspect and the text has been decreed to deal with problems. The Legislator's aim for us is to follow the meaning and the content and not to stop at the apparent meaning of the text. Therefore the *'illah* (reason) behind the ruling is taken into consideration when extracting a rule. In other words, it is the legislative side of the text that is taken into consideration when viewing a verdict. This verdict, if adopted by the *Khaleefah*, becomes law and everyone is obliged by it and to execute it.

Therefore, the submission of all people living in the Islamic State to the *Shari'yah* is conclusive and irrevocable. For the Muslims, it is their belief and their embracing of Islam which covenants them to abide by all its laws because the submission to the belief means submission to all the rules which emanate from that *'Aqeedah*, so their embracing of that *'Aqeedah* obliges them to conclusively abide by all the laws brought by that *'Aqeedah*. Thus, for the Muslims, the *Shari'ah* is the legislative part of Islam. They are covenanted to carry out all of its rules, whether those related to their relationship with Allah, which are acts of *'Ibadah* (worship), or those related to their relationship with themselves, such as their morals and diet, or those related to their relationship with others, these being concerned with transactions and penalties.

The Muslims are united under the Islamic *'Aqeedah* and by the fact that the Qur'an and the *Sunnah* are sources of *Shari'ah*, whereas the principles and verdicts are derived from it. None of them has differed on this issue at all. However, due to *Ijtihad*, they have differed in the understanding of the Qur'an and the *Sunnah*, and as a result of this difference different schools of thought and sects emerged. This was due to the fact that Islam encouraged the Muslims to make *Ijtihad* and to the fact that there are natural variances in understanding. Therefore, differences emerged in the understanding of the *'Aqeedah*, the legislation, and methodology of *'Usul ul Fiqh*. The Messenger of Allah (saaw) had encouraged *Ijtihad* and stressed that if the *Mujtahid* (one qualified to extract rules) makes *Ijtihad* and he errs, he receives a reward and if he is right his reward is doubled. Therefore, it was never surprising to find the *Sunnah*, *Shi'ah*, *Mu'tazilah*, and other sects. Nor was it surprising to witness the emergence of several *Madhahib* such as the *Shafi'i*, the *Hanafi*, the *Maliki*, the *Hanbali*, the *Ja'fari*, the *Zaydi* and others. All these Islamic sects and *Madhahib* embraced one single *'Aqeedah*, i.e. the Islamic *'Aqeedah*, they were all commanded to follow the obligations and abstain from the prohibitions of Allah (swt).They were all under the obligation to abide by the *Shari'ah* and not by any particular *Madhahib* .

The *Madhahib* is only a particular understanding of the *Shari'ah* verdict which is followed by the *Muqallid* (the one who is not a *Mujtahid*) if he is unable to make his own *Ijtihad*. The Muslim is commanded by the Divine rule and not by the *Madhab*. He takes the rule by means of *Ijtihad* if he can, otherwise he takes it by following a *Madhab* if he is unable to make *Ijtihad*. Therefore, all the sects and *Madhahib* which embraced the Islamic *'Aqeedah*, and believed in the Qur'an and *Sunnah* - as the sole source of *Shari'ah* - are all Islamic. Their advocates are all Muslims and the Islamic laws are to be implemented on them. The State should not, therefore, interfere with these groups nor with the followers of various *Madhahib* as long as they do not deviate from the Islamic *'Aqeedah*, but if they deviated from the Islamic *'Aqeedah*, whether individually or collectively, this would be considered an act of *Irtidad* (apostasy) from Islam and the punishment of apostates would be carried out on them. The Muslims are compelled by all Islamic laws. Some of these laws are definite with only one valid opinion, like the cutting of the hand of the thief, the prohibition of usury, the obligation of *Zakah*, and the obligatory prayers being five, etc. These laws are binding on all Muslims following one single understanding, for they are definite and decisive.

There are several rules and thoughts on which the Muslims differed, due to each *Mujtahid* understanding an issue differently from the other. For example, the prerequisite of the *Khaleefah* or the taking of the tithe on the *Kharaj* land or the rental of land, amongst others. In the case of such laws, the *Khaleefah* adopts an opinion and obedience becomes compulsory on everyone. Everyone who holds a different opinion to that adopted by the *Khaleefah* should abandon that opinion and comply with the Imam's opinion. Thus the opinion of the *Imam* settles all the differences and the obedience to the *Imam* is compulsory on everyone. The Muslims are all obliged to execute the order of the *Khaleefah* concerning the opinions which he adopts and his opinion is binding on them, both publicly and privately. Whoever implements a Divine rule other than the one adopted by the *Imam* will be sinful. Once the *Khaleefah* enacts a *Shari'ah* rule it becomes binding upon all Muslims. The *Shari'ah* rule concerning one issue cannot be multiple for one person.

However, the *Khaleefah* should not adopt a particular law which concerns matters related to the *'Aqeedah*, because this would cause hardship on the Muslims. But if innovations and tendencies based on erroneous *'Aqa'id* emerged, the State would hold accountable the culprits with firm measures as long as these innovations do not lead to disbelief. If they did, the responsible individuals would be treated as apostates. Also, the *Khaleefah* should not adopt any particular law which concerns matters related to worship because this too would lead to a hardship for the Muslims.

Therefore, the *Khaleefah* should not adopt any particular opinion in matters of *'Aqeedah* as long as these were Islamic, and he does not adopt any particular law in matters of worship, except for *Zakat*, as long as these acts of worship are approved Divine laws. Other than that, the *Khaleefah* can adopt and enact any particular law related to transactions, ranging from buying and selling, renting, marriage, divorce, alimony, business partnership, custody, etc. He can also enact and adopt a particular law concerning the penal code, or concerning diet, clothing or moral issues, and the Muslims are obliged to obey him in whatever he adopts.

The *Khaleefah* has to implement the *Shari'yah* related to the acts of ritual worship. He punishes those who abandon the prayer and those who do not observe fasting in the month of *Ramadhan*. He implements all laws regarding acts of worship in addition to all of the *Shari'yah* and this is his duty. The obligation of prayer is not a matter open for *Ijtihad* and cannot be considered as a law being adopted, it is plainly the implementation of a Divine rule that has been conclusively established among everyone. As for the penal code, the *Khaleefah* adopts a law which all Muslims will be ordered to comply with, the same as for any other penal code. This is as far as the Muslims are concerned. As for the non-Muslims, these are the people who have embraced a creed other than the Islamic one, and they are classified under the following categories:

1) Those who claim to be Muslims while believing in some issues in their creed which contradicts the Islamic *'Aqeedah*.

2) The People of the Book.

3) The Polytheists, among whom are the *Majus* (fire worshippers), Hindus, Buddhists and all those who are not People of the Book.

These people will be left alone and there is no interference with their beliefs or their worship. They will be allowed to adhere to their own laws in matters of marriage and divorce according to their religion. The State will appoint a judge from their own people to settle their disputes based on their religion in courts belonging to the State. As for their diet and adornment, they will be treated according to their own rules within the public order. People other than the People of the Book will be treated in the same way. The Messenger of Allah (saaw) said concerning the *Majus*, "Treat them in the same way you treat the People of the Book."

As for transactions and penal code, they are implemented on Muslims and non-Muslims alike. Penal judgments will be passed on non-Muslims in the same way as on Muslims without any prejudice. All those who hold the citizenship of the Islamic State are obliged to comply with the *Shari'yah* related to transactions and penal codes regardless of their religion, race, or sect. They all have to abide by the *Shari'yah*. However, their adherence to the laws would be legislative and legal rather than religious or spiritual. They would therefore not be obliged to believe in them because that would constitute them being forced to embrace Islam; Allah (swt) says,

"No compulsion in the Deen." [Al-Baqarah, 2:256]

The Messenger of Allah (saaw) has forbidden the Muslims from interfering with or persecuting the People of the Book about their belief, but they would be obliged to comply with the Islamic laws from a legislative and legal point of view.

In conclusion, the Islamic State's domestic policy would be to implement the Islamic *Shari'ah* on all those who hold the State's citizenship, whether they were Muslims or non-Muslims. The laws would be implemented as follows:

1) All Islamic laws would be implemented upon the Muslims.

2) Non-Muslims would not be interfered with regarding their beliefs and worship.

3) The non-Muslims would be treated according to their beliefs in matters related to diet and adornment within the general frame work of the law.

4) Disputes related to marriage and divorce for non-Muslims would be dealt with by appointing judges from themselves in courts set up by the State and not in private courts; similar disputes between them and the Muslims would be dealt with according to Islamic law by Muslim judges.

5) The State will enforce all other *Shari'ah* matters related to economic, social, and legal transactions on every citizen Muslim and non-Muslim alike without prejudice.

6) All those who hold the Islamic citizenship are subjects of the State, their guardianship and the management of their affairs is the duty of the State, without any discrimination.

The Foreign Policy of the Islamic State

The foreign policy is the State's relationship with other states. This relationship entails looking after the foreign affairs of the *Ummah*. The Islamic State's foreign policy is based on a fixed concept that does not change. This is the propagation of Islam and the conveyance of the Message to every nation and every society. This is the very basis of the Islamic State's foreign policy. The basis never changes and never differs or varies no matter who rules the State. This basis has always been maintained and it has been carried out at all times, from the time when the Messenger of Allah (saaw) settled in Madinah to the last day of the 'Uthmani State.

The Messenger of Allah (saaw) set up the policy of the Islamic State on the basis of spreading Islam since the very first day he (saaw) arrived in Madinah. He (saaw) signed treaties with the Jews in order to concentrate on extending the Message in Hijaz. He (saaw) signed the treaty of al-Hudaybiyah with the Quraysh in order to spread the Message in the Arabian Peninsula. Finally, he (saaw) sent envoys to the countries outside the Peninsula with the aim of establishing relations based on the spreading of Islam, by inviting them to embrace it.

Afterwards, came his *Khulafa'*. They also established relations with all the other states on the basis of spreading Islam, and they too continued to carry the Message of Islam to the world. All the Muslim rulers who came to power competed in the spreading of Islam. The Ummayads were actually more successful in conquering other countries and spreading Islam than the Abbasids, and the 'Uthmanis conquered more countries and spread Islam more than the Mamluks. This disparity was due, however, to the priorities the State would give to its foreign policy among other factors. The spreading of Islam always remained the basis upon which the relationship with other states was established. This has never changed throughout the rule of all the *Khulafah*. The duty of the State is to implement Islam at home and to carry its Message to the world. Therefore, the task of the Islamic State has always been to carry the Message of Islam. What actually makes the conveyance and spreading of Islam the basis of the foreign policy is the fact that the Message is addressed to the whole of mankind. Allah (swt) says,

$$\text{وَمَآ أَرْسَلْنَٰكَ إِلَّا كَآفَّةً لِّلنَّاسِ بَشِيرًا وَنَذِيرًا}$$

"And we have not sent you (O Muhammad) except as a giver of glad tidings and a warner to all mankind, but most of men know not." [Saba', 34:28]

Allah (swt) also says,

$$\text{يَٰٓأَيُّهَا ٱلنَّاسُ قَدْ جَآءَتْكُم مَّوْعِظَةٌ مِّن رَّبِّكُمْ}$$

"O mankind! There has come to you a good advice from your Lord." [Yunus, 10:57]

He (swt) says,

$$\text{قُلْ يَٰٓأَيُّهَا ٱلنَّاسُ إِنِّي رَسُولُ ٱللَّهِ إِلَيْكُمْ جَمِيعًا}$$

"Say, O mankind! Verily, I am sent to you all as the Messenger of Allah." [Al A'raf, 7:158]

And He (swt) says,

$$\text{وَأُوحِيَ إِلَيَّ هَٰذَا ٱلْقُرْءَانُ لِأُنذِرَكُم بِهِۦ وَمَنۢ بَلَغَ}$$

"This Qur'an has been revealed to me that I may warn therewith you and whomsoever it may reach." [Al-An'am, 6:19]

142

He (swt) also says,

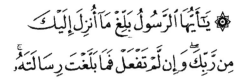

"O Messenger (Muhammad (saaw))! Proclaim (the Message) which has been sent to you from your Lord. And if you do not, then you have not conveyed His Message." [Al-Ma'idah, 5:67]

The Messenger of Allah (saaw) conveyed the Message to mankind, and when he (saaw) died Islam continued to be carried by the Muslims. The conveyance of the Islamic Message is in fact the continuation of the work that the Messenger of Allah (saaw) had initiated. The Muslims followed his (saaw) teachings and continued spreading the Message of Islam. The Messenger of Allah (saaw) said in his *Khutbah al-Wada'* (farewell speech), "Would the present tell the absent, for the absent may be more conscious than the listener." He (saaw) also said, "May Allah brighten a man who listened to my saying, understood it and conveyed it as he heard it."

This is why the conveyance of the Islamic call has become the basis of the Islamic State's relationship with other states during the lifetime of the Messenger of Allah (saaw) and in the days of his *Khulafah* after him. And this is the Divine rule which is decisive and conclusive, in evidence by the Book and the *Sunnah* and the general consensus of the *Sahabah*.

Therefore, the foreign policy of the Islamic State is to convey the Islamic Message to the world. This policy is implemented by a defined method that never changes, which is *Jihad*, regardless of who is in authority. Since the Messenger of Allah (saaw) founded the State until the end of the Islamic State, this method never changed. The Messenger of Allah (saaw) prepared the army soon after founding the Islamic State. He (saaw) initiated *Jihad* in order to remove the material obstacles that stood in the way of the Islamic *Da'wah*. The Quraysh was that material obstacle, so he (saaw) decided to remove it. Then he (saaw) went on to destroy the Quraysh's existence, the very existence

143

that stood in the way of the Islamic *Da'wah*. He (saaw) also removed and destroyed other obstacles until Islam engulfed the whole of the Arabian Peninsula. Then the Islamic State began knocking on the doors of other nations to spread Islam among them. It found that the existing ruling systems formed a material obstacle in the face of the *Da'wah*, thus they had to be removed in order to reach the people themselves and invite them to Islam so that they could visualize and feel the justice of Islam, observe the prosperity and decent living under its banner, and invite the people to a better life without compulsion or coercion. *Jihad* continued as a method of spreading Islam, and by the means of *Jihad* many countries were conquered. By means of *Jihad*, kingdoms and states were removed and Islam ruled the same people and nations. Islam was spread and was embraced by hundreds of millions of people after they had been ruled by it. The method used in implementing that foreign policy was *Jihad*. It has never changed and never will.

Jihad is the call to Islam which involves fighting, or the contribution of either money, opinions, or literature towards the fighting. It is an obligation, confirmed in the Qur'an and the *Hadeeth*. The Muslims never started the fight against an enemy before firstly proposing Islam or secondly the *Jizyah*. The Divine rule concerning *Jihad* is that if the enemy was surrounded they would be invited to embrace Islam and if they accepted then they would become a part of the Islamic *Ummah* and fighting them would be forbidden. If they refused Islam, then they would be asked to pay the *Jizyah* and if they paid it, their lives and assets would be safe and their country would become part of the Islamic State. They would enjoy the justice, equity, protection, guardianship and welfare enjoyed by the Muslims, and all their basic needs would be secured. Additionally, they would have to pledge allegiance to the State and the regime. If they rejected Islam and refused to pay the *Jizyah* then the fighting would be lawful.

Therefore, fighting the enemy would not become lawful until the call to Islam had been delivered to the people. The scholars have stressed that it is unlawful for us to fight those who have not received the Islamic call. Thus, public opinion about Islam, and the conveyance of a true image of Islam, together with attempts to allow the Islamic laws to reach the people in order to enable them to realize that Islam offers them a true salvation should precede any fighting. The Islamic State should undertake political work such as giving a clear picture of Islam and explaining its concepts, campaigning and advertising Islam. Such moves should include muscle flexing and displaying the might of the Islamic State, including the courage and resolve of the Muslims. The Messenger of Allah (saaw) would perform such maneuvers. He (saaw) would send envoys to the heart of the disbelieving countries. On one occasion he (saaw) sent forty men to the people of Najd to convey the Message of Islam. He (saaw) also displayed the might of the army in Madinah before he went to Tabuk. This was why the Messenger of Allah (saaw) said, "I was given the victory through the fear in the enemy, of a month's marching distance."

The Muslim army has always been feared and respected. For centuries, Europe always held that the Muslim army could never be defeated. However, political maneuvers are essential, especially those which help to spread the Islamic concepts and demonstrate the power of the State before resorting to armed struggle. Although *Jihad* is the fixed method that never changes in the spreading of Islam, the political maneuvers and other deliberate moves are all part of preparation, and is essential prior to actual combat. It is an important matter designed at determining the relationship of the State with other states, people and nations, whether these were economic or based on good neighborly relations or any other basis that may help to spread Islam.

Therefore, the political idea on which the State's relationship with other states is based on is the spreading of Islam among them and the carrying of the Message to them. The method that should be followed is *Jihad*. However, there are several ways and plans which the State initiates or adopts. It would for instance sign a good neighborly treaty with some enemies and fight others. The Messenger of Allah (saaw) approved such measures ever since he (saaw) arrived in Madinah. The State could declare war against all its enemies simultaneously. Abu Bakr did so when he sent the armies to Iraq and al-Sham at the same time. The State could agree to temporary truces, enabling it to create public opinion for a desired outcome.

That is what the Messenger of Allah (saaw) did when he (saaw) signed the treaty of al-Hudaybiyah. The State could also resort to local skirmishes as a means of terrorizing the enemy. This was the case when the Messenger of Allah (saaw) sent several expeditions out prior to the Battle of Badr, and when the Ummayads were in power they used the same tactics against the Romans, including summer and winter campaigns.

The State could also sign economic treaties with some countries, while at the same time not have trade relations with others, taking into account the interest of the *Da'wah* for Islam. It could have diplomatic relations with some countries and not with others. This would be according to a carefully designed plan to take the *Da'wah* in a favorable direction. The State could resort to propaganda and advertising in order to spread the *Da'wah*, or it could use the method of divulging the enemies schemes and cold war tactics.

The State's planning would be in accordance with the nature of the work to be undertaken and geared towards the benefit of the Islamic *Da'wah*. These plans have always helped the spreading of Islam and eased the task of *Jihad*, therefore they are necessary in implementing the foreign policy. Public opinion about Islam and the Islamic State has always been necessary to spread Islam by its fixed method, which is *Jihad* in the way of Allah.

Jihad to Carry Islam

The mission of the Islamic *Ummah* in this life is to carry the Message of Islam to the whole of mankind. The Muslims had to be in touch with the world. The Islamic State was thus obliged to carry out this task which Islam has decreed in order to convey the Message. It was inevitable that the State would conquer other countries and achieve this with great success. These conquests were merely the implementation of an Islamic obligation, which is the conveying of Islam to people in a manner that would catch their imagination by implementing its rules on them and spreading its concepts among them.

Therefore, the Islamic conquests were not designed to exploit and colonize people, nor were they made to take advantage of the resources of their land. The only aim was to carry the Message of Islam to them in order to save them from the miserable lives that they were leading and the corrupt regimes that they were ruled by.

The Islamic State was established on a very strong basis, an establishment that saw it grow and expand, spread and conquer other countries. The seed of its establishment was destined to bear a universal State, not a local one, because its *'Aqeedah* is a universal one. It is an *'Aqeedah* for mankind and its system is global, designed, as it was, for all humans.

Therefore, it was only natural for it to spread and to liberate other countries, the nature of its establishment makes this inevitable. There was the Messenger of Allah (saaw) taking the second *Ba'yah* of 'Aqabah from the Muslims who pledged to fight alongside him all and sundry even if it led to the loss of their wealth and the death of their nobles. They pledged themselves to him in complete obedience in ease and in hardship, to tell the truth at all times. In Allah's service they would fear the censure of none, pledging themselves to the Messenger of Allah (saaw) to fight to the death in the way of protecting the Islamic *Da'wah* and for their faithful service their reward would be Paradise. Those were the seeds of the army of the Islamic State that carried the Message of Islam. Bearing all these factors in mind, why was this army established? What was its task? Was it not to carry the Message of Islam? Was that not the only reason for which they came and gave their pledge and were ready to die for its cause?

The Messenger of Allah (saaw) had designed the plan of the conquests before his death. Once the Islamic State was established in the Arabian Peninsula, he (saaw) sent envoys to Chosroes and Caesar, part of his plan designed to spread the Message of Islam beyond the Peninsula which took place in the seventh year of Hijrah. He (saaw) also sent envoys to other kings and princes inviting them to embrace Islam. His plan was also reflected in launching the raids of Mu'tah and Tabuk and in the preparation of Usama's army. The *Khulafah* who succeeded him as heads of the State pursued his plan and executed it by conquering first the countries he (saaw) had sent envoys to, inviting them to Islam.

Other conquests soon followed, again always following the same method and principle. That is why the Islamic State was never selective in the countries it conquered, it never made any difference to the Muslims how difficult or easy was their task. And although Egypt was relatively easy to conquer and its resources were considerable compared with the harsh Saharan climate of North Africa with its poverty, the Muslims never took those factors into consideration because their ultimate goal was to spread Islam. This necessitated the liberation of every country regardless of its poverty or wealth and regardless of the resistance put up by its people. Carrying Islam to the other nations is not motivated based on the wealth or the poverty factor, nor will the acceptance or the refusal of the people stall the carrying of the Message. The main aim is simply the conveyance of Islam, to establish it as an intellectual leadership from which a way of life emanates. This Message should be carried to all mankind in all countries.

The Qur'an has outlined for Muslims the reasons for fighting and the obligation of *Jihad*, stressing that it should only be in the way of Islam and in carrying its Message to the world. The verses came strong and fast, commanding the Muslims to fight in the way of Islam.

Allah (swt) says in *Surah al-Anfal,*

$$\text{وَقَـٰتِلُوهُمْ حَتَّىٰ لَا تَكُونَ فِتْنَةٌ وَيَكُونَ ٱلدِّينُ كُلُّهُۥ لِلَّهِ}$$

"And fight them until there is no more Fitnah and the Deen will be for Allah Alone" [Al-Anfal, 8:39]

And He (swt) says in *Surah al-Baqarah,*

$$\text{وَقَـٰتِلُوهُمْ حَتَّىٰ لَا تَكُونَ فِتْنَةٌ وَيَكُونَ ٱلدِّينُ لِلَّهِ ۖ فَإِنِ ٱنتَهَوْا۟ فَلَا عُدْوَٰنَ إِلَّا عَلَى ٱلظَّـٰلِمِينَ ١٩٣}$$

"And fight them until there is no more Fitnah and worship is for Allah (alone). But if they cease, let there be no transgression except against Az-Zalimun (the transgressors)" [Al-Baqarah, 2:193]

Allah (swt) says in *Surah al-Tawbah,*

$$\text{قَـٰتِلُوا۟ ٱلَّذِينَ لَا يُؤْمِنُونَ بِٱللَّهِ وَلَا بِٱلْيَوْمِ ٱلْأَخِرِ وَلَا يُحَرِّمُونَ مَا حَرَّمَ ٱللَّهُ وَرَسُولُهُۥ وَلَا يَدِينُونَ دِينَ ٱلْحَقِّ مِنَ ٱلَّذِينَ أُوتُوا۟ ٱلْكِتَـٰبَ حَتَّىٰ يُعْطُوا۟ ٱلْجِزْيَةَ عَن يَدٍ وَهُمْ صَـٰغِرُونَ}$$

"Fight against those who don't believe in Allah, nor in the Last Day, nor forbid that which has been forbidden by Allah and His Messenger, And those who don't aknowledge the religion of truth (i.e. Islam) among the people of the scripture (Jews and Christians), until they pay the Jizya with willing submission, and being subdued." [At-Tauba, 9:29]

These verses, among others, have commanded the Muslims to perform *Jihad* and indicated to the Muslims the aim behind the conquests. It was these verses that motivated the Muslims to liberate other countries.

Therefore, the carrying of the Message of Islam was the basis on which the Islamic State was founded and for which the Muslim army had been prepared. *Jihad* was decreed and this was the method followed in the conquering of other countries. The carrying of the Message is what would bring the Islamic State back to the Muslims.

Consolidation of the Islamic Conquests

The Muslims liberated many countries and ruled them by Islam. Islam has commanded them to hold the reins of power and leadership. They are forbidden from being ruled by non-Muslims. Allah (swt) says in *Surah al-Nisa*,

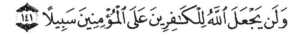

"And never will Allah grant to the disbelievers a way (triumph) over the believers." *[An-Nisa, 4:141]*

Allah (swt) has bestowed the *'Izzah* upon the Believers. He (swt) says in *Surah al-Munafiqeen*:

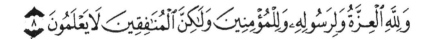

"But honor belongs to Allah, His Messenger (Muhammad (saaw)) and to the Believers, but the hypocrites know not." *[Al-Munafiqun, 63:8]*

However, Allah (swt) did not give them the might, nor had He given them the rule and the leadership until they had acquired an Islamic mindset. This mentality carried the idea of viewing the task of ruling as a means to implement Islam and propagate its Message, and not to possess a lust for power. Until they had acquired an Islamic mentality (having the ability to understand what the rule entailed and its responsibility before Allah) the authority to rule and look after the people's affairs was kept away from them. The splendor of Islam was reflected in the actions of those rulers and in their words and it reached the people that they ruled over through the implementation of the *Shari'ah*. This inevitably resulted in convincing these people to the extent that they embraced Islam in crowds. The might, leadership and the rule then belonged to them too. Their countries became an Islamic household and part of the Islamic State.

The Islamic conquests were asserted by ruling the conquered countries according to Islam, followed by the people's adoption of the Islamic belief until the conquests of countries by the Islamic State was a given until the Day of Judgment. It detached its people from their former condition and ruling authority and transformed them from disbelievers to Muslims and their country from *Dar ul-Kufr* to *Dar ul-Islam*. This state of affairs remained intact until Islamic rule was destroyed. However, its people remained Muslims and their land remained Islamic even after the Islamic rule had perished and the authority of the State dissipated. Although the Islamic State is currently absent, the countries originally conquered by the Muslims continue to be Muslim lands and the people still remain Muslims, and this land still has potential for the return of Islamic rule and the spreading of its authority over its territory.

Several factors have actually consolidated the Islamic conquests permanently and implanted the seeds of Islam to the Day of Judgment.

Some of these factors made the governace of the liberated lands simple from the very beginning such as the nature of the Islamic legislation. Other factors prepared the people to enter Islam such as the behaviors of the rulers while other factors contributed to the implantation of the seeds of Islam into the hearts and minds of those who embraced it forever such as the nature of the Islamic *'Aqeedah*.

In summary, these factors can be summarized by the following:

1. Islam is a rational *'Aqeedah*. It compels whoever embraces it to believe in it rationally through the agency of the intellect. Thus, the moment a human being embraces Islam, he turns into a thinking person. This is so because his attention would be turned towards the creatures and universe created by Allah (swt), thus enabling him to realize the existence of his Creator and thereby encouraging him to-

wards gaining the knowledge of His rules, to extract them and solve his problems accordingly. Therefore, Islam will conclusively become a part of the person and this will motivate him to understand its rules and implement them.

2. Islam obliges a Muslim to acquire knowledge and to become acquainted with the Islamic culture. It is not enough for the Muslim to simply profess the two *Shahadatain* (witnesses of faith) in order to become both knowledgeable about Islam and understand it. He should comprehensively study Islam and begin to develop a clear vision about the purpose of man, life, and the universe and the manner in which Islamic regulates these. This knowledge broadens the Muslim's horizons and develops his perception, thereby enriching his mentality, making him a teacher of others.

3. The nature of the Islamic ideology and its *Shari'yah* necessitate that they should be progressively acquired, i.e., it should affect the manner in which the individual learns and processes information from the society he lives in. The Muslims learned about Islam in order to implement it. This is why the Muslims were always eager and zealous towards Islam. They had an all encompassing thought, rich knowledge, and broad horizons because the Islamic *'Aqeedah* was deeply rooted in their hearts and minds. They also received the Islamic rules and opinions after a great deal of study and research and because the practical implementation of Islam was dominant.

The Muslims did not learn Islam for the sake of soaking up knowledge because this would have rendered them as mobile books containing information about Islam. This would have made them intellectual sponges, soaking up knowledge at each turn but not acting upon the information in order to change and subsequently order society. The information (like water) would eventually dry up and the individual would not make an impact up on society. They also did not merely listen to Islam as a form of advice. This would have turned them into shallow minded individuals, unable to relate the belief to the daily affairs of life. The Muslims made sure that they avoided these two dangerous paths, i.e. learning about Islam for information or taking it as mere advice. The Muslims restricted their learning of Islam and its rules to the method decreed by Islam, which is the clear and enlightened understanding of Islam in order to implement it in all walks of life.

4. Islam is progressive. It leads the Muslims to new heights and sets them on the path of perfection. It obliges the Muslim to perform certain actions, the performance of which would lead the Muslim to a level of perfection where he can enjoy spiritual superiority, peace of mind and true happiness. The human being, once raised to such a level, will remain there and will not degrade. However, if the reaching of such a level of perfection were hard to achieve, the maintaining of such a level is even harder, therefore, the actions performed by the Muslims have to be consistent and permanent, and not temporary. This enables the human being to maintain the attained level of superiority and progress.

These actions constitute acts of worship, some of which are obligatory and others complimentary. Fulfilling the obligations by all people would lead to realizing a common level of progress. Performing what is beyond the obligatory actions encourages people to strive towards perfection.

Performing these acts of worship is not a tough task, nor is it a tiring or shattering experience, nor does it entail deprivation of life's pleasures and an abstention from its joyful aspects. It does not lead to the suppression of instincts and consequently to the contradiction of human nature. No, the performance of such acts of worship, especially the obligatory ones, is an easy task and well within the capability of every human being, no matter what his strength and will-power. Acts of worship do not prevent him from enjoying life. To perform the complimentary acts of worship is a *Mandub* (desirable matter), the Muslims perform them with great zeal and eagerness, knowing that by doing so they will gain the pleasure of Allah (swt).

5. The Muslims conquered other countries in order to convey the Message of Islam. As a result, they felt that they were envoys of compassion and guidance. They would enter a country, rule it according to Islam and as soon as the people embraced Islam, they would enjoy the same rights as the Muslims. They would then become obligated to carry out the same duties that the Muslims were charged with. The newly conquered land would enjoy the same rights that the State provided for other Muslim regions and would become an integral part of the Islamic State because the Islamic ruling system is a system of unity. That is why the people of conquered countries never felt they were being colonized, nor did they ever sense the slightest signs of colonization. Therefore, it comes as no surprise that people embraced Islam in large numbers, more so after they had witnessed true Islam being implemented.

6. The Islamic ideology and rules are not exclusive. It is permitted to teach them to all people and it is in fact an obligation to teach them to everyone so that they can taste the sweetness of Islam and realize its true nature. The Messenger of Allah (saaw) would send governors, judges and teachers to rule people by Islam and to teach them its rules. The Muslims who came after him (saaw) conquered many countries and set up rulers and teachers who would teach the people *Fiqh* and the Qur'an. The people welcomed Islamic education with open arms until their culture became Islamic. This included those who chose not to embrace Islam.

7. The Islamic *Shari'ah* is a universal and comprehensive. Therefore, the Muslims never needed to study the laws of the country that they were about to conquer. They never needed to try and accommodate or compromise between the laws they had brought to solve life's problems and the laws in existence within that country. They would conquer a country and introduce the *Shari'ah* as a complete system, implementing Islam from the very first day they entered a country. Their method was radical in the sense that there was no phased approach to implement the system, such as implementing laws A, B, and C but not D, because implementing law D would result in con-

troversy, turn people away from Islam, or was too difficult to adhere to. This type of gradualism did not exist. There were no patches here and there.

The Muslims would not allow the status quo to prevent them from applying the system of Islam. They conquered the country with the sole aim of conveying Islam to its people in order to change their corrupt state of affairs and turbulent way of life. This necessitated the uprooting of the old structure and replacing it with a new structure in a most comprehensive manner. That is why it was easy for the Muslims to rule the newly liberated people from the very first day. Their rule would be completely and firmly established. They never suffered any legislative crisis nor did they undergo a transitional period. They had their Message and it was based on an *'Aqeedah* from which the system, legislation and rules emanated. It was and is a *Shari'ah* that is valid for implementation upon any human race, anywhere and at anytime.

Molding People into
one Ummah

The Messenger of Allah (saaw) passed away after the entire Arabian Peninsula had entered into the fold of Islam and polytheism had been abolished. The Peninsula was under the Islamic domain, ruled comprehensively by Islam according to its *'Aqeedah* and the system that emanated from it. He (saaw) died only after Allah (swt) had perfected the *Deen*, completed His favor unto the Muslims and chose for them Islam as that *Deen*. This included the invitation of neighboring nations and people to Islam by sending envoys to their kings and rulers as well as by dispatching expeditions to raid the Roman frontiers of Mu'tah and Tabuk.

Then came the *Khulafah al-Rashidun,* and the conquests continued. Iraq was inhabited by a mixture of Arabs and Persians who professed the faiths of the Christians, Mazdakyya and Zoroastrians and this was the first country to be conquered. Persia followed next and al-Sham after that. Persia was inhabited by Zoroastrians, Jews and Christians and ruled over by the Persians while al-Sham was a Roman colony where the Roman culture and Christianity were predominant. Syrians, Armenians, Jews, Arabs and a few Romans lived there. Egypt was conquered after this and it too was inhabited by a mixture of people, such as the Copts, Jews and Romans. North Africa followed suit and this was where the Berbers lived under Roman dominance. Along came the Ummayads and they conquered Sind, Khawarizm and Samarqand, joining them to the Islamic State in the process. Al-Andalus was then conquered and became a *Wilayah* of the Islamic State.

The inhabitants of these countries varied in the ethnicity, language, religion, traditions, customs, laws and culture. They naturally differed from each other in mentality and attitude. Therefore, the process of molding these countries together and of uniting them into one single *Ummah*, adopting the same *Deen*, language, culture and laws was a colossal task. Success would be a tremendous and extraordinary achievement. This happened solely through Islam and was only achieved by the Islamic State. Once those people were identified by the banner of Islam and ruled by the Islamic State. They became a single *Ummah*, which is the Islamic *Ummah*. This feat was due to the effect of Islamic rule and Islamic *'Aqeedah*. Many factors led to the successful molding of these disparate people into one *Ummah*, the most important of which were the following four factors:

1) The teachings of Islam.

2) The cohabitation of the Muslims with the liberated people in their daily life and work.

3) The quick embracing of Islam by the people of the conquered countries.

4) The radical change in the life of those who embraced Islam and their transformation from a dismal situation to a better one.

The teachings of Islam oblige Muslims to call for Islam and spread its guidance wherever and whenever possible. This necessitates *Jihad* and the conquest of other countries in order to enable people to understand it and contemplate the truthfulness of its rules. It also gives the people the choice between embracing Islam or retaining their faith if they so wished, provided that they submit to its rules related to matters of transactions and penal code. This last point is important because it would develop harmony in the people's actions and dealings once the system and rules that deal with their problems became unified, and it would also serve to make the non-Muslims feel like Muslims by being part of the society, sharing the same system, enjoying the peace of mind and the guardianship of the State.

The teachings of Islam necessitate that the ruled people should be looked upon from a human point of view and not a racial, tribal or sectarian one. Therefore, the Islamic laws related to social and penal matters must be equally implemented upon every citizen, with no difference between the Muslims or non-Muslims.

Allah (swt) says in *Surah al-Ma'idah*,

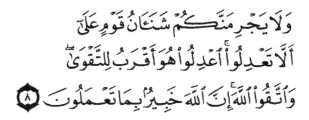

"And let not the emity and hatred of others make you avoid justice. Be just: That is nearer to piety, and fear Allah. Verily, Allah is Well-Acquainted with what you do." *[Al-Ma'idah, 5:8]*

All people are equal in the eyes of the law. The ruler looks after the people's affairs and rules over them. The judge settles people's disputes without any prejudice. He looks upon them from a human point of view with the aim of solving their problems and settling their disputes. The ruling system in Islam introduces true unity and equality between the different regions of the State.

Islam commands the rulers to guarantee the basic needs of all the *Wilayat* of the State with grants provided by the treasury, regardless of the amount of revenues being collected from each *Wilayah*, and regardless of whether these levies cover the expenditure or not. Islam commands a single financial policy by collecting levies for the treasury from all the *Wilayat*, thus helping to mold the conquered countries into *Wilayat* and making them into one State. This is what the Islamic ruling system would and did inevitably achieve.

The mixing of the Muslim with the indigenous people was one of the major factors that led to those people entering Islam and integrating with other Muslims. After conquering a country, the Muslims would take up residence there and begin teaching the people Islam and Islamic culture. They lived in neighboring houses, they shared in all of life's affairs and became subjects of one country, being ruled by the same laws. There never existed two different segregated communities divided into conquerors and conquered, winners and the defeated. They were all citizens of the State who helped each other in their daily affairs. The conquered people looked upon the rulers as being a different type of people whom they had never encountered before. They witnessed the equality with which they treated them by placing themselves on the same level and serving them and managing their affairs. They experienced fine treatment by rulers of high qualities and this made them adherent towards the rulers and towards Islam. The rulers and other Muslims would marry women from the People of the Book (Jews and Christians), eat their slaughtered meat and their food. This served as an incentive for them to enter Islam because they witnessed the effect of Islam through the rulers and saw the light of Islam through the system being implemented upon them. As a result, these people became integrated and constituted a single *Ummah*.

The entering of the indigenous people into Islam was not limited to a time period or a country. The people of each country embraced Islam en masse. People continued to enter into Islam until most of them were Muslims, and thus Islam was not merely confined to Muslim conquerors. By entering into Islam, the people of the conquered countries integrated with the conquerors and became one single *Ummah*.

The comprehensive change that Islam caused in those who embraced it led to the raising of the intellectual level of those new Muslims. This developed in them the Islamic *'Aqeedah* which became an ideological basis upon which all concepts were founded and measured. As a result, Islam took them from an emotional based belief (faith) to a rationally founded belief. It transformed them from the worship of idols, icons, other human beings, and fire, and the belief in the trinity and other similar types of worship, which led to a steep decline in the intellectual level, to the worship of Allah (swt), which led and will continue to lead to the establishment of an enlightened mind. Islam made them believe in the Hereafter and led them to comprehend it in the way that the Qur'an and the *Sunnah* have presented it and the reward and punishment in it. So they conceived of it as being real and this led them to acquire a true meaning of this life thus being the path to another happier and eternal life. They held life with open arms and they did not neglect it. They took its means and enjoyed the pleasures and wealth that Allah (swt) - the One who provided the right criteria and perceptions of life.

Prior to the advent of Islam, their criterion of life was based on personal interest as the only controls to perform any action. After the acceptance of Islam, the criterion of their actions changed and came to be based on what is *Halal* and what is *Haram*. This criterion became the driving force behind their actions, and its guidelines were according to what Allah (swt) had commanded and prohibited. The aim of their actions became attaining Allah's pleasure. The value of the action became the objective behind the performance of the action. It would be spiritual if it were prayer or *Jihad*; material if it were buying or selling; moral if it was a trust or an act of compassion; humanitarian if one was being assisted in a crisis, etc. People began differentiating between the motive behind the action and the value of the action. As a result, their conception of life became different from their previous one. It became the true conception about the life measured by a criterion that Islam had set, this being the commands of Allah (swt).

Islam gave the people a true meaning of happiness. Happiness had been, in their original view, the satisfaction of their instincts and organic needs. It came to be transformed into gaining the pleasure of Allah (swt). This entails true happiness because true happiness means total and permanent peace of mind and this can never be achieved merely through satisfying the human desires and acquiring material pleasures. It can only be achieved by obtaining the pleasure of the Lord of the Universe.

This is how Islam affected the viewpoint of the people who embraced it. Their viewpoint about life and the actions which they performed in this life changed. Their order of priorities also changed, some went up in value and others came down. Life to the human being was at the top of his list of priorities to begin with and the ideology came second. Then Islam came and reversed the situation so that the ideology came to the top of the human being's priorities in life. As a result of this, the Muslims began to devote their lives to the service of Islam because they correctly considered that Islam was more precious than life and it was only a natural corollary for the Muslim to endure hardship and sacrifice in the way of Islam. Life's matters came to be placed in their appropriate order of priority. Life became honorable and dignified and the Muslim acquired a permanent peace of mind once he set his ultimate objective to that being the pleasure of Allah (swt).

The new Muslims' concept of the highest ideal changed therein. In the past the people had different and ever changing ideals. Now they acquired the one and only ultimate objective. This resulted in the changing of things that mattered to them and in changing the definition of virtue. The basis of virtues formerly included things like personal courage, individual decency and re-spectability, sectarian backing, boasting about wealth and noble descent, gen-erosity to the point of extravagance, faithfulness to the tribe or clan, merci-lessness in revenge and other similar acts. Islam changed all that. It made of all these qualities trivial, which the human could take or leave according to Allah's decrees, not according to the benefits they generated, nor to the pride or prestige which they entailed, nor because they were traditions or customs or a heritage one had to preserve. Islam mandated the submission to Allah's orders only. Therefore, Islam enjoined the submitting of the individual, tribal, popular, and national interests to the commands of Islam only.

This is how Islam transformed the mentalities and attitudes of the people who embraced it. It changed their personalities and their evaluation of man, life and the universe. It completely altered their criteria concerning all of life's matters. People began realizing that life held a special meaning which was perfection and nobleness. They acquired a supreme ideal which was securing the pleasure of Allah (swt), and that was the happiness which they vigorously pursued. Therefore, they became different creatures from those which they had once been.

These four major factors helped to detach all the people who embraced Islam from their former circumstances. Their concepts and visions of life be-came unified into one concept and one vision. The management of their af-fairs sprang from that concept. Their interests also became unified and they became one interest, i.e. the interest of Islam. Their goals in life became a single goal, which was the spreading of Allah's word. In total, the integration of these people into Islam was inevitable and they eventually became a single *Ummah*, the Islamic *Ummah*.

The State's Weakness: Causes & Factors

The Islamic State is based on the Islamic ideology and derives its strength solely from that ideology. It is its main cause of progress and prosperity and the basis of its existence. The Islamic State came into existence and established itself in a powerful fashion due to the strength of Islam. It consolidated large areas of the world in the space of less than a century despite the fact that horses and camels were its only means of transportation, and all its conquered peoples, and nations embraced Islam within a short period of time despite the fact that Its means of communication were limited to the word of mouth and pen. Islam made all this possible by being the driving force behind the State.

The enemies of Islam realized this and knew that the weakening of the Islamic State would be impossible as long as Islam remained strong and deeply rooted within the hearts and minds of the Muslims, and as long as the understanding of Islam remained sound and its implementation accurate and comprehensive. Therefore, the *Kuffar* resorted to finding the means which would weaken the Muslims' understanding of Islam and their implementation of its rules.

The methods which the enemies of Islam used to weaken its understanding were numerous. Some were related to the text and others to the language used in conveying and teaching it, still other methods used were related to Islam's relevance with reality. They set about adding false narrations to the *Ahadeeth* of the Messenger of Allah (saaw) which were never said, and they managed to fabricate and include in them non-Islamic meanings and concepts that contradicted Islam in the hope that these would be adopted by the Muslims and thus deviate them and alienate them from Islam. Indeed, they managed to do just that, and they spread these false *Ahadeeth* among the people. The Muslims came to be alarmed by this and they in turn divulged the evil schemes of those *Zanadiqah* (heretics). The Muslims smashed their evil ring and aborted their conspiracy. Scholars and *Ahadeeth* experts then rose to the challenge and began gathering and listing the *Ahadeeth* by relating each *Ahadeeth* to the narrator, his qualification, and the date each *Ahadeeth* was narrated, underlining each *Ahadeeth* and classifying it. The *Ahadeeth* was either classified as *Sahih* (genuine) and *Da'if* (weak) and were protected. The narrations of the *Ahadeeth* were restricted to the three generations after the *Sahabah* and no other narration reported after them was accepted. The narrators were all individually identified and the books of *Ahadeeth* were also classified accordingly until the Muslims were able to relate the authenticity of any *Ahadeeth* by relating its text and chain of narrators. The Islamic State dealt harshly with those *Zanadiqah* and most of them were actually executed for their part in falsifying and fabricating the *Ahadeeth* of the Messenger of Allah (saaw). Overall, the conspiracy did not have any damaging effect on Islam nor the State.

The enemies of Islam then resorted to attacking the Arabic language as this is the language[2] by which Islam and its rules are conveyed and they attempted to divorce it from Islam. They did not succeed at first because the Muslims went forward in their conquests armed with the Book, the *Sunnah* and the Arabic language and they would teach the people all three. The people embraced Islam and became fluent in Arabic and some of the non Arabs actually became distinguished *Mujtahideen* like *Imam* Abu Hanifah. Others became exceptional poets like Bashar ibn Burd and some became eloquent writers like Ibn al-Muqaffa'. The Muslims devoted a great deal of attention to the Arabic language. *Imam* Shafi'i disallowed the translation of Qur'an and disallowed praying other than in Arabic. Those who did endorse the translation of Qur'an, like *Imam* Abu Hanifah, in any case did not call the translated text Qur'an at all. Arabic remained the focus of attention because it is the fundamental part of Islam and a necessary prerequisite of *Ijtihad*. The understanding of Islam from its sources does not come about but in Arabic and the ex-

---

[2] Translator - Muslims witnessed during their history atempts of Shu'ubiyyah (anti-Arabism and Arabic language sentiments) in the days of Ummayds and Abbasids and attempts of some Persians to take over the State in the days of Abbasids. These movements left their effects on the Arabic language. Later on, in the modern history, the onslaught against Arabic language started having different shapes and it was fuelled by European nations.

traction of the *Shari'yah* cannot be accomplished except in Arabic. However, the attention, care and importance given to the Arabic language diminished by the end of the sixth century Hijri when the rulers, who did not appreciate and realize the importance of the Arabic language, came to power. They, therefore, neglected that area and as a result *Ijtihad* was stalled due to the lack of fluency in the Arabic language, one of the main ingredients in deducing the *Shari'yah*. At this stage, the Arabic language became separated from Islam and the State's understanding of the *Shari'yah* became blurred and as a consequence the implementation of the rules also became blurred. This contributed a great deal towards the ailing of the State. It became diminished in its ability to understand and tackle new issues, thus leading to its failure to solve the problems that arose or to solving them in an erroneous way. As a result, problems accumulated in the face of the State and this caused it to become overwhelmed.

This was as far as the Islamic texts and the language were concerned. As for the applicability of Islam to the realities of life, the dangerous trend of reconciling Indian philosophy with Islam emerged. The seeking of the Hereafter was achieved through asceticism and self deprivation and this led many people to turn away from life's pleasures and to adopt a passive life. They renounced their role of being active members of society and consequently this resulted in a big loss to the Islamic State and Muslims in general. As a result of this, the State lost many talented young men who could have devoted themselves to the Message of Islam, instead of resorting to asceticism and self deprivation.

Later, the cultural invasion by the West brought with it a culture alien to Islam, the West duped the Muslims by claiming that they took this culture from them and that the systems which it brought did not contradict the Islamic rules. The West had brought legislation which contravened the *Shari'yah*. This affected the Muslims to a great extent and led to the encroachment of Western culture and influenced the Muslims. The Muslims began to see life as being based on benefit. During the 'Uthmani *Khilafah*'s rule, some Western laws were adopted, a Western banking system was established, *Riba* justified, and the penal code stalled and replaced by Western penal codes. Despite the fact that *Fatawa* were issued to justify such acts they had a disastrous effect on the

State and led her astray from the Islamic rule. This deviation from Islam extinguished the strong *Iman* Muslims once had, took the State away from the right path, and subsequently led to its weakness and disintegration.

This was as far as understanding Islam was concerned, as for its implementation, many factors contributed to the misapplication of the *Shari'yah*. One such factor was the political parties, each one wanting to impose their own opinion and resorting to military means in order to seize authority and rule. The Abbasids did just that by seizing Persia and Iraq and using them as a platform until they had managed to capture total power and restrict the function of ruling to the clan of *Banu* Hashim. Then came the Fatimids. They took over the *Wilayah* of Egypt and established a state there so as to use it as a support point with the ultimate aim of transferring the rule of the Islamic State to the sons of Fatimah, daughter of Allah's Messenger (saaw). Their action caused a setback to the Islamic State and stalled the *Jihad*, while it resulted in the establishment of a second power vying for control over the *Khilafah* despite the fact that the Islamic State is a state of unity and it is forbidden for the Muslims to have more than one *Khaleefah* at the same time. The Messenger of Allah (saaw) said in reference to this, "If a pledge of allegiance is taken for two *Khulafah*, kill the latter of them."

These factors contributed greatly to the weakening of the State, as well as leading to a suspension of the conquests and thereby resulting in neglect towards conveying the Message of Islam.

However, what in fact led those political parties to resort to that type of methodology in order to seize power, was as a result of what took place during the rule of the Ummayads. The Ummayads introduced the method of handing over the *Khilafah* to the heir apparent, who was then given the *Ba'yah*. This turned the *Ba'yah* into a mere protocol and killed the hope of reaching the position of ruling by its means. Mu'awiyah for instance passed on the authority to his son and took the *Ba'yah* for him later. Subsequently, every *Khalifah* followed the same trend, taking an oath for their heirs and then asking the people to give them the *Ba'yah*. The people were restricted to giving the *Ba'yah* to whoever the *Khalifah* had nominated, and rarely giving the *Ba'yah* to anyone else. This method pushed those political parties to resort to force in order to seize power. Despite the fact that Abu Bakr adopted the method of nomination, its misapplication by the Ummayads led to those problems arising. Abu Bakr had in fact consulted the Muslims over this issue and as a result 'Umar and 'Ali emerged as the two candidates. Nomination was then given to 'Umar and he was elected as *Khalifah* after the death of Abu Bakr. 'Umar took the *Ba'yah* from the *Ummah*. This was actually in accordance with the *Shari'yah*. The *Khulafah* of Bani Umayyah misapplied this rule and nominated their sons, brothers or relatives. In some cases, they even nominated more than one person. Such misapplication led to the deprivation of the Muslims from giving the *Ba'yah* to whoever they wished and this in turn led to the weakening of the State. At first, this did not have much effect on the State because it was so powerful, but the signs of cracking soon emerged.

Misapplication was not simply confined to the State. The *Wilayat* came to be infected by the same malaise. The Abbasids' silence over the action of 'Abd al-Rahman al-Dakhil in Andalus ensured this. His action led to the amputation of a big part of the State when he ruled Andalus independently, as did the governors who succeeded him, some of them even acquired the title of *Amir al-Mu'mineen*. Although, Andalus did not declare total independence from the Islamic State. It was, nevertheless, ruled separately and this resulted in weakness creeping into the State's structure.

Eventually this facilitated its seizure by the disbelievers while the Islamic State was at the height of its glory and at its most formidable strength. The State could do little to save Andalus' downfall and this was due to the disintegration of Andalus' administration. That occurred on the Western front. In the East, the *Wulaa'* were given general and wide mandatory powers which triggered their ego. They began to operate their *Wilayat* according to their own way and the *Khaleefah* agreed to this state of affairs. He was content with the praise which he received from their pulpit and by the mention that decisions were taken on his behalf or by the issuance of currency bearing his name or with the continued receipt of *Kharaj* revenues from them. These *Wilayat* became small independent entity. This was the case with the *Wilayat* of Saljuqiyyeen and Hamdaniyyeen and many others. This too became a contributory factor in the weakening of the State.

Following this period came the 'Uthmanis and the power shifted to them. The 'Uthmani *Khilafah* united most of the Muslim lands under its leadership. They initiated *Jihad* throughout Europe and resumed the conveyance of the Message of Islam. However, this outburst in activity was only backed by the solid *Iman* of the first 'Uthmani *Khulafah* and the military might of the army, and not on a clear understanding of the Islamic concepts and comprehensive implementation of Islam. Therefore, these conquests did not achieve what the conquests of old had achieved, and the strength of the rulers did not embrace all areas of the Islamic State. Consequently, the State soon waned, eventually collapsing until it finally ceased to function. This was as a direct result of the factors mentioned coupled with the many conspiracies brewing against the State.

The factors which contributed to the weakness of the State can be summarized into two main reasons: the weak and defocused understanding of Islam and the resultant misapplication of its Divine rules. Therefore, only a clear understanding of Islam would bring back the Islamic State. The maintenance of the State would rely on its strength of safeguarding such a clear understanding, and the proper implementation of its *Shari'yah* at home and the conveyance of its Message of Islam to the world.

The Disintegration of
the Islamic State

The intellectual debilitation of the Islamic State began in the fifth century A.H. At this time, some scholars called for the phasing out of *Ijtihad*, proclaiming that the doors of *Ijtihad* were closed and that all of man's problems had been addressed. This signaled the downfall of the State. Although there were still some *Mujtahideen* left, deintellectualization had already taken root and this greatly affected the State. By the time the crusaders launched their campaign, the State was in no position to face the challenge. The State became engaged in continuous battles with the crusaders, lasting two centuries. The crusaders emerged victorious at first and managed to occupy parts of the Islamic State. Then the State managed to recapture the occupied lands and vanquish the crusaders. Rule and authority were taken over by the Mamluks who neglected the Arabic language and the intellectual and legislative side of ruling. The door was slammed in the face of *Ijtihad* and the understanding of Islamic concepts weakened considerably. Scholars were forced to be content with *Taqleed* (imitation) and the ailment worsened.

This, however, only affected the State from within, since the State remained strong and its international standing remained intact. The Islamic State remained a superpower feared by all other nations, consolidating the largest and strongest part of the world at the time. The 'Uthmani State took control of most of the known world. In the 10th century Hijri (16th century CE), it united Arab lands under its rule and its dominion stretched over vast expanses of territory. The 'Uthmani State concentrated on its military might and the expansion of its authority as well as the glamour of its rule and power. It also focused its efforts on the conquests and neglected the Arabic language (despite the fact that it is essential in order to understand Islam and one of the conditions necessary in order to effect *Ijtihad*). The 'Uthmani State never paid attention to Islam from the intellectual and legislative point of view, consequently its level of thought and ability to extract rules for unprecedented situations was lacking. At the time, this weakness was not noticed by the Islamic State because it was at the apex of its glory, power and military might. Its ideology, legislation and culture when compared with that of Europe was superior in every respect. This comparison reassured the State and served to make its weaknesses seem both bearable and negligible. Europe was still plunged in total darkness, chaos and unrest. Europe attempted to launch a renaissance but it failed each time. The 'Uthmani State was in a much better situation compared with Europe and as a result it viewed itself as being superior in its culture and system of ruling. This caused the 'Uthmani State to ignore the internal malaise that it was suffering from.

What turned the 'Uthmani State's attention from internal problems was its sweeping victory over Europe, its seizure of the Balkans and the Southeastern part of Europe. This victory sent shock waves to the rest of Europe and everyone became resigned to the fact that the Islamic army could never be defeated and that nobody could ever successfully face the Muslims. This was when the issue of the Eastern Question first surfaced. Its meaning then was to abort the danger of the 'Uthmani invasion headed by Mohammed al-Fateh in the 9th century Hijri (15th century). The invasion continued until the end of the 11th century Hijri under the leadership of Sulayman al-Qanuny (The Magnificent). The conquests were concentrated up until the middle of the 12th century Hijri (18th century) during which time the continuity of the struggle remained a major source of strength to the Islamic State.

The strength of the *'Aqeedah* of the Muslims and the specific concepts that they carried - although those concepts were not clear in their minds - had given the State a great moral boost and this helped to maintain their military might. Additionally, the presence of the Islamic ruling system, despite its misapplication, and the state of affairs in Europe contributed to the continuity and superiority of the Islamic State. At that time the Islamic State could have attempted to understand Islam properly and devoted much more effort to the teaching of the Arabic language and the encouragement of *Ijtihad*. The State could have devoted more effort to understand the intellectual and legislative side of Islam so that it established a strong foundation with which to launch its conquests. This would have enabled the State to liberate the rest of the world through Islam. The State would have been in a position to strengthen its structure and inundate the world with Islamic culture and in the process save the world from corruption and mischief. However, none of this actually happened. Encouragement of the Arabic language was limited to giving the Arabs a few teaching posts and other minor positions of jurisprudence which had little effect on improving the knowledge of the Arabic language and had no effect in awakening the intellect. In order to revive the Arabic language, the State should have made it the official language, as should have always been the case. But this was not carried out. Again, because nothing was done on the intellectual and *Fiqhi* (jurisprudence) fronts the feeble and misguided efforts of the State resulted in the status quo continuing and the State remaining on the wrong track.

As soon as the second half of the 12th century Hijri (18th century) came the trend was reversed and the internal weakness became apparent because the State was founded on the remains of the misapplied Islamic system. The rule as a whole was more within the Islamic system's milieu rather than being an Islamic system itself. This was due to the lack of understanding of Islam and its misapplication due to the lack of *Ijtihad* and *Mujtahideen*. In the 13th century Hijri (19th century) the scales of history swung between the Islamic State and the non-Islamic countries. The awakening of Europe had just begun and this became evident. Meanwhile, the consequences of the intellectual stagnation coupled with the misapplication of the Islamic system finally caught up with the Muslims.

The 19th century CE witnessed an intense intellectual revolution in Europe. Considerable efforts were made by European philosophers, writers and intellectuals and a comprehensive change in the European concepts occurred with the aim of uniting the people of Europe. Many movements were established and these played a great part in the emergence of new opinions about life. Some of the most significant events that occurred were the change of the political and legislative systems. The specter of the despot monarchy gradually disappeared to be replaced by republican systems based on representative rule and national sovereignty. This had a tremendous effect towards triggering the awakening of Europe from its slumber. The industrial revolution also had a telling effect on the European scene. There were numerous scientific discoveries and inventions springing from the minds of Europe. These factors boosted Europe's intellectual and material progress. This material and scientific progress resulted in swinging the scales of power in Europe's favor at the expense of the Islamic world.

On the international scene, the issue of the Eastern Question came to be altered so that it was no longer simply a question of containing the impending Islamic danger to Europe, but whether the Islamic State should be left as it was or whether it should be divided up. The European countries had different opinions due to the differences in their interests. This change in the Eastern Question and in Europe's fortunes - reflected in its intellectual and scientific progress (e.g., the Industrial Revolution) - triggered a political swing between the Islamic State and the disbelieving states in favor of fragmenting the Islamic State.

The cause of the political revolution in Europe stemmed from intellectuals that sought to establish a new way of life. They adopted a specific viewpoint concerning life and embraced a new doctrine. Based on this revised outlook, they founded a system. This led to the change of thoughts and the set of values, creating a general transformation in their lives and this catapulted the industrial revolution into motion. Instead of looking and reflecting deeply on its ideology, instead of stimulating new concepts and resorting to *Ijtihad* to solve its problems according to the rules emanating from its *'Aqeedah*, instead of taking up science and industry, the Islamic State fluttered and became perplexed about how to react to Europe's change of fortunes. It remained idle due to this confusion and this further led to its backwardness in science and industry. It therefore lagged behind other European countries in terms of material progress and prosperity.

The 'Uthmani State was the Islamic State, the Islamic *'Aqeedah* was the basis of the State and its systems, the concepts of Islam were its concepts and the Islamic viewpoint about life was its viewpoint. It should have in fact looked into the new concepts that were emerging from Europe and measured them against its own ideological criterion. It should have studied the new problems from an Islamic perspective and given its verdict on those concepts and problems with the help of adequate *Ijtihad* according to the Islamic viewpoint. Finally, the validity of such concepts would have to be judged. But the State did none of this simply because in their minds, Islam was not clear. It did not have any well defined thoughts because it did not take the Islamic *'Aqeedah* as an intellectual foundation on which all concepts are to be based. The *'Aqeedah* became lifeless because its lifeblood, *Ijtihad* had stopped flowing. The Islamic culture - the collection of concepts concerning life - was not crystallized in the minds of the Muslims. The culture was not linked to the State's actions. This led to a steep intellectual decline, thereby causing regression.

As a result, the Islamic State was taken aback by the intellectual, cultural and industrial revolution they witnessed in Europe. However, they did not react because they were intellectually paralyzed, as they could not come to a decision about adopting or rejecting Europe's achievements or culture. They could not differentiate between what is allowed to be taken from science, discoveries and industry and what is forbidden to be taken from a particular culture, since the latter determines the viewpoint about life. They became stagnant and it was this which led to the backwardness of the Islamic State while the European progression gained momentum.

The Muslims failed to realize the contradiction between the Islamic and European concepts. Another cause was their failure to distinguish between science, industry and inventions which Islam encourages Muslims to acquire, regardless of the source, and culture and ideology which can only be adopted from Islam.

The 'Uthmanis did not properly understand Islam. Such blindness led the *Ummah* and the State to live haphazardly. Meanwhile its enemies held onto a specific system and carried it out. Europe became the possessor of an ideology, regardless of the validity of its creed, and the Islamic *Ummah* with its correct ideology was incipiently being relegated to live in the shadow of Europe's ideology. The Islamic ideology, seemed remote from the people's lives and a thing of the past because the *Ummah* resided in a State where it was misapplied. Despite the fact that the Messenger of Allah (saaw) said, "I have left with you two things, if you hold on to it, you will never go astray, the Book of Allah and my *Sunnah*" and despite the fact that the State was Islamic and the *Ummah* was Muslim, and despite its vast intellectual repository and wealth of *Fiqhi* knowledge being accessible to everyone, the State did not grasp the meaning of that *Hadeeth* and did not take the necessary steps to return to the roots of Islam, i.e., the *'Aqeedah*. The State did not make use of this wealth, a wealth which no other nation possessed, possesses, or will ever possess.

Indeed the Islamic State did not benefit from this wealth because as soon as *Ijtihad* was stalled and intellectual activity ceased the Islamic concepts became blurred in the minds of the Muslims and Islamic cognizance declined. Books and other cultural and intellectual artifacts were kept on shelves and only very few learned people and scholars were left in existence. The desire to study and research diminished. The large amount of cultural and intellectual wealth within the State and society was not sought after because the State never encouraged the pursuit of it. Intellectuals sought knowledge for the sake of knowledge, or they sought knowledge to earn a living. Rare indeed were the ones who sought knowledge to benefit the Ummah and the State. Consequently, the scientific, cultural and legislative momentum did not exist and the understanding of Islam was in disarray. The Muslims understood Islam in a spiritual sense rather than intellectually, politically and legislatively.

The original idea of Islam and the method by which this idea is implemented had become vague. The Muslims could not correctly perceive the Qur'an and the *Sunnah* and began to think that Islam was merely a spiritual religion. They began comparing Islam with other religions from a spiritual point of view, instead of looking at Islam as being an *'Aqeedah* and a complete way of life. It therefore came as no surprise when the Muslim *Ummah*, under the leadership of the 'Uthmani State, stood idle and confused before the European revolution. It remained visibly behind without being affected by the economic progress which Europe was enjoying nor by the multiple inventions that took place there, nor by the industrial revolution that had been launched all over the continent. The effect that this European material progress had on the State was somewhat minimal and never resulted in any notable benefit nor did it generate any material progress or any gain. Most Muslims perceived Europe's achievements as being contradictory to Islam and called for the prohibition of adopting such elements of progress.

A vivid example of this was when the printing press was invented and the

State decided to print the Qur'an. Some scholars prohibited its printing and they began issuing *Fatawa* prohibiting anything new and of accusing anyone who studied the natural sciences of being a disbeliever. They accused every intellectual of being a *Kafir* and *Zindiq*.

Conversely, a small group of Muslims at that time envisioned the need for adopting everything from the West, their science, education, culture and civilization. Those were the ones who had been educated in Europe or in missionary schools that had infiltrated the Islamic world. At first, that small band of Muslims made little impact on society. In the last years of the 'Uthmani State the notion stating that the West adopted its culture from Islam and that Islam does not forbid the adoption of what conforms to it and that which does not contradict it, was spread amongst the Ummah. The West succeeded in spreading this concept until it was adopted by the majority of the Muslims, especially the educated ones - the scholars and jurists, who came to be known as "modern scholars" or "reformists".

However, due to the real contradictions between the Western and Islamic cultures and because of the obvious differences between the Western and Islamic concepts about life, the attempts to harmonize the teachings of Islam with Western culture were doomed to failure. The reformists lost their way and in the process alienated themselves from Islam. Their misguided pro-Western approach failed because they could not correctly perceive the Western concepts and they neglected in the process the inventions, science and industry as they moved further away from Islam. The Ummah relied heavily on those reformists and as a result, confusion was exacerbated. The State was unable to take a decisive stand and the Ummah rejected all means of material progress, ranging from science, inventions and industries. She became weak and unable to stand or defend herself. This weakness encouraged the enemies of Islam to mutilate the powerless Islamic State piece by piece.

The missionary invasion, disguised as scientific cooperation, began infiltrating the Muslim land. At the same time the various movements that emerged succeeded in destroying the structure of the State. The concept of nationalism was implanted and avidly encouraged by the West, taking root in the Islamic State, such as the Balkans, Turkey, Arab regions, Armenia, Kurdish reqions and many other places.

In 1914, the State was on the verge of collapse. It entered the First World War and emerged defeated. Then, finally it was destroyed in 1924. Therefore, the Islamic State disintegrated and the dream that had eluded the West for many centuries was finally fulfilled. The West wanted to destroy the Islamic State in order to destroy Islam. With the disintegration of the Islamic State, the system in the Muslim land became non-Islamic and the Muslims have lived ever since under a non-Islamic banner. Since that time they have lived under disbelieving regimes ruled over by laws of disbelief, they have become unsettled and their situation has deteriorated.

The Missionary Invasion

Europe began its invasion of the Islamic State in the name of science and it appropriated large budgets for that purpose. In fact, the invasion was covertly colonial, but disguised as missionary work in the name of science and humanitarian aid. This invasion was designed to enable the departments of political intelligence and cultural colonization to settle in Muslim countries until they became the heart and spearhead of the Western colonial juggernaut. Colonization began when the Muslim world opened its gates to Western culture via the guise of missionary associations, which were mainly French, English and American.

As a result of this, both French and English influence infiltrated the Muslim world via these missions. They actually became the driving force behind nationalist movements, encouraging Pan-Arabism and Pan-Turkism, as well as in control of orienting the educated Muslims towards the West. There were two main objectives behind this. The first was to separate the Arabs from the 'Uthmani State, which they named Turkey in order to stir up racism, further ripping at the fabric of the Islamic State. The second was to alienate the Muslims from the real bond of Islam, since they had no knowledge of any other bond.

The missionary institutions managed to achieve the first stage of their scheme, but the second remained unfulfilled. It was left to the nationalist orientation of the Turks, Arabs, Persians and others to be the remaining wedge to split the unity of the Muslims and to veil them from their guiding principle. The missionary associations went through several phases and their effect was telling all over the Islamic world. The weakness and decline we suffer today is a result of these associations. It was the colonialist powers who positioned the first brick of the barrage which they placed in the path of our advancement and which came between us and our ideology.

The Europeans established missionary societies in the Islamic world due to their unsuccessful campaigns against the Muslims, who exhibited patience, strength, and courage in *Jihad* during the crusades. When the crusaders clashed with the Muslims on the battlefield, they were relying on two factors according to their own calculations and they held out high hopes on those two factors, leading them to exterminate Islam and the Muslims forever.

The first factor was their reliance on the Christians living in the Muslim world, especially in al-Sham and who numbered many. These Christians were very religious people and the Europeans regarded them as brothers in faith. They thought that they would conspire against the Muslims and spy for them under the pretext that they were waging a religious war.

The second factor was that the Europeans were relying on their large numbers combined with their formidable strength, knowing all the while that the Muslims were divided and at odds with one another as the disintegration of their unity had already begun. The Europeans thought that once they had defeated the Muslims, they would subjugate them for good and destroy them, and their *Deen* would merely become a collection of rituals. However, their hopes were dashed and their predictions faltered. They were stunned and amazed when they saw the Arab Christians fighting alongside the Muslims on the battlefield, unaffected by the propaganda launched by the Europeans. What the Europeans had not understood and had consequently overlooked was that the Arab Christians lived alongside the Muslims in the Islamic homeland, enjoying the same rights as the Muslims and fulfilling the same duties towards the State. The Muslims would eat of their food, marry the Christian women and share in the daily matters of life together with the Christians, as it was Islam that safeguarded their rights.

All the *Khulafah* and governors adhered to that rule and duly implemented it in the Islamic State. Al-Qurafi and Ibn Hazm stated,

"That it would be our duty to protect the people of the *Dhimma* if aggressors attacked our land, and we should die protecting them if necessary. Any neglect of such a duty would be a breach of the rights of the *Dhimma*."

Al-Qurafi also said,

"The Muslims' duty towards the *Dhimma* would be to act gentle and lenient towards their weak, help their poor, feed their hungry, clothe them and talk to them gently. The Muslims should accept and endure the harm of their neighbors even if they were able to repel the harm, this was as a mercy to them and not out of fear of or glorifying them. They should give good advice in all matters, repel anyone harming them, protect their assets, families and honor and all their rights and interests, and do right by them like any generous and pious Muslim should do."

With this in mind it was only natural for the Christians to fight alongside the Muslims. The Europeans' surprise was even greater when the second factor which they had relied on failed to materialize. They occupied al-Sham and defeated the Muslims comprehensively, committing the worst atrocities in the process. For example, they were the first to initiate a mass evacuation of Muslims and this trend continued throughout their wars with the Muslims. They thought that everything had gone well for them and that the Muslims would never again stand against them. However, the Muslims remained determined to expel them from their land, and despite the fact that the crusaders occupied Muslim lands for about two centuries, during which times they established kingdoms and principalities, the Muslims eventually managed to expel them from it.

The Europeans searched for the secret behind this turn of events and found that it was embedded in Islam, its *'Aqeedah* being the source of the formidable power which the Muslims possessed, coupled with its rules, which safeguarded the rights of the non-Muslims. This was the main reason behind the cohesion between the citizens of the Islamic State. In their time, the colonialist disbelievers thought of new ways by which they could invade the Islamic world. They deduced that the best way would be by way of a cultural invasion through missionary work, this was in order that they might gain the support of the Christians and initiate doubt among the Muslims vis a vis their *Deen*.

This, it was hoped, would raise the doubts of the Muslims in their *Deen* and shake their *'Aqeedah*, with the aim of creating divisions between them and other citizens of the Islamic State, thereby weakening the power of the Muslims.

The colonialists managed to execute their plan. At the end of the 16th century they established a missionary center in Malta and made it their headquarters from which they conducted their missionary onslaught on the Muslim world. To begin with, missions were sent out from there. After a while they saw the need to expand their activities and so they moved to al-Sham in 1625 and tried to establish missionary movements there as well.

However, their activities remained very limited and they did not progress beyond establishing a few small schools and publishing a few religious books. In fact they suffered a great deal of persecution, opposition and hostility from everyone. They managed to function until 1773 when the missionary activities of the Jesuits were abolished and their institutions shut down, except for some insignificant missions like those of the 'Azaryin' missionaries which, despite their continuing presence, reduced the effect of the missionaries and their missionary work to a non-existent level. Their influence came to be confined to Malta until 1820 when the first missionary center was established in Beirut and the missionary work began again in earnest. They faced great difficulties at first, but they persisted with their activities. Their first area of concern was religious preaching and religious culture, their education program remained limited and weak.

In 1834, the missionary expeditions spread out all over the region of al-Sham, a college was opened in the village of Antoura in Lebanon and the American mission transferred its print shop from Malta to Beirut in order to print and distribute its books.

The noted American missionary Ely Smith was very active at this time, he had been working in Malta as a volunteer in charge of the mission press and had arrived in Beirut in 1827. After one year there, fear and boredom drove him out and he returned to Malta. He next returned to Beirut in 1834 and together with his wife they opened a school for girls. His area of work broadened and he devoted his life to working in al-Sham, Beirut in particular. All these efforts and the efforts of many others helped revive the missionary movement. An opportunity presented itself to the missionaries when Ibrahim Pasha adopted the syllabus for primary education and implemented it in Syria. The syllabus was inspired by the Egyptian educational system which in turn was taken from the French system. The missionaries took advantage of this opportunity and contributed to the educational movement from the missionary point of view, expanding their printing works in the process. On the back of all this the missionary movement prospered. They succeeded in making the citizens of the Islamic State boil with anger against each other in the name of religious freedom and managed to initiate among the Muslims, Christians and Druze various kinds of religious activities related to the *'Aqeedah*.

When Ibrahim Pasha retreated from al-Sham, unrest, fear and anarchy broke out and people became divided among themselves. The foreign delegates, especially the missionaries, seized the opportunity and due to the meager influence of the 'Uthmani State in al-Sham, began igniting civil strife. After a period of just one year, in 1841, serious disturbances broke out in the mountains of Lebanon between the Christians and the Druze. The situation deteriorated and under the pressure and influence of the foreign states the 'Uthmani State was talked into designing a separate ruling system for Lebanon, dividing the province into two parts. One part would be occupied by the Christians, while the Druze would occupy the other. The 'Uthmani State appointed a governor over both parts, aiming to avoid any clashes between the two sects. This system did not succeed, however, because it was not natural. Britain and France became involved in the dispute and incited civil strife wherever the official authorities attempted to quell the trouble.

The British and the French used these clashes as a pretext to interfere in Lebanon's affairs. The French sided with the Maronites and the British sided with the Druze, this led to the renewal of disturbances in 1845. The scenes were horrifying and the attacks were extended to include Churches and monasteries. Theft, killing and pillage became common practice, prompting the 'Uthmani government to send her foreign affairs in charge to Lebanon in order to use his mandatory powers to quell the trouble once and for all. He, however, could not achieve anything significant, although he managed to appease the tension a little. Meanwhile, the missionaries intensified their activities and in 1857 the Maronites began calling for a revolution and armed struggle.

The Maronite clergy incited the farmers against the feudal lords and they attacked them fiercely in the North of the country, thus the revolution was ignited and it spread to the South. The Christian farmers now rose against the Druze feudal lords and the British and the French backed their respective allies. Civil strife spread rapidly all over Lebanon as a result of this. The Druze began to indiscriminately kill all Christians, whether they were clergy or ordinary people until thousands of Christians were either dead or displaced and homeless, such was the ferocity of these clashes.

The waves of disturbances and violence spread to the rest of al-Sham. In Damascus, a fierce campaign of deep hatred was waged between its Muslim and Christian inhabitants which finally led to the Muslims attacking the Christian district in 1860 resulting in them committing a massacre. This was accompanied by pillaging and mass destruction until the State was forced to militarily intervene in order to put an end to the disturbances. Although the State managed to restore calm and order, the Western countries saw it as an opportunity to interfere in al-Sham and so they sent their warships to its shores.

In August of the same year, France sent a division of her infantry to Beirut which began the task of quashing the revolution. This was how the 'Uthmani State was infested by civil strife in Syria and Lebanon. Its true cause was the Western states who were trying to meddle in the internal affairs of the 'Uthmani State. This they did and they managed to force the 'Uthmani State to design a special ruling system for Syria, dividing her into two *Wilayat* and giving Lebanon special privileges. From these events, Lebanon became separated from the rest of al-Sham and it was granted local autonomy, governed by a local administration headed by a Christian ruler and assisted by an administrative council representing the local residents. Since then, foreign countries have managed the affairs of Lebanon and have made it the center for their activities. Lebanon therefore became the bridgehead from which the foreign powers infiltrated into the heart of the 'Uthmani State and its Muslim lands.

Meanwhile, the missionaries adopted a new policy. The missionaries did not content themselves with just building and running schools, printing presses, and clinics, but went further to establish associations. In 1842, a committee was set up to establish a scientific association under the auspices of the American mission. The committee's work lasted for five years until it had managed to establish an association called the "Association of Arts and Sciences." Its members included Nasif al-Yaziji and Butrus al-Bustani, (Lebanese Christians taken on board because they were Arabs) Americans Eli Smith and Cornelius van Dyke, and Briton Colonel Churchill. The objectives of the association were vague at first. It had the tendency to teach science to adults, as well as teaching youngsters at school. The association encouraged adults and youngsters alike to learn Western culture, sculpting their minds according to the missionary plan.

However, despite the tremendous efforts put in by the association it only managed to recruit fifty active members in the whole of al-Sham over a two year period. They were all Christians, mainly from Beirut, and no Muslim or Druze joined the association. Colossal efforts were made to expand and activate the work of the association but to no avail. The association collapsed after five years from its initial establishment without reaping any significant results except for the desire of the missionaries to establish more associations. Therefore, another association was founded in 1850 and it was named the "Oriental Association." It was founded by the Jesuits under the guardianship of the French Jesuit Father Henri Debrenier and all its members were Christians. It followed in the footsteps of the "Association of Arts and Science" lasting only a short time before collapsing as its predecessor had done.

Afterwards, several associations were established, but all were doomed to failure and they collapsed as before. A new association was founded in 1857 which adopted a slightly different method, no foreigners whatsoever were allowed to join and its founders were all Arabs. Somehow, it managed to succeed and some Muslims and Druze actually joined. The association accepted them because they were Arabs. Its name was the "Syrian Scientific Association." It became successful owing to its activities, Arabic affiliation, and because of the absence of foreigners among its membership. Its members managed to recruit other people to join and they gathered support for the association until 150 members had enrolled in it. Among its administrative staff were some noted Arab personalities such as Mohammed Arsalan from the Druze and Hussein Bayham from the Muslims. Personalities from all Arab Christian sects joined, the most noted of them being the son of Ibrahim al-

Yaziji and the son of Butrus al-Bustani. This association had in fact outlasted all the others. Its program was designed to accommodate all sects and to serve as the spark for Arab nationalism. However, its covert objective was colonial and missionary draped in the name of science. It was a shadow organization manifesting itself in the spreading of Western culture and education.

In 1875, the "Secret Association" was formed in Beirut, it was actually based on a political idea. It began encouraging the concept of Arab nationalism. Its founders were five young men from amongst those who had been educated in the Protestant college in Beirut. They were all Christians whom the missionary parties had managed to affect. Following the establishment of this association, a small number of members were recruited by them. The association seemed to be calling, through its declarations and leaflets, for Arab nationalism and political independence for the Arabs, especially those in Syria and Lebanon.

However, its actual work and its real program was concerned with an entirely different objective. Its aim was to cast strange desires and false hopes into the hearts of the people. It called for Arab nationalism and encouraged animosity towards the 'Uthmani State, dubbing it the Turkish state. It worked towards separating religion from the State and making Arab nationalism as the basis of life. The association always championed Arabism. Those in charge repeatedly accused Turkey in their literature of snatching the Islamic *Khilafah* from the Arabs, of violating the Islamic *Shari'ah*, and of abusing the *Deen*. This neatly demonstrates the true nature of the association and the real objective for which it had been founded, i.e. to cause agitation against the Islamic State. It was chartered with creating suspicion and skepticism about the *Deen* and to establish political movements based on non-Islamic principles. The fact is that these movements had been initiated by Western powers. It was they who established them, monitored their progress and managed them. They also wrote reports about their activities. For instance, the British consul in Beirut sent a telegram to his government on 28th July 1880 saying, "Revolutionary leaflets came into circulation, Midhat is suspected to be the source, despite this, the situation remains calm. Details in the post."

This telegram was dispatched in the wake of a leaflet distributed on the streets of Beirut and posted on the walls there. The telegram was soon followed by several letters sent by the British consuls in Beirut and Damascus.

The letters were accompanied by copies of the leaflets which the association had distributed and should therefore rightly be regarded as reports on the movement set up in the Protestant college which began its activities in al-Sham. The association's activities were more evident in al-Sham, although they took place in other predominantly Arab areas as demonstrated by what the British commissioner in Jeddah wrote to his government in 1882. In a report about the Arab movement, he stated, "However, news has reached me that even in Makkah itself some intellectuals have begun talking about freedom, it seems to me from what I have heard that a plan has been designed aiming at uniting Najd with the land between the two rivers, i.e. the South of Iraq, and appointing Mansur Pasha as ruler, as well as uniting 'Asir and Yemen by appointing 'Ali ibn 'Aabid to rule over them."

Britain was not the only interested party, France too displayed a great deal of interest. In 1882, one of the French officials in Beirut voiced the French concern by saying,

"The spirit of independence is well spread and I noticed during my stay in Beirut the dedication of Muslim youths in establishing schools and clinics and in reviving the country. What is worth mentioning here is that this movement is free of any sectarian influence, this association welcomes the membership of the Christians and relies on them to participate in the nationalist activities."

A Frenchman wrote from Baghdad,

"Everywhere I went, I was faced with the common feeling, on the same scale, of hatred for the Turks. As for the concept of initiating collective action to get rid of this much hated situation, this is very much under way. In the horizons a wind of Arab movement is gathering strength and is about to be born. This people who have been oppressed for a long time are about to proclaim their natural status within the Muslim world and direct the destiny of this world."

Missionary work in the name of religion and science was not merely confined to the focus of the attention of the US., France and Britain, but extended to most of the non-Islamic states, including Czarist Russia who sent missionary expeditions and Prussia (Germany) who sent a group of 'sisters' (the nuns of Carodt) to participate with other missions. Inspite of the difference of opinion among the various missions and Western delegates regarding their political programs, which took into consideration their international interests, their objective was the same; the preaching of Christianity and the spreading of Western culture in the East coupled with the arousal of the suspicions of the Muslims towards their *Deen*, pushing them to resent it and to regard their history with contempt while leading them to praise the West and its way of life.

The missionaries carried out their preaching according to their great hatred of Islam and the Muslims. They disdained the Islamic culture and its way of life and they regarded the Muslims as backward barbarians, which remains the ill-considered opinion of nearly every European. The results that they achieved are reflected today in the concentration of disbelief and colonialism in our lands.

The Crusaders' Hatred

One of the French learned writers Count Henri Decastri wrote in his book entitled 'Islam' in 1896,

"I cannot imagine what the Muslims would say if they heard the tales of the mediaeval ages and understood what the Christian orators used to say in their hymns; all our hymns even those which emerged before the 12th century emanated from one concept which was the cause of the crusades, these hymns were filled with hatred towards the Muslims due to the total ignorance of their religion. As a result of those hymns and songs, hatred against that religion became fixed in people's minds, and the erroneous ideas deeply rooted, some of which are still carried nowadays. Everyone used to regard the Muslims as polytheists, disbelievers, idol worshippers and apostates."

This is how the Christian clergy in Europe described the Muslims and their *Deen*. The allegations in the mediaeval ages were horrible and these were used to incite the feelings of hatred and animosity against the Muslims. The Christian world became affected and the crusader wars took place. After lasting two centuries resulting in the defeat and the humiliation of the Christians, the Muslims began to reconquer the West in the 15th century when the Islamic State entered Constantinople. Then in the 16th century the Muslims swept across southern and eastern Europe and carried Islam to its peoples. Millions of the inhabitants of Albania, Yugoslavia, Bulgaria and other countries embraced Islam in the process. Once again the crusader animosity was revived and the Orientalist concept emerged, which was concerned at the time with resisting the Muslim armies, halting the Islamic conquest and lessening the threat of the Muslims.

This deeply rooted animosity in the minds and hearts of the Europeans prompted all Christians in Europe to send their missionaries to the Muslim land in the name of science and culture. The missions took the shape of schools, clinics, associations and clubs. The Europeans devoted almost unlimited resources and huge efforts to the missionary work. They combined their efforts and methodology despite their differences in policy and interests. People and states were united behind the missionary effort since it was conducted by their consuls, ambassadors, delegates and missionaries.

The crusader hatred harbored by the Westerners, especially in Europe and more so by Britain, and their deeply rooted animosity and wicked malice were the cause of our eventual humiliation in our homeland. General Allenby said in 1917 when he entered al-Quds,

"Only today the crusades have ended."

This was simply a genuine expression of what he really felt. It reflected the hatred and malice he harbored and the same could be said about every European that fought in the battles - cultural and military - against the Muslims, and Allah (swt) says,

قَدْ بَدَتِ ٱلْبَغْضَآءُ مِنْ أَفْوَاهِهِمْ وَمَا تُخْفِى صُدُورُهُمْ أَكْبَرُ

"Hatred has already appeared from their mouths, what their breasts conceal is far worse." [Al-'Imran 3:118]

What Allenby said was indeed most loathsome, and what his country, Britain, harbored was even greater without a doubt; this goes without saying for every European.

This malice and hatred has existed ever since the days of the crusades and it is still perpetuated today. What we face in terms of oppression, humiliation, colonization and exploitation - in addition to the political aspect - is in fact an act of brutal revenge on the Muslims. Indeed it is particular to the Muslims.

Leopold Weiss wrote in his book Islam at the Crossroads,

"Verily the renaissance, or the revival of science and European arts which owed a great deal to Islamic and Arabic sources, used to be attributed to the material contact between East and West. Europe has indeed benefited a great deal from the Islamic world, but she never acknowledged or recognized this favor, nor did she show any gratitude by easing her hatred to Islam, in fact this hatred grew stronger and deeper over the years and at times reached uncontrollable proportions. This hatred engulfed the popular feeling and was triggered each time the word Muslim was mentioned. The hatred became a part of their popular heritage until it took root in the heart and mind of every European man and woman, and more astonishing though was that it remained alive even after all the stages of cultural change that took place. Then came the era of religious reform, when Europe became divided into sects, and each sect stood in the face of other sects, armed to the teeth, ready for battle; however, animosity towards Islam remained the same within every sect. Soon after, a time came when religious fervor diminished but the hatred of Islam remained as strong as ever, a clear example of this was delivered by the French philosopher and poet Voltaire, although he was an arch enemy of Christianity and the Church in the 18th century, he also was at the same time expressing his feelings of hatred and arrogance towards Islam and the Messenger of Islam; after a few decades, there came a time when the Western intellectuals began exploring foreign cultures and looked upon them with some kind of sympathy and openmindedness, however when it came to Islam, the traditional disdain began infiltrating their scientific researches in an extraordinary factional way; and the wide gap which history dug up between Europe and the Islamic world remained unbridged, then the contempt for Islam became an integral part of the European mentality."

It was on this basis that the missionary associations mentioned above were established. Their aim was to preach the Christian religion and to arouse suspicions in the Muslims about their *Deen*, thereby leading them to hold it in disdain within their hearts and to blame their own failures on it.

On the other hand, the aim of the associations was also political and the consequences were in fact horrendous on both accounts until they reached unexpected proportions. The missionary movements were founded on the basis of wiping out Islam by libeling it, by creating problems and misgivings about it and about its rules, in order to come between the people and the way of Allah (swt), and to alienate Muslims from their *Deen*. Behind these missionary movements came the Orientalist movements who had the same target and the very same objective.

Efforts and resources were unified throughout the whole of Europe and a crusade was waged against Islam for the second time; this time it was a cultural war which poisoned the mind by what they had distorted from the Islamic laws and Islam's high values, the poisoning of the young Muslim minds by what they alleged about Islam and the history of the Muslims in the name of scientific research and scientific fairness. It was in reality the cultural venom which was far more dangerous than the crusader wars. The missionaries carried out the spreading of their poisonous filth in the name of science and humanity. They used to do it in the name of Orientalism. As Weiss stated,

"The reality is that the first Orientalist of modern times were Christian missionaries working in the Muslim countries, the distorted picture they fabricated allegedly from Islamic teachings and history was expertly designed to guarantee a negative reaction and influence the European opinion towards the idol worshippers, i.e. the Muslims; however this twisted concept continued despite the fact that Orientalist studies had been liberated from the missionary influence, stripping the Orientalism from any religious and ignorant fervor that would misguide it. As for the Orientalist' hostility to Islam, this was an inherited instinct and a natural characteristic derived from the effects of the crusader wars."

This inherited animosity is the one that supports the hatred in the hearts of Westerners against the Muslims. It is the one that portrays Islam, even in Muslim countries, to Muslims and non-Muslims as being the bogeyman, or this demon which would destroy the progress of humanity. This is in fact to conceal their real fear of Islam, for they know that if Islam were deeply implanted in the hearts and minds of the people it would signal the end of the hegemony of the disbelieving colonial powers over the Islamic world and the return of the Islamic State to once again resume the carrying of the Message of Islam to the world - and indeed it will return *Insha'Allah* - for the sake of humanity and the West itself. The work of the missionaries would eventually turn into grief and sorrow for them; Allah (swt) says,

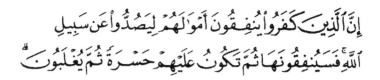

"Verily, those who disbelieve spend their wealth to hinder (people) from the path of Allah, and so will they continue to spend it; but in the end it will become an anguish for them." [Al-Anfal, 8:36]

The inherited animosity is the one that supports any anti-Islamic movement. You will find the Western scholar researching Taoism, Hinduism, Buddhism, or Communism without any hatred or prejudice at all. Whereas, if he were to research Islam malice, hatred, and contempt would soon appear despite the fact that Muslims were defeated by the colonial disbelievers. The Western clergy, backed by the colonialists, still actively conspire against Islam and they will never abate from libeling Islam and the Muslims and from degrading Muhammad (saaw) and his Companions, or from injecting slander into the history of Islam and of the Muslims. All this is to get their revenge and to strengthen the hold of the colonialists.

The Effects of the Missionary Invasion

The missionary invasions were regarded as the avant-garde which paved the way for European colonialism to conquer the Islamic world politically after first conquering it culturally. Through conquering Istanbul and the Balkans and by bringing Islam to Europe the Islamic intellectual leadership was carried by the Muslims to the countries of the West. When that leadership faltered the Muslim countries became the target of the West, which consequently carried its intellectual leadership to the Muslim world where it encountered fertile ground for its culture and its concepts about life; these were sowed in different ways under the name of science, humanism and religious preaching. The West did not stop there either, as well it libeled the Islamic culture and the Islamic concepts about life by directing its onslaught against Islam. This adversely affected the educated class and the politicians, in fact it deeply affected all those who carried the Islamic culture, and in time it came to affect the majority of the Muslims.

As for the educated people, the colonial powers had designed in their missionary schools, before the occupation, and in all the other schools after the occupation, their own educational syllabus and cultural programs according to their particular philosophy and culture and their own special concepts about life. They made the Western personality the basis of this culture and of their renaissance, history and environment the main sources of the material which we Muslims eagerly overflow our minds with. Neither did they stop at that, but they went as far as interfering with the details of the syllabi making sure that no partial items stepped out of line nor contradicted the general principles which represented their philosophy and culture. This was the case even concerning the Islamic *Deen* and history lessons; both these syllabi had been designed on a Western basis and according to Western concepts.

Even today the Islamic *Deen* is taught in Islamic schools as a spiritual and moral subject conforming to the Western concept of religion. It is taught in a way which is far from reality and far removed from the real facts of life. The life of the Messenger of Allah (saaw) is taught to our youth in a way which is cut off from the Prophecy and the Message. It is taught in the same way that the lives of Napoleon or Bismarck are taught, for instance. As a result, this does not create in their hearts any of the proper emotions or concepts. The subject of worship and morals, which is included in the religious syllabus, is presented from a self-interest point of view. Thus, the teaching of the Islamic *Deen* has likewise come to be set upon the same course as the Western concepts of personal benefit and interest.

Educating the Islamic history has also been similarly stained due to ill-intention and misunderstanding, and has been blackened in the name of historical fairness and scientific research. What rubs salt into the wound is the fact that some of the educated Muslims have taken up the teaching of history and the editing of historical works according to the missionary method and syllabus. Consequently, all the educational syllabi have been designed according to Western philosophy, and, through following its syllabi. This has made most of the intellectuals Westernized. They digested the culture, loved it, and led their lives according to its concepts until most of them became averse to the Islamic culture and critical of it when and where it contradicted Western culture.

Those Muslims became Westernized in their culture, a culture controlled by the Western viewpoint. They were faithful to that culture, to the extent that they idolized the foreigner and adopted his culture. Many of them assumed the Western character, they became hateful of Islam and Islamic culture, in the same way that the Westerner was. They believed that Islam and the Islamic culture was the cause of the decline of the Muslims, as they had been led to believe by them. Consequently, the missionary expeditions achieved great success when they managed to pull across to their side the intellectual Muslims who then fought alongside them against Islam and the Islamic culture.

The situation spread even further to include not only those educated in Europe and in foreign schools, but also to those carrying the Islamic culture as well. They were stunned and incensed with the colonial Western powers' actions in libeling their *Deen*, and so began their response to the libel. Their response was initiated without realizing whether such was either right or wrong in the first place. In their eagerness to defend Islam from the libel of the foreigners they did not check their reply. They were certain that Islam was being wrongly accused, but all the same they began the dangerous process of twisting the Islamic texts in order to make them comply with Western concepts.

As a result, their reply was weak and in effect, it was this which proved very helpful to the missionary invasion, rather than the reply itself. What is even worse is that the Western culture, which is contradictory to the Islamic culture, became part of their concepts which they readily accepted and unjustly and wrongfully attributed to Islam. Most of them began by saying that the West had taken its culture from Islam and the Muslims, and then they started twisting the Islamic rules to suit that culture, despite the flagrant contradiction between the Islamic and Western cultures.

Therefore, once they had demonstrated to themselves that their *'Aqeedah* and culture were consistent with the Western culture they came to accept the Western culture in its entirety. This meant that they had accepted the Western culture and abandoned their Islamic culture. This was precisely what the colonialist wanted and what the West was aiming for when it concentrated its missionary work and its colonial expeditions.

By having their intellectuals educated in Western schools and colleges, and through their lack of understanding of Islam relative to those who had an Islamic education, the Muslims by and large inherited the Western concepts about life. Their countries were, thus, swamped by the materialistic Western culture in the society which led the society to be solely run according to the Western culture and its concepts.

Most of the Muslims did not realize that the democratic ruling system and the economic Capitalist system were both systems of disbelief. They were neither moved nor shocked when their disputes were settled by other than what Allah (swt) had revealed despite the fact that they most certainly knew that Allah (swt) says,

"And whosoever does not judge by what Allah has revealed, such are the Kafirun (i.e. disbelievers)." [Al-Ma'idah, 5:44]

All this was because of the Western culture, based on the separation of religion from the state, which was predominant amongst their societies, and because the materialistic Western concepts were widespread. They felt that if they just believed in Allah (swt) and observed the prayers, then they would have accomplished their Islamic duties. Meanwhile, they thought that they could conduct their life's affairs according to their own desires and with what they thought was best. This did not trouble them in the slightest because they had been infected by the Western concept which states that one should, "Render unto Caesar what is Caesar's and unto God what is God's." Conversely, they were unaffected by the Islamic concepts which make Caesar and all he possesses firmly under the domain of Allah (swt). Allah's orders encompass all things as well as the prayer; they encompass buying and selling, renting (indeed all business transactions), the Judicial and education systems; simply everything, but the Muslims were no longer affected by these concepts. If only they had read what Allah (swt) says,

وَأَنِ ٱحۡكُم بَيۡنَهُم بِمَآ أَنزَلَ ٱللَّهُ

"And so judge (you O Muhammad (saaw)) between them by what Allah has revealed." [Al-Ma'idah, 5:49]

And His saying,

إِذَا تَدَايَنتُم بِدَيۡنٍ إِلَىٰٓ أَجَلٍ مُّسَمًّى فَٱكۡتُبُوهُ

"When you contract a debt for a fixed period write it down." [Al-Baqarah, 2:282]

And His saying,

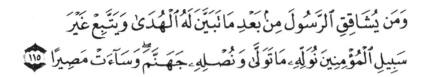

"And whoever contradicts and opposes the Messenger (Muhammad (saaw)) after the right path has been shown clearly to him, and follows other than the believers way. We shall keep him in the path he has chosen, and burn him in hell - what an evil destination." [An-Nisa, 4:115]

And by Allah's saying,

۞ وَمَا كَانَ ٱلْمُؤْمِنُونَ لِيَنفِرُواْ كَآفَّةً
فَلَوْلَا نَفَرَ مِن كُلِّ فِرْقَةٍ مِّنْهُمْ طَآئِفَةٌ لِّيَتَفَقَّهُواْ فِى ٱلدِّينِ
وَلِيُنذِرُواْ قَوْمَهُمْ إِذَا رَجَعُوٓاْ إِلَيْهِمْ لَعَلَّهُمْ يَحْذَرُونَ ١٢٢

"And it is not (proper) for the Believers to go out to fight (Jihad) all together. Of every troop of them, a party should only should go forth, that they (who are left behind) may get instructions in (Islamic) religion, and that they may warn their people when they return to them, so that they may beware (of evil)." [At-Tauba, 9:122]

Certainly, they were never affected by the concepts carried in the verses contained in the Qur'an even if they read them. Instead, they read these verses as Qur'anic verses stopping at that. Whereas, a Muslim really reads the Qur'an knowing that it is alive and that he should use the concepts in his life by attempting to implement them in it. However, they read these verses in circumstances whereby Western concepts were predominant and accordingly they indulged in the spirituality of the verses. When it came to the concepts and the meanings of these verses they erected a mental block. All this was because the Western culture and concepts effectively controlled them, holding sway over them. This is as far as the majority of the people were concerned and those who held an Islamic or foreign education.

As for the politicians the tribulation was far greater and the catastrophe far worse due to them. Ever since the colonial powers had gathered these politicians, tempting them to stand against the 'Uthmani State by promises of big rewards, they conducted themselves according to what the Westerners had designed for them. In the days of the 'Uthmani State, they sided with the Westerner and helped him against their State. This being expressly forbidden in Islam, yet still they somehow managed to do it and they felt proud of it. They boasted about their achievement during every occasion and anniversary which they chose for themselves to celebrate. At that time, instead of struggling against the ruling faction in order to redress the situation and shake up the State, they went along with its enemy, the disbelievers, against the State. The bitter irony was that the disbelievers eventually ended up taking over their country. Then, instead of seeking the people's help against the disbelievers, they sought the help of the latter against their own people. They were affected by the disbelievers to the point whereby they lost their Islamic personality. Their concepts became poisoned by certain political and philosophical opinions and this in turn poisoned their viewpoint about life and ultimately about *Jihad* itself (this being the ultimate purpose of the State). This spread to poison the whole of the Islamic atmosphere and confuse the concepts in every aspect of life.

Compromising through negotiations replaced *Jihad*. The politicians believed and adopted the principle of, 'Take, then demand' - which is considered better for the colonialist than a huge army in the land - and seeking the help of the disbelieving colonialist became common practice and a standard rule. They relied on him without realizing that any assistance they sought from the disbeliever was considered a grave sin and political suicide. They also resorted to working through the narrowness of regionalism, and made it their own political atmosphere. Not realizing that this very regionalism makes political work fruitless because regionalism - no matter how large the region is - cannot fulfill all the political and non-political duties that a true life needs. They did not stop at that either, but they made their personal interests the focus of their attention and gave the foreign countries their general center of attention. Therefore, they lost the natural center of attention, which was their ideology. By losing it, they lost the chance of succeeding in their quest, no matter how hard they worked at it and however faithful they were.

Therefore, all the political movements became futile, and every awakening in the *Ummah* turned into a contradictory, confused movement like that of the slaughtered animal, which finally ends with a motionless, despair and surrender. This is so, because the leaders of the political movements lost their natural focal attention. Thus, it became natural that the *Ummah* loses this focal attention. Accordingly, the concepts of the politicians were poisoned with the erroneous, as well as with the foreign ideologies. As a result, movements were established in the Muslim lands in the name of nationalism, socialism, regionalism, communism, spiritual *Deen*, morals, education and preaching. These movements worsened the situation and added to the complexes of which the society suffers.

The result of all these movements was the failure and to revolve around themselves, because they went according to Western concepts, affected by the Missionary invasion; and they directed the *Ummah* in matters which brought no fruit or good. They also enabled imperialism to get strong hold and remain there. Thus, the success of the Missionary invasion was unmatched.

The Political Siege of the Islamic World

The real cause behind the invasion of Andalus was the revenge which Europe yearned for ever since their humiliating defeat in the crusader wars. After the crushing blow they were dealt by the Muslims, and after they had been chased away from Muslim lands, the Westerners carried a grudge against the Muslims. Their hearts were filled with hatred and malice towards the Mulsims. They would not dare repeat their venture in the East, for they knew that the Muslims would be able to repel any offensive there. They thought that revenge would be easier to obtain in Andalus. In time, Europe directed its onslaught to Andalus and savagely ripped it apart using guillotines and crematoriums on its inhabitants. It was more savage than by beasts, being one of the most despicable of many shameful acts carried out by the West. Nevertheless, they were encouraged by the neglect of the Muslims in supporting Andalus.

The Muslims were strong enough at the time and in a position to militarily assist that *Wilayah* (province) against its Western foes. However, the Muslims slackened and left Andalus an easy prey. This encouraged the West to think even further about revenge and had it not been for the might of the Muslims, especially the 'Uthmani State, the raids would have come strong and fast on the rest of the Muslim lands. It was the sheer might of the Muslims and the conquest of large parts of Europe by the invading 'Uthmanis which caused great fright among the Westerners and pressed them to think twice about embarking on any rash venture against the Muslims lest they get defeated in the style of the crusades.

The Western invasion had to be delayed until the second half of the eighteenth century. Only then had stagnation hit the Islamic world. Thus, with the Muslims abandoning the conveyance of the Islamic message internationally and with the fervor of Islam having waned in their hearts and minds it was only then that their grandeur and might diminished in the eyes of their enemies. Following this, the cultural and missionary invasions of the Islamic world intensified, accompanied by the political invasion that carved up the Muslim lands.

During the rule of Catherine (1762-1796), Russia fought the 'Uthmanis and defeated them. In the process, a large area was sliced off of their land. The Russians took the city of Azov and the al-Qaram Peninsula (the Crimea), as well as the whole of the Northern coast of the Black sea. They founded the city of Sevastopol as a military base in the Peninsula and built the commercial port of Odessa on the Black Sea in the South of the Ukraine. Russia became a major concern for the foreign policy of the 'Uthmani State by assuming sovereignty over the Roman emirates and considering herself the protector of Christianity within the 'Uthmani State.

In 1884, Russia cut the whole of Turkistan from the Islamic State, and then completed its occupation of all of Qafqas. However, Russia was not the only state to challenge the 'Uthmanis, the rest of the Western powers did so too. On July 1st, 1798, Napoleon attacked Egypt and quickly occupied her. In February, 1799, he attacked the southern port of al-Sham and seized Gazza, al-Ramlah and Yafa. He stood near the fort of Akka (famous in the crusades as Acre), but his onslaught faltered and so he returned to Egypt, then to France and his venture finally failed in 1801. However, despite the fact that his campaign proved unsuccessful and abortive, it deeply affected the 'Uthmani State. In its aftermath, most of the countries of Europe queued up to attack the Islamic world and occupy parts of its land. The French occupied Algeria in 1830, and worked towards occupying Tunisia until they did so in 1881. They occupied Marrakesh in 1912. The Italians occupied Tripoli in 1911 and this marked the separation of North Africa, which was no longer under Islamic rule, from the 'Uthmani State. It came to be ruled by the disbelievers and was directly colonized by them.

The Westerners did not stop there but continued to complete the consolidation of their occupation of the remaining parts of the State. Britain occupied Aden in 1839 and expanded its covenant to include the Lahaj and the other nine Protectorates which spread from the Southern Yemeni border to the East of the Peninsula. The British had long before seized India, therefore, stripping the Muslims from their authority over it in the process. They specifically con-

centrated their oppression on the Muslims, who had been the people in authority in India, the British thus seized that authority and colonized India.
Then they began a process aimed at weakening the Muslim stand in general.

In 1882, Britain seized Egypt and in 1898 Sudan. Meanwhile, Holland
occupied the East Indies; Afghanistan was put under Anglo-Russian pressure
and so was Iran. The Western onslaught on the Islamic world intensified until
it was felt that it was about to fall under Western hegemony altogether and
that the crusaders' campaign had been resumed and was achieving success
after success. Steps were taken to resist this Western invasion and to minimize
its heavy pressure. Resistance movements broke out in several places. A revolution erupted in Algeria, the Muslims of China rose up in arms, as did the
Mahdyyun in Sudan. The Sanusyya revolution also erupted. This actually
proved that there was still some kind of vitality left within the Islamic world
despite its decline and weakness. However, all these attempts completely failed
and they never did manage to salvage the Islamic world.

The West, in addition to its military invasion, set about dividing the Islamic world culturally and politically, and went on to sever other parts of the
Islamic world and worked tenaciously towards destroying the 'Uthmani State,
for this was the Islamic State that represented the Muslims world-wide. With
this purpose in mind the West established ethnic and nationalist groups. To
begin with, they incited the people of the Balkans to rebel in 1804. Such re-
bellions as these were financed by the West and they eventually led in 1878 to
the Balkans gaining their independence.

The foreign powers also incited Greece to rebel in 1821 until this rebellion, thanks to their intervention, ended in Greece gaining its independence
from the 'Uthmani State in 1830. It was at this stage then that the Balkans
followed suit, until the shadow of the 'Uthmani State no longer engulfed Crete,
Cyprus and most of the Mediterranean Islands which it had once governed
over. Most of the inhabitants of these places were subsequently expelled from
their homes and forced to flee due to the savagery of the disbelievers. They
sought refuge in the Arab countries which were still Muslim land and remained part of the Islamic State. The Circassians, the Bushnaks, the Chechens
and others are the sons of those heroes who refused to yield to the rule of the

disbelievers and fled with their *Deen* to the safety of the Islamic household and Islamic rule.

The Westerners went even further and secretly encouraged and supported separatist movements among the Muslims themselves within the State, i.e. between Arabs and Turks. They backed the nationalist movements and helped to establish Turkish and Arab political parties such as the "Turkyya al-Fatah Party" (Young Turks), the "Union and Progress Party", the "Arab Independence Party", and the "Covenant (Al-A'hd) Party", amongst others. This resulted in the State's body being violently shaken from within and it began to crumble, coupled with foreign invasions. The disbelieving forces found it very promising to direct their onslaught against the Islamic world, seizing the rest of its land and destroying the Islamic State by wiping it out of existence. This was at the start of the First World War which the 'Uthmani State was forced into and which ended in its defeat. The allies emerged as the victors and they divided the Islamic world between them as war booty. All that remained of the Islamic State was Turkish land which came to be known as Turkey and which remained at the end of the war in 1918 at the mercy of the Western forces until 1921, when she in turn managed to gain her independence from them after giving the allies guarantees that she would abandon the Islamic system of government.

The Destruction of the
Islamic State

In the wake of the First World War, after a truce had been declared and once allies had secured their sweeping victory, the 'Uthmani State was destroyed and fragmented into small statelets. The allies seized all the Arab lands, Egypt, Syria, Palestine, TransJordan and Iraq, stripping them from the State so that all that remained in the hands of the 'Uthmanis was Turkey, and even she had been invaded by the allies. British warships seized the Bosporus and the British army occupied parts of the capital, Istanbul, all the Dardanelle fortresses, and most of the strategic points throughout the whole of Turkey.

The French meanwhile had also occupied parts of Istanbul and their Senegalese soldiers filled its streets. The Italian army occupied Bira and the railways, and the allied forces took over the running of the police, the national guard and the ports. They stripped all the fortresses of their weaponry and discharged part of the Turkish army. The "Union and Progress Party" was dissolved and both Jamal Pasha and Anwar Pasha fled the country. The rest of its members went underground. A puppet government was then formed, headed by Tawfeeq Pasha, to execute the orders of the occupying forces.

The *Khalifah* at the time was Waheed al-Deen, who forged the situation and deemed that he should deal with it in a wise manner. He dissolved the parliament and assigned the Prime Minister's post to one of his most faithful friends, Farid Pasha, who backed him in his policy of being lenient with the allies lest they destroy the country, which it was more than especially vulnerable to, now that the war had ended. He executed his plan and the situation remained as such for a while with the allies dominating and Turkey in a state of lull. This continued until 1919, when things began to change and the position of the allies weakened. A series of crises hit Italy, France and Britain at home, serious enough to threaten their internal stability, and soon differences emerged between them. This was evident in Istanbul, where they fought over the booty, each of them wanting the lion's share of military positions and economic advantages. At this point, Turkey was in a position to seize a last chance and save her existence. Now that a rift had occurred between the allies and their weaknesses were revealed, a point was reached whereby each one of them began inciting the Turks against the other, and in the process they gave the Turks assistance.

The peace conference, which they had been planning, had not yet taken place and its conditions not laid down. Therefore, a glimmer of hope appeared on the horizon and people began to believe that they could organize a serious resistance movement. More than ten secret associations were established in Istanbul. Their aim was to acquire weapons and depots under the control of the enemy and send them to secret organizations within the country. Some officials were also involved in this work. Ismat, a deputy in the War Ministry; Fawzi, the Chief of Staff; Fathi, the Interior Minister; and Ra'uf, Minister of the Navy were amongst those who helped these movements. Thus, the task of secretly resisting the enemy was taken up by the many associations formed with that purpose in mind; the "Union and Progress Party" also became very active again. These movements were joined by some of the military until eventually they came to be unified under one movement headed by Mustafa Kemal. He established a movement to fight the allies and expel them from the country and he vowed to fight the *Khalifah*'s army if it stood in his way.

Mustafa Kemal's success in this quest was remarkable. Having realized that the central government and the authority in Istanbul were under the enemy's control he decided to establish a national government in Anatolia. So he organized a national conference (rally) in Sywas, where the policies and means to safeguard Turkey's Independence were discussed. The conference adopted a few resolutions and an executive committee was formed, to be headed by Mustafa Kemal. The conference sent a warning to the Sultan demanding the removal of Prime Minister Farid and the holding of free parliamentary elections. Under such pressure, the Sultan was forced to submit to the conferences' demands, and so he dismissed the Prime Minister and appointed Ali Redha as his successor, then he ordered new elections to be held. The delegates from the conference entered the elections as a group with a manifesto designed to salvage the country and they achieved a sweeping majority in the new parliament.

After their success they moved on to Ankara and established their head-quarters there where they held a meeting and proposed that the parliament should meet in Istanbul and their Council of Representatives should be dissolved since its members had now become official deputies. However, Mustafa Kemal strongly opposed these two proposals saying, "The Council of Representatives should continue until the parliament's commitment and integrity is made clear and until its policy becomes known. As for the move to the capital, this would be sheer madness, for if you did this you would be under the mercy of the enemy. The British still control the country and the authorities will undoubtedly meddle in your affairs and perhaps arrest you. The parliament should therefore convene here in Ankara so that it remains independent." Mustafa Kemal persisted and defended his opinion strongly, but failed to persuade the deputies to hold the parliament's sessions in Ankara. The deputies duly went to the capital and expressed their loyalty to the *Khalifah*, and continued on with their work. This was in January 1920.

The *Khalifah* tried to impose his will on the deputies but they resisted and showed their willingness to hold on to the country's rights. When pressure from the allies mounted on them, they rallied public opinion for the covenant which they had agreed upon during the Sywas conference. The covenant included the conditions according to which they were prepared to accept peace. Most important of these conditions was that Turkey should become a free and independent state within specified borders. The allies, especially the British, rejoiced, for this was exactly what they had been aiming at. Moreover, they wanted it to come from the Turks themselves.

It is worth mentioning here that all the countries which the 'Uthmani State used to rule over as *Wilayat* in her capacity, as the Islamic State, had each had, in the wake of the First World War, a covenant drawn up for them by the allies and which proclaimed for them the independence of the part which the allies wanted to keep separate. Iraq, therefore, had a covenant comprising the independence of Iraq, as did Syria, Palestine, Egypt and so on. Thus, it was only natural for the allies, especially the British, to rejoice at this Turkish Nationalistic Covenant, for it was exactly what they wanted; the dismembering of the 'Uthmani State and its division into statelets lest it return again as one strong State. Their dream of destroying the Muslims' State looked as though it would now come to fruition.

Had it not been for the covenants, which the allies managed to set up everywhere, the situation would have taken a different turn. The reason for this was because the 'Uthmani State was a single entity which considered all of its *Wilayat* as part of it. It had adopted a system of Unity (i.e., a federation) and not Union (i.e., a confederation) and so there was no difference in the State's policy between Hijaz or Turkey, nor between the district of al-Quds and the district of Iskandarona. All of them were part of one single State.

In addition, the situation should have been further complicated by the conditions imposed on the defeated powers at war's end. This was because the defeat of Turkey was similar to that of Germany, since they were allies in the war together, and the conditions of peace laid down on one country should have applied to the other. Thus, if the people of Germany resisted the idea of having to part with as much as a handspan of their land, and fought against their country being dismembered, so should have been the case for the 'Uthmani State, and she too should never have been dismembered. The allies were aware of these realities and took them into account. However, when the 'Uthmanis themselves requested their country to be dismembered, a request sought by Arabs and Turks alike, the allies leaped at the chance and ardently encouraged such moves; especially in the State's center (Turkey) where most of the rule within the State originated and where it was represented.

Therefore, the allies considered the covenant to be their final victory. The Turks were thus allowed the freedom of resistance, once it had been published, and the allies then began to pull their troops out from every corner of the land. The British and the French troops were removed from the country. Concomitantly, the Turks began gathering strength. A resistance movement was formed which eventually turned into a revolution against the *Khalifah*, thus forcing him to send in an army to crush the movement. This it managed to do until all the people stood by the Sultan except those in Ankara where the stronghold of the revolution was. Eventually, Ankara itself was on the brink of defeat. In the face of the *Khalifah*'s army, the surrounding villages fell one after the other and then joined it. Mustafa Kemal and those with him were placed in a very critical situation, but Mustafa Kemal was determined to fight on and so he incited the nationalists. They responded and gathered strength. Rumors were spread in the Turkish provinces and villages that the British army was about to occupy the capital, arrest the nationalists and shut down the house of parliament by force.

Rumors about the *Khalifah* and his government supporting the occupation were also spread. The situation soon changed. People began deserting the *Khalifah* and public opinion shifted towards the nationalists in Ankara. Men and women drifted towards Ankara volunteering to defend Turkey. Many soldiers deserted the *Khalifah*'s army and joined the army of Mustafa Kemal, who by then had become a hero for the Turks and a symbol of their hopes. His position gathered strength and almost the entire country came under his control. He issued a leaflet calling for the election of a national Council of Representatives that would position Ankara as its headquarters. The election took place and the newly elected members convened, calling themselves the National Assembly. They considered themselves the legitimate government. They voted Mustafa Kemal as president of the Council of Representatives. Ankara became the center of the national government and all the Turks approved of it. Mustafa Kemal then moved and destroyed what remained of the *Khalifah*'s army, putting an end to the civil war. He then concentrated on fighting the Greeks, and several bloody battles ensued. The Greeks had the upper hand at first but soon the balance shifted in Mustafa Kemal's favor.

By August 1921, he launched a swift and successful attack on the Greeks who at the time occupied Izmir and other parts of the Turkish coasts. In the beginning of September, he sent for Ismat to meet Harrington and work out the details. At that meeting, the allies agreed to expel the Greeks from Tarees and to withdraw themselves from Istanbul and the whole of Turkey. If we closely followed Mustafa Kemal's moves, we deduce that the allies agreed to his demands only when they secured a promise that he would destroy Islamic rule in return. This was made clearer when the National Assembly discussed with him the future of Turkey in the wake of the victories he had achieved. He replied, "I do not believe in a league of Islamic countries, nor in a league of the 'Uthmani people, and each one of us is free to embrace any opinion he wishes. However, the government should adhere to a fixed and devised policy based on realities. A policy that carries one single objective, that is to protect the country and its independence within its natural borders. Sentiments and illusions should not affect our policy, and damn to the dreams and the myths, they have in the past cost us dearly."

By this declaration, he wanted to forge the independence of Turkey on the basis of being a country for the Turkish people and not the Islamic *Ummah*. Some of the deputies and politicians asked him about how the government of the new Turkey should be shaped, for it would be inconceivable for her to have two governments as was the case at that time: a transitional government with power and Ankara as its headquarters and an official yet nominal government in the capital headed by the *Khalifah* and his ministers. The politicians insisted upon Kemal that he should clearly state his opinion about this issue. He did not answer them and concealed his intentions. Instead he began to incite public opinion against *Khalifah* Waheed al-Deen, accusing him of collaborating with the British and the Greeks. People were enraged against the *Khalifah* and amidst the public euphoria behind him, Mustafa Kemal called for a meeting of the National Assembly to outline his plan regarding the Sultan and the government. He had known all along that he was capable of convincing the deputies to remove Waheed al-Deen and strip the *Khalifah* of authority, but he could not be so daring as to risk a direct attack on the *Khilafah*, since this would have triggered Islamic sentiment. He did not therefore dissolve the *Khilafah* and avoided tackling the issue head on. Instead, he slyly suggested stripping the *Khalifah* of all power.

Thus, the Sultanate could be dissolved and Waheed al-Deen removed. As soon as the deputies heard this they became speechless, and quickly realized the dangerous implications of the proposal which they had been asked to endorse and they moved to first debate the issue at hand. Mustafa Kemal was exceedingly apprehensive and fearful of such a debate, so he asked instead for a motion (vote) regarding the proposal to take place. He received the backing of eighty of the deputies, who were from among his personal supporters.

However, the National Assembly refused to grant him his wish and alternatively referred the proposal to the legal committee to look into. When the committee convened the next day, Mustafa Kemal attended and watched the course of events closely. The committee, comprising of scholars and lawyers, debated the issue for a few hours and soon realized that the proposal violated the *Shari'ah* texts, since in Islam there is nothing called religious authority and temporal authority, "Sultana and Khilafah", are one and the same. The concept of separating the *Deen* from the State does not exist in Islam and had never existed throughout its history. There was an Islamic System and the State implemented the System. Inevitably, the legal committee could not find any justification for such a separation nor could it find a reason for conducting a debate on the issue because the Islamic texts are clear-cut and decisive (not open to interpretation) about this issue. Not surprisingly, the committee rejected the proposal.

However, Mustafa Kemal was determined to separate the *Deen* from the State by separating the Sultanate from the *Khilafah*, which was the fulfillment of the aims of the allies; the destruction of the remains of the Islamic State by the hands of its own people. His colonialist culture, which makes him imitate the Westerners in their separation of the temporal power from the spiritual one drove him to separate the Sultanate from the *Khilafah*, just as the Church had come to be separated from the state in the West. When Mustafa Kemal realized that the debate of the committee was taking a course different to his, he lost his temper and leaped off his seat, he stood on a chair fuming with rage and interrupted the debate of the committee by shouting, "Your excellencies! The 'Uthmani Sultan has seized the authority of the people by force, and it is by force that the people have decided to regain it. The Sultanate must be separated from the *Khilafah* and dissolved, this shall take place whether you agree or not, all there is to it is that some of your heads will fall in the process." He spoke like a dictator, then the meeting of the committee broke up. The National Assembly was immediately called for to meet and discuss the proposal.

Throughout the debate, Mustafa Kemal realized that the majority of the deputies were against the proposal, so he gathered his supporters around him and called for a vote on the proposal by raising hands once. The deputies objected to this and said, "If it is absolutely necessary to vote, let this take place by calling out the name of each deputy." Mustafa Kemal rejected this and shouted out menacingly, "I am confident that the National Assembly will endorse the proposal by general consensus and it will be sufficient to take votes by raising hands only." The proposal was put to the vote and only a few hands were raised. However, the result was declared as though the National Assembly had accepted the proposal by a clear majority. The deputies were stunned by this and some of them leaped from their seats protesting and shouting, "This is not true, we did not agree!" The supporters of Mustafa Kemal shouted back at them and restrained them, insults were exchanged then the President of the National Assembly declared the result of the vote once more stating that the National Assembly had approved by a clear majority the dissolution of the Sultanate. The meeting was adjourned. Mustafa Kemal left the conference center surrounded by his supporters. When Waheed al-Deen, the *Khaleefah*, received news of this he fled the country and soon after his nephew, 'Abdul Majid, was nominated as the *Khalifah* of the Muslims, albeit stripped of any authority. The country, however, remained without a legitimate ruler.

If the Sultanate was separated from the *Khilafah*, who then was the legal ruler? Mustafa Kemal had all along been very anxious to separate the Sultanate from the *Khilafah*, and he did so without revealing the structure of government which Turkey was to adopt. With the dissolution of the Sultanate it had become necessary to decide the format of the new government. Would Mustafa Kemal form the government and become the President of a constitutional government while keeping the *Khalifah* as the authoritative figure? If so, then would not the decision to dissolve the Sultanate have been ineffectual in the first place?

Mustafa Kemal refused to form a government and did not reveal his intentions. Backed up by his power and authority, through which he had control over the people, he went on to form a party which he called the "People's Party". His intention was to gain public opinion in his favor because despite his power, the sweeping majority in the Council of Representatives were still against him even after the declaration of the separation of the Sultanate from the *Khilafah*. This led him to consider disclosing the shape of the new government which he had decided to form, declaring Turkey to be a republic with himself as its President. He started by initiating a smear campaign against the National Assembly and this produced an embarrassing political crisis, thus leading to the resignation of the government in office. The government tendered its resignation to the National Assembly creating a power vacuum. Amidst the deepening crisis, some of the deputies suggested to the Council of Representatives that it should appoint Mustafa Kemal as the head of the government in order to solve the crisis. At first he pretended that he held no ambitions for the job, then he agreed and went up to the stand to address the National Assembly.

In his speech he said to the deputies, "You have sent for me to come to the rescue at this critical hour. However, the critical situation is of your own doing. Therefore, this state of affairs is not a passing incident, but a fundamental error of judgment in the system of our government. The National Assembly has at the moment two functions, legislative and executive. Each deputy wants to take part in every ministerial decision and stick his nose into every government department and every decision made by a minister. Your excellencies, no minister can become familiar with his job and responsibility, and accept a post in such circumstances. You have to realize that a government founded on this basis is impossible to establish, and if it were established, you would not call it a government, but shambles, and we have to appreciate this state of affairs. Therefore, I have decided to turn Turkey into a republic, with an elected President." Once he had finished his speech, it was soon realized that he had already prepared a decree, making Turkey a republic and electing himself as the first President of the Turkish republic. He turned himself into the lawful ruler of the country.

However, things did not run as smoothly for Mustafa Kemal as he had wished. For one thing, the Turkish people are Muslim and what Mustafa Kemal did contradicts Islam. A feeling that Mustafa Kemal intended to destroy Islam spread, fueled by Kamal's own personal actions. In his private life, he held Islam in contempt, violating all the Divine *Shari'ah* rules, mocking everything that Muslims hold in high esteem and sanctity. People soon realized that the new rulers of Ankara were damned *Kafireen* and they began to gather around the *Khalifah* 'Abdul Majid. They attempted to hand him back the authority and make him the effective ruler so that he could get rid of these apostates. Mustafa Kemal sensed the growing danger and realized that the majority of the people despised him, accusing him of being a *Zindiq* and *Kafir*. He thought long and hard about the matter and as a result intensified his smear campaign against the *Khalifah* and the *Khilafah*, inciting the fervor of the National Assembly, until it adopted and enacted a law stating that any opposition to the republic and any siding with the Sultan would be considered an act of treachery, carrying the death penalty. Mustafa Kemal then began to talk about the disadvantages of the *Khilafah* at every meeting, especially the National Assembly. He started to prepare the ground to abolish the *Khilafah*. Some of the deputies countered this threat by speaking out about the diplomatic advantages of the *Khilafah*, they were met in turn by a fierce attack from Mustafa Kemal. He said to the National Assembly, "Was it not because of the *Khilafah*, Islam and the clergy, that the Turkish peasants fought and died for five centuries? It is high time Turkey looked after her own interests and ignored the Indians and the Arabs. Turkey should rid itself of leading the Muslims."

Mustafa Kemal pursued his smear campaign against the *Khilafah*, highlighting its disadvantages to the Turkish people. He also smeared the *Khalifah* himself by portraying him and his supporters as the real traitors and as British puppets. Mustafa Kemal did not stop there, but went on to sponsor a terror campaign against those who championed the *Khilafah*. His reaction towards one of the deputies who openly declared the obligation of holding onto the *Khilafah* and safeguarding the *Deen* was to hire someone to kill him the very night that he was meant to speak. So one of his followers assassinated him that night while he was on his way back home from the National Assembly. Another deputy delivered an Islamic speech, so Mustafa Kemal summoned him and threatened him with hanging if he opened his mouth again.

Mustafa Kemal spread terror everywhere. In time, he ordered the Governor of Istanbul to scale down the protocol and ceremonial display that surrounds the *Khalifah*'s cortege during *Salat ul Jumu'ah*. He also cut down the *Khalifah*'s salary to the minimum and exhorted his followers to desert him. When some of Mustafa Kemal's moderate supporters witnessed this, their Islamic feelings began to run high again and they feared the annulment of the *Khilafah*. They proposed to Mustafa Kemal the idea of appointing himself as *Khalifah* over the Muslims. He flatly refused. Then he was visited by two delegations, one from Egypt and the other from India, asking him to appoint himself as *Khalifah* of the Muslims, pleading with him repeatedly but to no avail. Mustafa Kemal had by now prepared the way to ring the death knell and deal his final blow to the *Khilafah*.

Hatred and contempt for foreigners, the enemy and their supposed ally the *Khalifah* was spread by Kemal amongst the people, the armed forces and the National Assembly. Inciting the feeling of hatred towards foreigners was merely a ploy intended to accuse the *Khalifah* of being their ally. When public opinion had shifted towards him and with feelings against the *Khalifah* running high, Mustafa Kemal presented to the National Assembly on March 3rd, 1924 a motion stating the annulment of the *Khilafah* and the removal and expulsion of the *Khalifah*, thereby formally separating the *Deen* from the State.

Some of the words which he said when he presented the motion to the deputies were as follows, "At what cost should the threatened republic be safeguarded and be established on a strong scientific basis? The *Khalifah* and the legacies of *"Ahl ul Uthman"* must go, the ancient religious courts and their laws must be replaced by modern courts and modern laws, the schools of the clergy must give way to secular government schools." He then went on to attack the *Deen* and what he called religious men. Displaying real dictatorial authority, he adopted the motion himself and secured the National Assembly's approval without any debate. He then sent an order to the Governor of Istanbul stating that the *Khalifah*, 'Abdul Majid, should leave Turkey before dawn the following day. The Governor himself, went with a group of policemen and soldiers to the *Khalifah*'s Palace at midnight. They forced him to get into a cart and escorted him to the border not allowing him to take more than one suitcase containing some clothing and a little money.

This is how Mustafa Kemal abolished the Islamic State and the Islamic System, and in its place established a Capitalist state and a Capitalist system. By destroying the Islamic State, he fulfilled the dream of the disbelievers which they had nurtured ever since the Crusades.

Preventing the Establishment of the Islamic State

In the wake of the First World War, the allies occupied all the lands of the Islamic State. Their main aim was to destroy the State for good and then ensure that it would never rise again. Once they had destroyed the Islamic State, they set about making sure that the Islamic State could not be reestablished in any part of its lands. They designed several plans and used several methods to make certain that the Islamic State would never return to existence, and they are still working towards that objective.

Following a carefully designed plan, the disbelieving colonial powers set about strengthening their grip on the Muslim lands, from the very first day that they occupied the Islamic world. In 1918, they occupied the countries which were still under the rule of the 'Uthmani State and established military rule within them until 1922. They concentrated their stranglehold over them through mandatory rule or self autonomy. Then came 1924. In that year, many steps were taken by the enemy, especially Britain, in order to quell any moves; whether directly or indirectly, aimed at reviving the Islamic State.

In that year, Mustafa Kemal abolished the *Khilafah* System in the 'Uthmani State due to direct pressure from the colonial disbelievers and turned Turkey into a 'democratic' republic. He thus destroyed the specter of the *Khilafah* and with it the last vestige of hope for the Islamic State to stage a comeback. In that year, al-Hussein ibn 'Ali was expelled from Hijaz and imprisoned in Cyprus as he had an eye on the *Khilafah*. In the very same year, the British, through their collaborators, intervened to make sure that the *Khilafah* conference held in Cairo was called off and doomed to failure. Again, in that same year, the British worked hard to dissolve the *Khilafah* movement established in India, making sure that the movement's ambitions were aborted and its tendency was transformed into a nationalist and sectarian one. Still in the same year, and following pressure from the colonial disbelievers, literature written by some of al-Azhar's scholars calling for the separation of the *Deen* from the State, claiming that Islam does not contain any fundamentals for government or ruling, and portraying Islam as a theological (*Kahanuty*) religion with no basics or teachings about ruling and the State, was published. Yet again in that same year and the following one, some Sophist sponsored debates and arguments over two topics took center stage in the Arab countries: Which of the two leagues would be better, the Arab league or the Islamic league? Newspapers and magazines focused their attention on this issue, despite the fact that both leagues had a damaging effect and that their very existence presented an obstacle in the face of any attempt to reestablish the Islamic State. Nevertheless, the colonial disbelievers managed to bring about this debate in order to direct attention away from the real issue, which was the Islamic State. These moves, therefore, managed to distance the people's minds in the Muslim lands away from the concept of the *Khilafah* and the Islamic State.

Prior to their occupation the colonial powers began spreading nationalistic slogans amongst the Turkish youth by claiming that Turkey had been burdened with the running of the affairs of non-Turkish people and that it was high time she left those people to their own fate. Political parties also worked towards spreading Turkish nationalism and called for Turkey's independence from the non-Turkish countries. The disbelievers spread the same concepts among Arab youths and encouraged Arab nationalism. They described Turkey as being an occupying force and called on the Arabs to rid themselves of being occupied by the Turks, and likewise, political parties calling for Arab unity and Arab independence were formed. They soon filled the vacuum which was once graced by Islamic concepts. Consequently, the Turks gained their independence on the basis of nationalism, and the Arabs began working towards achieving autonomy on a nationalist geographic basis. The concepts of nationalism and patriotism spread rapidly throughout the nation, and the Muslims prided themselves on these concepts.

The colonial forces did not stop at that, but went further by spreading erroneous concepts about the Islamic ruling system and Islam, portraying the *Khilafah* as being a papal and priestly rule. This reached the point whereby the Muslims were embarrassed to mention the word *Khalifah*, or to proclaim the concept of the *Khilafah*. At this time there arose a popular conception amongst the Muslims that any proclamation of the word *Khilafah* was backward and pointed up rigidity, and that it should not be uttered by any educated person.

It was amidst this highly nationalistic feeling, which had gathered momentum within society, that the disbelievers dismembered the Islamic State. Parceling it up into little statelets, and encouraging local communities to strengthen these divisions. The 'Uthmani State was divided into several states, these being: Turkey, Egypt, Iraq, Syria, Lebanon, Palestine, East Jordan, Hijaz, Najd and Yemen. Politicians in these statelets, both the collaborators and those with good intentions, began to hold conferences in every country, demanding their independence, i.e. independence for the country that the disbelievers had founded to the exclusion of the other statelets. On this basis the State of Turkey was founded, as were the states of Iraq, Egypt, Syria etc. Then a national homeland for the Jews was founded in Palestine, which was then subsequently turned into an independent entity. It was used by the disbelievers as a political bridgehead to the Muslim World and to draw the attention of the Muslims away from the colonial disbelievers, i.e. the Western countries such as Britain, the United States and France, and for it to constitute one of the obstacles which stand in the way of the return of the Islamic State. This geographical situation and the general scene were both designed to ensure that the Muslims would never be able to liberate themselves.

The disbelievers set about implementing the Capitalist system in Economics and the Democratic system in Government. They also introduced Western laws in their Administrative and Judicial systems. They spread their culture and their concepts about life, and earnestly attempted to establish their viewpoint about life so that their way of life became the one that the Muslims adopted and followed. They have in fact succeeded in this quest. They turned Egypt into a Sultanate, then a parliamentary monarchy was established. In Iraq, a parliamentary monarchy system was established. Syria and Lebanon became republics and in East Jordan an emirate was established, while Palestine was put under mandatory rule which ended in the establishment of a parliamentary democratic system for the Jews. The remainder of Palestine was joined to East Jordan and turned into a parliamentary monarchy. In Hijaz and in Yemen, dictatorial monarchies were established, and in Turkey a presidential republic was formed. Afghanistan was fitted with a hereditary monarchy. The colonial disbelievers encouraged Iran to maintain the Imperial system while India remained a colony, until eventually it was divided into two states. The colonial disbelievers, therefore, managed to impose their system on Muslim land, and by so doing the concept of reestablishing the Islamic rule gradually waned in people's minds.

Furthermore, each local community was encouraged to hold on to the system that the disbelievers had established for it and they worked towards achieving total independence from all other countries that comprised the Muslim world. Thus, an Iraqi became a foreigner in Egypt. The rulers of each statelet became more keen to safeguard the Capitalist democratic system than the founders of the system itself. They became surrogates, watching over and guarding the system and constitution that the colonial powers had set up for them.

The colonial disbelieving powers implemented Western laws directly on Muslim land. Previously, they had attempted to implement them through their collaborators in the Muslim countries. The disbelievers initiated their attempts to introduce Western laws in the first half of the 19th century. They began encouraging people in Egypt to adopt French civil laws so as to replace the *Shari'ah*, succeeding in doing so and Egypt began implementing the French Judicial system in 1883. The old French civil law was translated and enacted, it became the newly adopted system in Egypt replacing the *Shari'ah* in the courts. A similar move began within the 'Uthmani State in 1856 with the aim of introducing Western laws there. However, this move was not as easy as in Egypt because the *Khilafah* itself was based in the 'Uthmani State.

However, due to the disbelievers' persistence, and the response of their collaborators, they succeeded in introducing the penal code and new non-Islamic legal and commercial laws by securing *Fatawa* which stated that these *Kufr* laws did not contradict Islam. The concept of codification then took root and *Al Majalla* (Code issued in 1868 as a canon for transactions compiled from the weak opinions of many *Madhahib*, which justified the situation) was adopted as a law. *Al Majalla* was codified as law. The court system was divided into two: 1) a *Shari'yah* court, using *Shari'yah* rules. 2) civil court, using a.) Western laws, justified by some *Fatawa* stating that these laws did not contradict Islam. b.) *Shari'ah* laws after being codified as a law in imitating western process. This was concerning the law. As for the constitution, moves aimed at drafting a new constitution for the State, using the French constitution as its source, were made in conjunction with the movement for new codification. These moves nearly succeeded in 1878 except for the fierce resistance of the Muslims who stood up to them and stopped them in their tracks. However, the colonial disbelievers' persistence, coupled with the success of their collaborators and those who were seduced by their culture, enabled the movement for the drafting of a constitution to emerge once more and this time succeeded in its task. The constitution was put into practice in 1908 with its adoption and implementation of the new legislation. All Muslims lands, with the exception of the Arabian Peninsula and Afghanistan, came to be directly governed by Western laws[3]. Thus, the *Shari'ah* laws were abandoned and this meant that *Kufr* rule was enforced and the rule of Islam discarded.

What helped the rule of *Kufr* to strengthen its grip over the Muslims was the fact that the colonialists had based their strategy on changing the Islamic State's education policy. They designed a new educational program for the Muslims. The objective of this curriculum was to produce individuals with a Western personality, i.e., someone with a capitalistic/secular outlook to regulating life's affairs. These programs, including those in Islamic universities, are still in force today throughout all the countries of the Muslim world. As a result, we have many teachers that ensure the safety of these educational programs. They take up influential posts, carrying out the wishes of the disbelievers. The education policy was founded on two principles.

The first principle was to separate the *Deen* from the temporal affairs of life, which would naturally lead to the separation of the *Deen* from the State. This measure was also designed to ensure that young Muslims would fight off the re-establishment of the Islamic State as it would contradict the basis upon which they had been educated.

---

[3] Translator - This was true until 1952 when this book was published. However, now all Muslims lands are governed by Western laws.

The second principle was to make the personality of the colonial disbeliever the main source of emulation for young Muslims. This would then readily facilitate their minds to be imbued with his culture and information. Such a move entailed giving respect to the *Kafir*. It entailed glorifying him, and an attempt to emulate and befriend him, despite the fact that he was a colonial disbeliever. It also entailed holding the Muslims in contempt and disdain so that he was kept away from him. The feelings of disgust displayed towards him thus prevented anyone taking or learning anything from him and naturally compelled them to fight the reestablishment of the Islamic State.

The colonialists felt that the school syllabus, which they had designed and closely monitored, was not enough. They went further by establishing missionary schools based on their colonialist principles. In addition, cultural centers were tasked with the spreading of misguided political orientations. Consequently, the intellectual atmosphere in these various "learning" centers led to the *Ummah* being fed with the culture that led her away from thinking about reestablishing the Islamic State and prevented her from working towards that cause.

Separating the *Deen* from life's affairs became a widespread concept amongst intellectuals. For the rest of society, it was manifested as a separation of the *Deen* from politics, or the regulation of their daily affairs and concerns. As a result, some of the intellectuals claimed that the cause behind the decline of the Muslims was their attachment to the *Deen* and they claimed that the only path to their revival would be through nationalism. Others claimed that the cause behind the Muslims' decline was the absence of morals. On the first count, nationalistic political parties were established, claiming that they had an Islamic basis. This was merely a colonialist ploy. On the second count, several groups were formed on the basis of morals, preaching and spiritual guidance. These began to work towards moral excellence of the individual, and not to get involved in politics. It was the presence of these parties and organizations that proved to be the effective obstacle in the efforts made to reestablish the Islamic State. They distracted the minds of the Muslims. In addition, these parties were also established on a colonialist basis that contradicts Islam, and because of this they inadvertently prevented the reestablishment of the Islamic State.

To safeguard the newly adopted political programs, new laws were drafted. Some laws were enacted to bar the establishment of Islamic political parties and movements. There were laws that included certain clauses which imposed a democratic system on political parties and movements, and specified that they should not restrict their membership to any particular sect. This meant that it became against the law to establish any Islamic groups or parties in Muslim countries lest the Islamic State should be reborn. Muslims had no right to establish any party or movement except charity organizations or other similar organizations. They were restricted from indulging in political work on the basis of Islam. Some of the laws that were introduced considered establishing Islamic political parties a serious crime that deserved punishment. The political programs propagated in the Muslim world, with the help of the adopted laws, were therefore, focused on preventing the reestablishment of the Islamic State.

The colonialists did not stop there but went on to occupy the Muslims with trivial matters, aiming to distract them from thinking about the Islamic State. They encouraged Islamic conferences which served as a diversion from the real work, i.e. the Islamic call and the resumption of the Islamic way of life under the umbrella of the Islamic State. Such conferences served as an effective way for the Muslims to vent their frustrations and provided a safety valve to channel one's Islamic emotions. Decisions would be made at these conferences, published in the newspapers, and announced on radio stations, but never executed.

Writers and lecturers were also encouraged to present the Islamic State as a threat. They promoted the concept that Islam does not contain a ruling system. Books and essays, written by some hired Muslims, were published carrying these colonialist concepts in order to lead the Muslims astray, divert them from their *Deen*, and from working towards the resumption of the Islamic way of life according to the rules of that *Deen*.

Since destroying the Islamic State, the colonialists have persevered in their bid to place obstacles in the way of the re-establishment of the Islamic State. They have concentrated their efforts to prevent its formation again after first having abolished it from the face of the earth.

The Neglected Duty

The structure of the Islamic State is based on eight pillars: the *Khalifah*; the Delegated Assistants; the Executive Assistants; the Commander of *Jihad*; the Judiciary; the *Wulaa'*; the Administrative System; and the *Majlis Al Ummah*. The structure of the State would be complete if these seven elements were in place. If any of these elements were absent, the structure would be incomplete, though the State would still remain Islamic. Any defect or shortage would not upset its status as long as the *Khalifah* remained viable, since it is he who is the foundation of the State. As for the principles of the ruling system in the Islamic State, there are four:

1. The sovereignty belongs to the *Shari'ah*.

2. The authority belongs to the *Ummah*.

3. The appointment of *one Khalifah*.

4. The *Khalifah* alone reserves the right to adopt the *Shari'ah* rules, i.e. to enact them as laws.

If any of these principles were missing, the ruling system would become non-Islamic. Therefore, these four principles must be enforced. The basis of the Islamic State is the *Khalifah* and anyone other than him is a deputy to him or an advisor for him; the Islamic State is a *Khalifah* who implements Islam and the office of *Khilafah* or *Imamah* is to have full disposal over the affairs of Muslims. It is not part of the doctrines (*'Aqa'id*) of Islam, but part of the *Shari'ah* rules because it is part of the branches related to a human's actions.

The appointment of the *Khalifah* is an obligation upon the Muslims. They are forbidden from spending more than two nights without giving a *Ba'yah* to him. If the Muslims did not appoint a *Khalifah* within three days they would all be sinful until they had appointed a *Khalifah*. The sin would not fall until they had exhausted their efforts to appoint a *Khalifah* and continued to endeavor to appoint him.

The obligation of appointing a *Khalifah* has been confirmed by the Qu'ran, *Sunnah* and the general consensus of the *Sahabah*.

Allah (swt) ordered the Messenger (saaw) conclusively to rule among the Muslims whatever was revealed to him. Allah (swt) says,

$$ فَٱحۡكُم بَيۡنَهُم بِمَآ أَنزَلَ ٱللَّهُ وَلَا تَتَّبِعۡ أَهۡوَآءَهُمۡ $$

"So judge between them by what Allah has revealed, and follow not their vain desires." [Al-Maidah 5:48]

$$ وَأَنِ ٱحۡكُم بَيۡنَهُم بِمَآ أَنزَلَ ٱللَّهُ وَلَا تَتَّبِعۡ أَهۡوَآءَهُمۡ $$

"And so judge between them by what Allah has revealed and follow not their desires," [Al-Maidah 5:49]

Any address to the Messenger (saaw) is considered an address to the entire *Ummah* as long as there is no daleel restricting the order to the Messenger (saaw). And there is no such daleel, therefore, Muslims are mandated to establish this ruling. Establishing the *Khilafah* is the establishment of this ruling.

As for the *Sunnah*, the Messenger of Allah (saaw) said, "He who died not knowing the *Imam* of his time has died a death of *Jahiliyyah*." Ahmed and al-Tabarani extracted from the Hadeeth of Mu'awiyah the following: The Messenger of Allah (saaw) said, "Whoso dies while there was no *Ba'yah* on his neck dies a death of *Jahiliyyah*." Muslim reported in his *Sahih* on the authority of Ibn 'Umar that he said, I heard the Messenger of Allah (saaw) say, "Whoso takes off his hand from allegiance to Allah will meet Him on the Day of Resurrection without having any proof for him, and whoso dies while there was no *Ba'yah* on his neck dies a death of *Jahiliyyah*." Hisham reported on the authority of 'Urwa, who reported on the authority of Abu Salih, who reported on the authority of Abu Hurayrah that the Messenger of Allah (saaw) said, "Leaders will take charge of you after me, where the pious one will lead with his piety and the impious with his impiety, so listen to them and obey them in everything which conforms with the truth. If they acted rightly it is to your credit, and if they acted wrongly it is counted for you and against them."

As for the *'Ijma'* of the *Sahabah*, they made the appointment of a *Khalifah* their top priority in the wake of the departure of the Messenger of Allah (saaw). This is according to that which has been narrated in the two *Sahih Ahadeeth* about the events in the courtyard of Banu Sa'idah and also in the wake of the death of each subsequent *Khalifah*. The general consensus of the *Sahabah* concerning the obligation of appointing a *Khalifah* has been transmitted by way of *Khabar Mutawatir* (continuous report). The *Sahabah* agreed that it was the most important of all obligations. This is considered to be a conclusive evidence. It has also been confirmed by means of *Tawatur* that the *Ummah* should at no time remain without a *Khalifah*. It is obligatory upon the whole *Ummah* to appoint a *Khalifah*, i.e. to establish him in office or to govern her affairs. The command is addressed to the entire *Ummah*. This took effect from the moment of his (saaw) departure and will continue to the Day of Judgment.

The extent of the obligation to reestablish the *Khalifah* and awareness of this obligation among the *Sahabah* is clearly reflected in their actions following the death of the Messenger of Allah (saaw). They delayed the burial of the Messenger of Allah (saaw) until a *Khalifah* had been given the *Ba'yah* to head the State. It is also clearly reflected in the action of 'Umar ibn al-Khattab, in the wake of his stabbing while the agony of death neared; when the Muslims asked him to nominate a successor. At first he refused, when they persisted he nominated six candidates from which a *Khalifah* was to be elected. He also set a deadline of three days for the six to reach an agreement. He gave instructions stating that in the case of the six not coming to an agreement within the three days, the one who opposed the decision should be killed. Indeed, he ordered the killing of the one who sat in opposition despite the fact that the six were all people of *Shura* and senior *Sahabah*. The six were in fact 'Ali,

'Uthman, 'Abd al-Rahman ibn 'Auf, al-Zubayr ibn al-'Awwam, Talhah ibn 'Ubaydullah and Sa'd ibn Abi Waqqas. That one of these *Sahabah* could have been killed, should they have been unable to reach an agreement concerning the election of a *Khalifah*, serves as an oppressively clear evidence that the appointment of a *Khalifah* is compulsory.

Besides, numerous *Shari'ah* duties depend on the presence of the *Khalifah*, such as the implementation of Islamic rules, the execution of the penal code, guarding the frontiers, educating the society, training and equipping the Armed Forces, settling disputes and keeping law and order, in addition to looking after other matters and regulating the economic and societal transactions which take place between individuals and collective entities. Thus the appointment of a *Khalifah* is compulsory.

Seeking the post of *Khalifah* and competing for it is not undesirable, the *Sahabah* competed for the post in the *Saqeefah* and the people of *Shura* also competed for the office. Nobody condemned or disowned this action. On the contrary, the general consensus of the *Sahabah* regarding the competition for the post of *Khalifah*, is clearly established, confirming that it is lawful and acceptable.

Muslims are forbidden from appointing more than one *Khalifah*. Imam Muslim reported on the authority of Abu Sa'id al-Khudry that the Messenger of Allah (saaw) said, "If a bay'ah has been taken for two *Khulafah*, kill the latter of them." In another *Hadeeth*, he (saaw) is reported to have said, "Whoso pledged allegiance to an *Imam* giving him the clasp of his hand and the fruit of his heart shall obey him as long as he can, and if another comes to dispute with him you must strike the neck of that man." In another narration, the wording was as follows, "...strike him with the sword whoever he may be." The command to kill the other one would come into effect if he did not comply and retreat. If a group of people, who met all the requirements necessary for the post of *Khilafah*, were given the *Ba'yah* then it would be the one with the majority of votes who would become *Khalifah*, whoever opposed the majority would subsequently be considered a rebel. This would apply if the nominees were gathered together in person, but if the *Khilafah* had been contracted to one man who fulfilled the requirements of the *Khilafah* and the majority of the Muslims gave their *Ba'yah* to another, then the first man should become *Khalifah* and the second man should be turned down.

The requirements for the *Khilafah* office are Islam, manhood, freedom, competence, maturity, sanity and justice, i.e. the candidate should be Muslim, male, mature, sane, free, competent and just. As for the condition of being a Muslim, this follows because of Allah's saying,

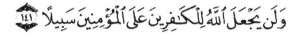

"And never will Allah grant to the disbelievers a way (triumph) over the believers." [An-Nisa, 4:141]

As for the condition that the *Khalifah* must be a man, it is derived from the *Hadeeth* of the Messenger of Allah (saaw), who said, "A nation (*Ummah*) will never be successful if they are headed by a woman?" The conditions of maturity and sanity must be met because the insane and the minor need tutors and guardians to look after their welfare. Therefore, if one cannot rule one's own affairs, he is obviously unable to run other affairs beyond his own. As for justice, this must be fulfilled because the duty of the *Khalifah* is to implement the rules of the *Deen*, and if he could not implement them upon himself then he could not be trusted to implement them upon others; for one cannot give what one does not possess. Justice has been made a condition which the *Khalifah* must fulfill because if he were a *Fasiq* then he would be unfit for the *Khilafah* and he could not remain in office. Trustworthiness is a condition laid down in the contract and it must be observed throughout.

As for the freedom, since the slave does not have the authority upon himself, therefore, he would not have authority over others. As for the competence, its is a requirement since asking an incompetent person to do things beyond his capacity is invalid. This leads to the undermining the legislation and the rights of the people, which is not allowed.

These are the set conditions for the post of *Khalifah*, as for the other conditions which the scholars have mentioned, such as bravery, knowledge and belonging to the Quraysh or a descendant of Fatimah among others, these are not necessary conditions for the contract of the *Khilafah* and none of the evidences put forward to back such claims have proven to be reliable and therefore cannot be considered as conditions. Every male Muslim who is mature, sane, trustworthy, free and able is fit to be given the *Ba'yah* by the other Muslims in order to become their *Khalifah* and no other conditions are needed nor should be laid down.

Reestablishing the Islamic State is a duty upon all the Muslims because this has been confirmed by the *Sunnah* and the general consensus of the *Sahabah*. It is obligatory upon them to live in an Islamic homeland and to have possess Islamic citizenship, yet they cannot achieve this unless they establish the Islamic State. Thus, the Muslims would remain sinful until they began to work towards reestablishing the Islamic State so that they could give their *Ba'yah* to a *Khaleefah* who would implement Islam and carry its Message to the world.

Obstacles in Establishing the Islamic State

Reestablishing the Islamic State is by no means an easy or straightforward task. There are several colossal obstacles facing the re-establishment of the Islamic State which first need to be removed and dismantled, and there are several major difficulties standing in the way of the resumption of the Islamic way of life which also need to be overcome. This is so because the issue is not merely the existence of just any state, nor the founding of a state simply calling itself Islamic. The issue is in fact the existence of the Islamic State which implements Islam as a system emanating from the Islamic *'Aqeedah*, a State which implements Islam according to the *Shari'ah* rules, since these are the rules of Allah (swt). Thus, the Islamic way of life would initially be resumed at home and the Islamic Message would come to be conveyed to all the peoples abroad.

This Islamic State should be founded upon the Islamic concepts and emotions, grounded in the Islamic *'Aqeedah*. The Islamic mentality, nurtured by Islamic thought and rationally shaped by the Islamic ideology and method should be present in its citizenry. The incentives to adhere to the *Shari'ah* should originate from the inner self. This Islamic disposition would ensure the voluntary implementation of the system and its rules with passion, zeal and peace of mind.

This State must be Islamic both at the level of the *Ummah* and that of the people in authority. It must be Islamic in all aspects of its life, securing the resumption of the Islamic way of life in a manner which would enable her to carry its Message to the whole world. This in turn would enable the non-Muslims to witness the light of Islam from within its State so that they enter the *Deen* of Allah (swt) in flocks.

This is why the difficulties which stand in the path of resuming the Islamic way of life are numerous. They should be assessed and a clearly laid out plan should be made in order to overcome them.

The most serious of these obstacles are:

1. *The presence of the non-Islamic concepts in the Islamic world.* This is so because the Islamic world - while undergoing a period of decline with the level of thought being low, knowledge scarce and rationality very weak due to its state of decline - was invaded by non-Islamic concepts, which contradict the Islamic concepts and are based on an erroneous understanding of what existed prior to the life of this world, life as we know it, and the life to come after the life of this world comes to its conclusion. These concepts found fertile ground free of any resistance and they became deeply rooted, thus the mentality of the Muslims, especially the intelligentsia, came to be infested by these concepts. A mentality largely influenced by imitation emerged which lacked any sense of creativity and which was unprepared to accept the Islamic ideology nor was it able to realize the essence of this ideology, especially the political side of it. The Islamic call must be a call to resume the Islamic way of life. The non-Muslims should be called to Islam by presenting the Islamic thoughts to them and the Muslims should be called to work towards the resumption of the Islamic way of life by properly explaining Islam to them. This would entail divulging the shortcomings of non-Islamic concepts and their dangerous consequences and thus the *Da'wah* should take its political course with endeavors made in order to acculturate the *Ummah* with the Islamic outlook on the reality before and after life, as well life itself, which necessitates a discussion of life's political aspects. This is how the first obstacle would be overcome.

2. *The presence of the educational programs which the colonial powers set up and the method by which these educational systems are implemented in the schools and universities.* Those who take up positions in Government, the Administration, the Judiciary, the teaching profession, medicine and students of other professions who gradu-

228

ate from such institutions have adopted a distinctive mentality that works in harmony with the plan which the colonialists have laid down. This is clearly reflected in the ruling system as we see it today whereby the colonial employees were replaced by Muslim ones whose task was (and is) to safeguard the laws, the culture, the policies and the systems which the colonial powers had established, and to defend them as the colonialists did, nay with even greater vigor! The way to overcome this obstacle would be to divulge these actions to those rulers, civil servants and all the people so that the ugly face of colonialism comes to the surface and so that they cease protecting those policies and systems allowing therefore the *Da'wah* to find its way to those Muslims.

3. *The continued application of the educational curriculum according to the basis which was laid down by the unbelieving colonialists, and according to the method which they selected, a matter which made the majority of the graduated young people and those in the educational institutions proceed in a direction contradictory to Islam.* We do not mean the scientific and industrial part of the educational curriculum, as these are universal which do not relate to a specific *Ummah*. We mean here the culture which affect the viewpoint towards life, as they are responsible for making the educational programs stand as an obstacle in the face of resuming the Islamic way of life. These subjects include history, literature, philosophy and legislation. History reflects the practical interpretation of life; literature reflects emotional conditions; philosophy is the basic thought upon which the viewpoint towards life is built; and legislation is the practical solutions to life's problems and the tool which regulates the organization of and transactions between individuals and communities. These comprise the culture with which the disbelieving colonialists fashioned the Muslim mentality with. Some felt Islam as unnecessary in their life and the life of their *Ummah*. It made some of them hostile to Islam, denying its capability to solve life's problems. Therefore, it is necessary to change this mentality, by acculturating today's young people outside the schools and universities with concentrated education that entails probing discussions about the Is-

lamic thoughts and rules.

4. *Lending culturally based subjects, such as sociology, psychology and education science unnecessary respect and erroneously classifying them as universal sciences.* Most people recognize these disciplines as being scientific and that the facts which these studies establish have come by way of experimentation. As a result, they treat them with high regard and they consider the findings of such studies to be indisputable. In so doing, they turned to them in order to solve their life's affairs and taught them in our schools and universities as sciences. Consequently, whatever the psychiatrists, sociologists and educationalists say is taken as a reference above the authority of the Qur'an and *Hadeeth*, or at best, these studies have been mixed with the Islamic texts and thus we carry erroneous concepts and viewpoints.

It has thus become extremely difficult for people to accept anything which contradicts this state of affairs. This categorically leads to the separation of the *Deen* from life's daily affairs in both the public and private arena and stands in the way of reestablishing the Islamic State. The truth of the matter is that these disciplines cannot be considered as scientific endeavors, as they are drawn from observation and inference and are not based on experimentation. Implementing them upon people cannot be defined as experimentation, but merely repetitive observations carried out on different persons in different situations and circumstances, and therefore they are just observations and inferences and nothing like the experiments carried out in laboratories where something is tested. Thus, they are classified as culturally based studies and not scientifically based. The findings are always doubtful with some considerable margin of error. Furthermore, these disciplines are based on false premises because they are based on viewing the society from an individualistic point of view.

Therefore, their outlook, progresses from the individual to the family, group, and then to society on the basis that the society is defined as a group of individuals. This leads to the understanding that societies are independent and that what is valid for one society is not necessarily valid for another. In reality, society is comprised of the human (individual), concepts, emotions, and systems, and what is valid for the human in terms of concepts and solutions in one place should be valid for him everywhere else. These concepts and solutions would transform several societies into one single society for which the concepts, emotions and systems would be valid. The shortcoming of education and sociology is due to the fact that those two disciplines are built upon this misinterpretation of the makeup of society.

Furthermore, psychology influences sociology and education. Psychology is an erroneous discipline for two reasons: It considers the brain as being divided into segments with each of these segments having a distinct function or aptitude and claiming that some brains have certain aptitudes which other brains may not have. The truth of the matter is that the brain is one unit and the disparity of thoughts is natural due to the disparity of things and the previous information retained by the mind. There is no aptitude in one brain which is not found in another, but all brains contain the ability to think about every matter whenever the tangible reality, the senses, and previous information were made available to the brain. Brains differ in their ability to assess and link information and in the ability of the senses; similar to the natural variation in eyesight. It would be possible therefore to feed any person with any type of data and he would have the ability to digest such data. Thus, the claims which psychologists make about those aptitudes are groundless. Psychology considers the instincts to be numerous, some of which have been discovered and others which are yet to be discovered.

Some theorists went on to establish false theories based on this concept about instincts. In reality, if we observe the reaction of human beings, one can perceive through the senses that the human being possesses vital energy which has two aspects: one which needs to be satisfied, otherwise the human being would perish, and the other which needs to be satisfied, otherwise the human being, although he would survive, would become agitated and troubled. The first one represents the organic needs, such as hunger, thirst, and the call of nature.

The second represents the instincts, which are the instinct of religiosity, kind, and survival. These instincts reflect the feeling of weakness, the feeling of the preservation of species and the feeling of survival, and there are no other instincts except these three. Anything other than these three instincts would be merely drives of these instincts. For example, fear, supremacy and ownership, which are drives that are part of the instinct of survival; sanctification and worship, which are drives of the spiritual instinct; and parenthood and brotherhood, which are aspects of the instinct of kind. Evidently, psychology's vision of human instincts is false and its claims about the brain are also incorrect, which in turn leads to the falsehood of the theories upon which it is based and consequently to the falsehood of education.

Sociology, education and psychology are cultural discipline are studied and propagated by the West contain ideas that contradict Islamic thought. To continue to hold them in high esteem and to refer to them as a reference constitutes an obstacle in the face of working towards establishing the Islamic State. We ought to demonstrate that these are cultural matters and not pure sciences, and that they are disputed subjects and their results are inconclusive. They are based on false premises that should not be running our lives.

5. *Society in the Islamic world is misguided by the non-Islamic way of life.* This is so because the political system upon which the society is based, as well as the principles upon which society as a whole stands, and the emotional trend which Muslims follow and their intellectual mode of thinking is based on concepts about life which are alien to Islamic concepts. As long as these fundamentals remain unchanged and as long as these erroneous concepts are not eradicated, it would be difficult to change people's way of life in society, political system, society's order, and the emotional and rational trends which control the Muslims.

6. *The widening gap between the Muslims and Islamic rule, especially in the areas of ruling and economy.* This makes the Muslims' vision of the Islamic way of life as something remote, and makes the disbelievers' illustration of the Islamic way of life negative due to the fact that the Muslims witnessed a period during which Islam had been misimplemented. Since 1924, they have been ruled by their enemy with a system which contradicts Islam in every department, specifically in ruling and economics. It is therefore imperative that people should realize that this transformation to the Islamic way of life must be comprehensive and not partial, and that the implementation of Islam must be simultaneous and comprehensive, and not gradually and in a partial or haphazard manner.

7. *The presence in the Muslim countries of governments founded on a secular basis, implementing the Capitalist Ideology and Democratic System upon the people, having strong political ties with Western countries, and founded on nationalism.* This makes the task of resuming the Islamic way of life difficult to achieve because it cannot be brought about unless it is comprehensive. Islam does not allow Muslim lands to be divided into statelets, but commands that the land be united under one single state. This entails the need for comprehensiveness in the *Da'wah*. This would be met by the resistance of the representatives of these regimes even if they called themselves Muslims. The *Da'wah* should therefore be conducted in every land even if it means enduring difficulties and hardship as a result of opposition from the regimes in the Muslim countries.

8. *The presence of strong public opinion in favor of nationalism, patriotism and socialism coupled with the rise of political movements based on nationalist, patriotic and socialist ideas.* This came about due to the fact that seizure by the West of Muslim lands, its resumption of power and its implementation of the Capitalist system over the land, triggered the tendency of self defense. This fueled the sentiments of nationalism and touched on the raw nerve of racism and tribalism in self defense and in defense of the family and tribe, and which led people to work and compete towards gaining the rule on that basis.

This led to the rise of some political movements which carried the banner of nationalism to repel the enemy from the land, and others which carried the banner of patriotism in order to confine the rule within the people. Then the corruption and shortcomings of the Capitalist system became flagrant and the call for socialism spread. As a result, groups carrying the banner of socialism were established in order to patch up the Capitalist system. These movements did not have any clear vision of the system of life, their strategy was not focused and this led them astray from Islam being a universal ideology.

How the Islamic State Would Rise

The strength of the Islamic thought coupled with its methodology would be sufficient to establish the Islamic State and to resume the Islamic way of life, provided that this thought is deeply rooted in the hearts and minds of the Muslims, and that it materialized itself in the Muslims in all walks of life. However, despite all this, some colossal tasks have to be carried out prior to the reestablishment of the State, and phenomenal efforts must be made in order to resume the Islamic way of life. Desire and optimism would not, therefore, be sufficient for the State to arise, nor would hope and enthusiasm be enough to secure the resumption of the Islamic way of life. The mother of all duties would be to duly assess these colossal obstacles which stand in the way of Islam in order to make their removal possible.

It is also important to warn the Muslims about the heavy load which awaits those who rise to this objective and to bring to the attention of the people, especially the intellectual ones. The serious consequences of any opinion which is voiced concerning this most serious issue, so that words and actions move together with awareness, determination, mettle, resoluteness and courage. Those who tread the path in order to resume the Islamic way of life should be aware that they would be carving their way into hard stone, but that with great resolve and dedication they would be able to break the stone. At the same time they should be aware that they would be treating a delicate matter.

However, their kindness would help them treat it perfectly. They should be aware that they would clash against major problems, yet they would overcome them. They should not deviate from the path because it is the path which the Messenger of Allah (saaw) traversed, and if the path is traversed correctly the positive results would be inevitable and victory would be certain without a shadow of a doubt. It is this path which the Muslims should tread carefully today, provided that the example of the Messenger of Allah (saaw) is carefully followed, and his (saaw) steps are carefully and correctly copied so that anyone who treads upon this path does not stumble, because every error in the analogy and every deviation from the path would introduce sterility and regression to the *Da'wah*. It therefore follows that holding conferences on the issue of the *Khilafah* would not of itself lead to the establishment of the Islamic State, nor would a federation of countries ruling Muslim peoples be a legitimate method to establish the Islamic State, nor would congresses of Muslim peoples help in the resumption of the Islamic way of life. None of these, nor anything similar to them, should be considered correct. Instead, they would merely represent rhetoric aimed at soothing the anger of the Muslims. Rather, these would contain their feelings and neutralize their zeal, and consequently lead them astray from the real task.

The only way to establish the Islamic State is to carry the Islamic Message and to work towards the resumption of the Islamic way of life, which necessitates taking the Islamic countries altogether as one unit because the Muslims are but one *Ummah*, which represents a human group bound by one *'Aqeedah* from which emanates her system. Any task carried out in any Muslim country, touching on the emotions and concepts, should therefore have its effects in all the other Muslim countries. Thus, it is imperative that all Muslim countries be considered as one and that the *Da'wah* is carried to all these countries so that it affects their respective societies. This is because the society which represents the *Ummah* would be like water in a pot, if a fire was lit under it the water would warm up and reach its boiling point. The boiling would cause the society to move and work. This is why the *Da'wah* should target the Islamic world so that work towards resuming the Islamic way of life could be initiated; this would be done by means of publishing books and leaflets, and by means of communication and all other means of publicity, especially contacts and discussion since they are one of the most successful methods of *Da'wah*.

However, the initiation of *Da'wah* in this open manner is merely a fuel for the society in order to convert frigidity into energy. It cannot reach the boiling point unless the practical *Da'wah* is confined in its political orientation within one single country from where the work would begin. The *Da'wah* would be launched from there to mushroom to other parts of the Islamic world.

236

This country, or several countries, would be taken as the support point where the Islamic State would be established. Following this would be expanding and establishing the greater Islamic State, which in turn would carry the Islamic Message to the whole world.

This is what the Messenger of Allah (saaw) did. He (saaw) conveyed his *Da'wah* to all the people and the steps of conveyance reached the practical phase. He (saaw) invited the people of Makkah and all the Arabs in the *Hajj* season. His *Da'wah* spread all over the Arabian Peninsula, as if he (saaw) had lit a fire under the society of the Peninsula, a fire which was aimed at releasing the energy in the Arabs as a whole. The Messenger of Allah (saaw) called the Arabs to Islam by directly contacting them and by inviting them to Islam during the *Hajj* season, and by visiting the tribes in their homes and calling them to Islam. The *Da'wah* reached all the Arabs as a result of the clashes which took place between the Messenger of Allah (saaw) and Quraysh, the echoes of those impacts reached the Arabs and triggered their curiosity and their desire to learn more about the *Da'wah*. However, although the *Da'wah* reached all the Arabs, the scope of the *Da'wah* was confined to Makkah, stretching to Madinah therefore the Islamic State was founded in Hijaz. Only then did the heat of the *Da'wah* and the victory of the Messenger of Allah (saaw) cause the boiling to result in real action, so that all believed and the Islamic State grew until it engulfed the whole of the Arabian Peninsula from where it launched its Message to the world.

We ought to adopt the carrying of the *Da'wah* and the work towards resuming the Islamic way of life as our method to establish the Islamic State. While we should consider the Muslim countries as one indivisible society and as a target for the *Da'wah*, we must concentrate our scope of work to one province or specific provinces where we undertake to educate people with Islam so that it springs to life within themselves and so that they live by it and for it, and we ought to create public opinion by Islam and for Islam so that a response is generated between the carriers of the *Da'wah* and society, a response which would be fruitful, effective and moving, and which would be able to transform the *Da'wah* into interaction and result in output. Interaction of this nature would be translated into a struggle aimed at establishing the Islamic State, which emanates from the *Ummah*, in that part of the Islamic world. The *Da'wah* would then have developed from being an idea in the mind to existing in society, and from a popular movement to a State. By then it would have concluded its stages and moved from the starting point to the launching point, and then to the point of support where it would be rooted in the State, which fulfills all elements of the State and the strength of the *Da'wah*. Following this, the practical task, which the *Shari'ah* commands the State and the Muslims who live outside its authority to fulfill, would have begun.

The duty of the State would be to rule comprehensively by that which Allah (swt) has revealed and to initiate the merging of other provinces with it and consider their affairs as part of the domestic policy (and not the foreign policy). It would therefore, initiate the conveyance of the *Da'wah* and the call for the resumption of the Islamic way of life all over the other provinces. It would lift the imaginary political borders which the colonialists drew up between them and who were responsible for making the rulers of those provinces the watchdogs of the borders. The State must therefore remove the borders even if the other provinces choose not to follow suit. Visas would be canceled, as would the customs checkpoints, and its borders would be left wide open to the citizens of the other provinces. This would make the citizens of the other Muslim provinces feel that this State was indeed the Islamic State, and it would make them witness the implementation and the execution of Islamic rule.

As for the duty of the Muslims, they should work towards turning their land where Islam is not implemented, and which is considered as *Dar al-Kufr*, into *Dar al-Islam*. This would be achieved by aiming to merge their household with the Islamic State by means of *Da'wah* and publicity. This would ensure that the whole of the society within the Islamic world had reached boiling point, which would drive it towards the right action and which would ensure in turn the unification of all the Muslims under one State. Thus, the greater Islamic State would be established, and so the Islamic State, which represents a universal intellectual leadership, would have come back into existence. By then it will have gained its stature and the weight necessary to enable her to convey its Message and to work towards saving the world from the evils it has been plunged into.

If the Muslim *Ummah*, had in the past, lived in a country which did not stretch beyond the Arabian Peninsula, and which at that time numbered only a few million, and despite that when she embraced Islam and carried its Message she represented a world superpower in the face of the two major camps at the time, whereupon she struck them both simultaneously, conquered their lands and spread Islam over almost the whole of the inhabited parts of the world at that time, then what are we to say about the *Ummah* today; numbering more than one billion, spread over countries that are geographically linked together; if she were a single state, stretching from Spain in the East to China in the West and from Turkey in the north to Malaysia in the south, occupying the best part of the world in terms of resources and strategic points, and carrying a single correct ideology to the world? She would undoubtedly constitute a front which would be stronger in every respect than the leading superpowers put together.

Therefore, it is the duty of every Muslim to work from this moment on to reestablish the Islamic State. Work should commence by carrying the Islamic *Da'wah* with the aim of resuming the Islamic way of life in all the Muslim countries. The practical scope of the *Da'wah* should be in one country or some selected ones in order to achieve the point of support so that this serious task can be resumed. Such a cause with its high objective, which the Muslim should aim to achieve by treading this practical and clear path and which he must follow, should be worth enduring all types of hardship and sparing no effort for. One should rely on Allah's help, seeking no reward for it except to gain the pleasure of Allah (swt).

A Draft Constitution of the Islamic State

GENERAL RULES

Article 1

The Islamic *'Aqeeda* constitutes the foundation of the State. Therefore, nothing is permitted to exist in the State's structure, system, accountability, or any other aspect connected with the State that does not take the Islamic *'Aqeeda* as its source. The Islamic *'Aqeeda* is also the source of the State's constitution and laws. Consequently, nothing related to them is permitted to exist unless it emanates from the Islamic *'Aqeeda*.

Article 2

Dar al-Islam is the territory where the rules of Islam are applied in all of life's affairs and whose security is maintained by sovereignty of Islam. *Dar al-Kufr* is the territory where *Kufr* rules are applied or whose security is not maintained by Muslims.

Article 3

The *Khalifah* adopts *Ahkam Shar'iyah* and enacts it as canons and a constitution. Once the *Khalifah* has adopted a *Hukm Sharii* (Islamic law), only that *Hukm Sharii* must be enacted and implemented. Every citizen must publicly and privately obey the adopted *Hukm Sharii*.

Article 4

The *Khalifah* does not adopt any *Ahkam Shar'iyah* pertaining to *Ibadat*, except in the case of *Zakat* and *Jihad.* He also does not adopt any specific opinions, or thoughts concerning the Islamic *'Aqeeda.*

Article 5

All citizens of the Islamic State enjoy the *Sharii* rights and obligations.

Article 6
All citizens will be treated equally regardless of their religion, race, color or any other factor. The State will not discriminate between citizens in any matter, such as ruling, judiciary or welfare.

Article 7
The State implements Islamic *Shar'iyah* on all citizens, whether Muslim or not, in the following manner:

a. All Islamic rules are applied on all Muslim citizens, without exception.
b. Non-Muslims are permitted to follow their own beliefs and acts of worships.
c. The *Murtadeen* will be treated according to the rules of *Murtadeen*, provided that they themselves have renounced Islam. If their ancestors are *Murtadeen* and they are born as non-Muslim, they are treated as non-Muslims according to their status as being either *Mushrikeen* or People of the Book.
d. In matters of food and clothing, the non-Muslims are allowed to follow their religions within the limits set by Islam.
e. Marital affairs, including divorce, among non-Muslims are settled in accordance with their religions. However, between non-Muslims and Muslims they are settled according to the rules of Islam.
f. All the remaining *Shar'iyah* matters and rules, such as: the application of transactions, legal, political and economic systems are implemented by the State on everyone, Muslim and non-Muslim alike. This includes the *Muahid*, the *Al Musta'min* and all who submit to the sovereignty of Islam. The implementation on these people is the same as the implementation on the citizens of the State. Diplomats are afforded the diplomatic immunity.

Article 8
The Arabic language is the language of Islam. It is the sole language used by the State.

Article 9
Ijtihad is *Fard Kifayah*. Every Muslim has the right to exercise *Ijtihad* if the necessary conditions to perform it are met.

Article 10

There is no clergy in Islam. All Muslims bear the responsibility for Islam. Therefore, the State will prevent anything that signifies the existence of a clergy among Muslims.

Article 11

The primary function of the State is to carry the Islamic *Da'wah*.

Article 12

The Qur'an, the *Sunnah*, *Ijma'a as-Sahabah* [the consensus of the Companions of Prophet Muhammad (saaw)] and *Qiyas* are the only sources for extracting *Ahkam Shar'iyah*.

Article 13

Every individual is innocent until proven guilty. No person shall be punished without a court sentence. Torturing is absolutely forbidden. Whoever inflicts torture on anyone shall be punished.

Article 14

All actions are controlled by *Ahkam Shar'iyah*, while all things are permitted unless there is an evidence of prohibition. Therefore, no action should be undertaken unless its *Hukm* is known.

Article 15

An action is *Haram,* if it is declared by the *Shar'iyah* to be *Haram*. The medium which leads to *Haram*, will be prohibited, if it most likely will lead an individual to *Haram*. Otherwise, the medium is permitted.

THE RULING SYSTEM

Article 16

The ruling system is unitary and not a federation.

Article 17

Government is centralized. The Administration is decentralized.

Article 18

There are four positions of ruling in the State:

a. The *Khalifah*
b. The *Mu'awin Tafweed* (deputed assistant)
c. The *Wali* (governor)
d. The *A'mil* (subgovernor)

All other officials of the State are employees and not rulers.

Article 19

The ruler or anyone who assumes a ruling position must be just, free (not a slave), male. He must be a Muslim.

Article 20

Questioning the rulers is a right for the Muslims and a *Fard Kifayah* upon the Muslim *Ummah*. Non-Muslim citizens have the right to voice their complaints for any injustices or misapplications of the Islamic rules upon them by the rulers.

Article 21

Muslims have the right to establish political parties. These parties are to question the rulers or in order to assume power through the *Ummah*. The parties are to be based on the Islamic *'Aqeeda*. Their rules must be based on the *Ahkam Shar'iyah*. The establishment of such a party does not require a license by the State. Any group not established on the basis of Islam is prohibited.

Article 22

The ruling system is founded upon four principles. They are:

a. Sovereignty belongs to the *Shar'iyah*, and not to the people;
b. Authority belongs to the *Ummah*;
c. The appointment of one *Khalifah* is an obligation upon all Muslims;
d. Only the *Khalifah* has the right to adopt the *Ahkam Shar'iyah*. Therefore, he enacts the constitution and laws.

Article 23

The State system is based upon eight institutions. They are:

1. The *Khalifah*
2. *Mu'awin Tafweedh* (the deputed assistant)
3. *Mu'awin Tanfeedh* (the executive assistant)
4. The *Amir* of *Jihad* (Commander of *Jihad*)
5. *Al Qada* (Judiciary)
6. *Wulah* (governors)
7. *Masalihud Dawlah* (An administrative system)
8. *Majlis al-Ummah* (tassembly of the *Ummah*)

THE *KHALIFAH*

Article 24

On behalf of the *Ummah*, the *Khalifah* carries out the authority of the *Ummah* and the execution of the *Shar'iyah*.

Article 25

The *Khilafah* is a contract of mutual agreement. Nobody is forced to accept it. No one is to be forced to select a particular person for it.

Article 26

Every sane Muslim of legal age, male or female, has the right to elect the *Khalifah* and to give him the *Ba'yah*. Non-Muslims have no right in this issue.

Article 27

Once the contract of the *Khilafah* has been completed through the *Ba'yah* of agreement from those who are qualified to give it, the *Ba'yah* of the remaining people is a *Ba'yah* of obedience and not a *Ba'yah* of agreement. Consequently, anyone in whom a potential for rebellion is perceived must be compelled to make this *Ba'yah* of obedience.

Article 28

Nobody can become a *Khalifah* without being appointed by the Muslims. No one can hold the authority of the *Khilafah* unless it is acquired according to the *Shar'iyah*, as is the case with any contract in Islam.

Article 29

The country which gives the *Khalifah* the *Ba'yah* of agreement must fulfill the following conditions:

a. The country must be independent and its authority solely relies on the Muslims, not on *Kufr* states;

b. The security of the Muslims in that state, internally and externally, must be maintained by the sovereignty of Islam and not by the power of *Kufr*.

The *Ba'yah* of obedience, as opposed to the *Ba'yah* of agreement, can be taken from any country without the need to satisfy the aforementioned conditions.

Article 30

The individual who is given the *Ba'yah* for *Khilafah* needs only to fulfill the basic conditions (listed in Article 31). He does not need to fulfill the preferred conditions, because what is necessary are the basic conditions.

Article 31

For an individual to become *Khalifah,* he must fulfill the following basic conditions: Male, Muslim , Free, Mature, Sane, Just.

Article 32

If the post of the *Khalifah* becomes vacant, due to death, resignation or dismissal, the appointment of a new *Khalifah* must take place within three days of the date when it became vacant.

Article 33

The *Khalifah* is to be selected in the following manner:

a. The Muslim members of the *Majlis al-Ummah* (assembly of the *Ummah*) nominate the candidates. The names of the candidates are announced to the public. Muslims are asked to elect one person from this list of candidates.

b. The results of the election are to be announced. The person who has acquired the majority votes will become known to the people.

c. The Muslims must give the *Ba'yah* to the candidate, who has attained the majority of votes as a *Khalifah* to apply the Book of Allah and the Sunnah of the Messenger (saaw) of Allah.

d. Once the *Ba'yah* has been completed, the name of the *Khalifah* will be announced, so that the news of his appointment reaches the whole *Ummah*. Along with his name, a statement will be issued indicating that he satisfies the basic conditions, which makes him eligible to be the head of State.

Article 34

Although the *Ummah* appoints the *Khalifah*, it is not empowered to dismiss him once the *Ba'yah* has been effected in the legally prescribed manner.

Article 35

The *Khalifah* is the State. He possesses all of the authority of the State. Therefore, he has the following powers:

a. The *Khalifah* issues *Ahkam Shar'iyah*. When he adopts and implements them, they become laws to be obeyed. They are not to be transgressed.

b. The *Khalifah* is responsible for domestic and foreign policies of the State. He is the Commander-in-Chief of the Military and the Armed Forces. He has the right to declare war, conduct peace, armistice or any other treaty.

c. The *Khalifah* has the authority to receive or refuse foreign ambassadors. He appoints and dismisses Muslim ambassadors.

d. The *Khalifah* appoints and dismisses *Mu'aween* and *Wulah* (governors). The *Mu'aween* and *Wulah* report to the *Khalifah* and to the *Majlis al-Ummah*.

e. The *Khalifah* appoints and dismisses *Qadi al Qudaa* (the Supreme Judge), the directors of all government departments, including commanders and generals of the Armed Forces; all of them report to the *Khalifah* and not to the *Majlis al-Ummah*.

f. The *Khalifah* must adopt the *Ahkam Shar'iyah* by which the State's budget is set. The *Khalifah* decides the revenue and expenditure of every sector.

Article 36

In the process of adopting the *Ahkam Shar'iyah*, the *Khalifah* is himself is bounded by the *Ahkam Shar'iyah*. Thus, the *Khalifah* is forbidden to adopt any rule that is not correctly deduced from the *Shar'iyah* sources. He is confined to the rules he adopts and to the methodology of deduction he chooses. Consequently, he is prevented from adopting a rule deduced by a method that contradicts the method he has adopted. Nor should he enact any directive that contradicts the rules he adopted.

Article 37

The *Khalifah* has the absolute right to conduct the affairs of the citizens according to his opinion and *Ijtihad*. He is allowed to adopt from the *Mubah* actions what is needed to conduct the affairs of the State. He is not allowed to violate any *Hukm Sharii* with the pretext that it is beneficial for the people. For example, he must not prevent citizens from importing products on the pretext of protecting the State's industries. He must not control prices on the pretext of preventing exploitation. He must not impose birth control on the assumption of the scarcity of resources. Furthermore, the *Khalifah* must not appoint any female or non-Muslim governor, because he thinks it is beneficial. The *Khalifah* must not forbid any *Halal* or legalize any *Haram*.

Article 38

There is no term limit for a *Khalifah*, as long as he abides by the *Ahkam Shar'iyah*, and implements them, and is capable of running the State's affairs. He remains the *Khalifah* as long as his condition does not change. If his condition changes in such a way that he can no longer remain the *Khalifah*, he must be dismissed immediately.

Article 39

There are three situations which can change the condition of the *Khalifah* and thus render him unqualified to continue as the *Khalifah*. They are:

a. If one of the basic conditions of the *Khalifah* changes; such as, he reverts from Islam, becomes insane or commits *Fusq* and so on. These are necessary conditions for the *Khilafah* contract, as well as the continuation of it.

b.   He is unable to undertake the responsibilities of the position of *Khalifah* for any reason.

c.   In the event of being incapacitated, whereby the *Khalifah* is rendered unable to conduct the affairs of the Muslims by his own opinions according to the *Ahkam Shar'iyah*. If the *Khalifah* is subdued by any force to an extent that he is unable to manage the citizens affairs by his own opinion according to the rules of the *Shar'iyah*, he is considered to be incapable of undertaking the duty for which he has been placed in charged, and therefore, he is no longer a *Khalifah*. This situation may arise under two circumstances, which are:

1.   When one of the entourage of the *Khalifah* exerts control over the management of affairs. If there is a chance that the *Khalifah* could rid himself of their dominance, he is given a warning for a specified period of time. After this period, if he fails to rid himself of their dominance, he must be dismissed. If it appears that there is no chance of the *Khalifah* freeing himself from their dominance, he is to be dismissed immediately.

2.   When the *Khalifah* becomes a captive by an enemy, whether actually captured or is influenced by that enemy. The situation in this case has to be examined. If there is a chance to rescue the *Khalifah*, he is given the time it will take to rescue him. When it appears that there is no hope to rescue him, then he is to be dismissed. If it appears from the outset that there is no hope of rescuing him then he is to be dismissed immediately.

Article 40

Only the Court of *Madhalim* decides if the condition of the *Khalifah* changed in such a way as to warrant his dismissal. Only the *Madhalim* Court has the authority to dismiss or to warn the *Khalifah*.

DEPUTED ASSISTANT

Article 41
The *Khalifah* appoints the deputed assistant who is given the authority to assist him in undertaking the responsibility of ruling. The *Khalifah* deputizes him to manage the affairs (with the deputy's opinion and *Ijtihad*).

Article 42
The deputed assistant has the same requirements as the *Khalifah*. These are: male, Muslim, mature, sane, free and just . In addition, he must be qualified for the tasks assigned to him.

Article 43
The appointment of the deputed assistant must include two items: to deal with all that entail ruling situations and to act on behalf of the *Khalifah*. Thus, in the appointment of the assistant, the *Khalifah* must pronounce a statement to the effect of "I appoint you on my behalf as my deputy" or any other statement that confers both deputation and general responsibility. If the person is not appointed in this manner he would not hold the authority of a deputy assistant and thus, would not be one.

Article 44
The function of the deputed assistant is to report to the *Khalifah* the actions he carried out and the issues he executed within the authority delegated to him. He should do this so that he will not be equal to the *Khalifah* in his responsibility. Therefore, his job is to report to the *Khalifah* and execute the directives given to him.

Article 45
The *Khalifah* must oversee the actions and decisions made by the deputed assistant. The *Khalifah* confirms what is sound and rectifies that which is wrong. This should occur, because the management of the *Ummah*'s affairs is entrusted to the *Khalifah*. It is related to his *Ijtihad*.

Article 46
Once the deputed assistant has managed a matter with the knowledge of the

Khalifah, he has the right to carry it out as acknowledged without any revision. If the *Khalifah* revises the matter and objects to what the deputed assistant has executed, the following considerations apply:

a.   If the *Khalifah* has objected to what the deputed assistant has carried out with regards to a rule implemented correctly, or a fund spent justly, then the view of the deputed assistant must be enacted, because that action is the original view of the *Khalifah*. In this case, the deputed assistant must not redress rules which he has implemented and funds which he has spent.

b.   If the deputed assistant has implemented something else, such as the appointment of a *Wali* (governor) or deployment of the army, then the *Khalifah* has the right to object and to overrule the decision of the deputed assistant. The *Khalifah* has the right to revise and redress his own decisions in such cases and hence those of the deputed assistant.

Article 47

The deputed assistant has general responsibilities. Therefore, he must not be assigned to a specific department or specific types of actions. He must undertake general supervision of the administrative system without engaging in the work himself.

EXECUTIVE ASSISSTANT

Article 48

The *Khalifah* appoints the executive assistant. His function is executive and not ruling. He is to execute the instructions of the *Khalifah* in both domestic and foreign affairs of the State. He is to relay to the *Khalifah* what is received from these spheres. This administrative office is a medium between the *Khalifah* and the others.

Article 49

The executive assistant must be a Muslim because he is one of the *Khalifah's* entourage.

Article 50

The executive assistant must remain in direct contact with the *Khalifah*, similar to the deputed assistant. However, the executive assistant is considered to be an assistant with respect to executive function only and not in ruling.

AMIR OF JIHAD

Article 51

The office of the *Amir* of *Jihad* consist of four departments. They are: Foreign Affairs, the Military and the Armed Forces, the Domestic Security, and the Industry. The *Amir* of *Jihad* is the supervisor and director of all four departments.

Article 52

The Department of Foreign Affairs handles the foreign policies which deal with the relationship of the *Khilafah* State with other states.

Article 53

The Department of Military and the Armed Forces handles all affairs related to the Armed Forces, such as: the Police, the Equipment, the Armament, the Logistics, Missions and other related activity. It also includes the Military Academies, Military Mission, and everything necessary to obtain the Islamic education and the general education of the Armed Forces. It also takes care of issues related to war and preparation of it.

Article 54

The Department of Domestic Security handles affairs related to security within the State. The Armed Forces are responsible for this function and they utilize the Police to accomplish this function.

Article 55

The Department of Industry directs all affairs related to industry. This includes heavy industry, such as the manufacturing of motors, engines and vehicle chassis; metallurgical industries, electronics and consumer industries. It also handles the affairs of privately owned factories that are engaged in military based production. All factories of whatever type should be established on the basis of the military policy.

THE ARMED FORCES

Article 56

Jihad is a *Fard* on all Muslims. Military training is compulsory. Every Muslim male, fifteen years and over, is required to undergo military training as a preparation for *Jihad*. Active participation in the army is *Fard Kifayah*.

Article 57

The Armed Forces consists of two services: those who are on active duty and are salaried from the State's budget, just like other employees, and the reserves, who comprise all Muslims capable of fighting.

Article 58

The Armed Forces are one force. The Police Force is a division of it, organized and trained in a particular way and provided with a special education.

Article 59

The Police Force maintains public order, supervises domestic security and enforces the laws.

Article 60

The Armed Forces will have flags and banners. The *Khalifah* gives the flag to whom he appoints as a Chief-of-Staff of the Armed Forces. The banners are introduced by the commanders of the divisions.

Article 61

The *Khalifah* is the Commander-in-Chief of the Armed Forces. He appoints the Chiefs-of-Staff, a General for each Corp and a Lieutenant General for each division. The brigadier and the Major General appoint the remaining ranks. Commissioned officers are appointed according to their military education and can be appointed by the Chiefs-of-Staff.

Article 62

The Armed Forces is one entity. It has units located in specific military bases. Some of these bases must be located in different *Wilayat* (provinces). Some should be situated in strategic locations and some must be striking forces with mobility. The bases are organized in numerous formations. Each one is given a number to accompany its name, such as the first army, the second army and so on. Some units can be given names of *Wilayat* or *'Imala* (districts).

Article 63
It is necessary to provide the Armed Forces with the highest possible level of military education. Its intellectual level should be elevated as high as possible. Every member in the Armed Forces should be provided with the Islamic education, so that he possesses a full awareness of Islam, in toto.

Article 64
Each base should have a sufficient number of commissioned officers who have attained the highest level of military knowledge and experience in formulating plans and directing battles. The Armed Forces as a whole should have as many commissioned officers as possible.

Article 65
It is necessary to provide the Armed Forces with all the necessary armaments, supplies and equipment that it requires to fulfill its duty as an Islamic Army.

THE JUDICIARY

Article 66
Judgment constitutes the binding verdict delivered by the judges. It settles the disputes between people, prevents that which infringes the community's rights, eliminates the disputes between the people and any government official whether it is a ruler or an employee. This includes the *Khalifah* or anyone else below him.

Article 67
The *Khalifah* appoints the Chief Justice. This judge must be a Muslim male, mature, free, and just. He must also be a jurist. He has the authority to appoint, dismiss and discipline the judges within administrative regulations. The remaining courts employees are under the department which administers the court affairs.

Article 68

There are three types of judges: *Qadi al Khusoomat* (the judge who settles the disputes between people, in transactions and punishments); *Qadi al Hisba* (the *Muhtasib* who judges on public violations); and *Qadi al Mahkomat al Madhalim* (the judge of the Court of *Madhalim* who settles disputes between the people and the officials of the State).

Article 69

All judges must be Muslim, mature, free, sane, just, and jurist. They must be aware of how to apply rules in different situations. Judges of the Court of *Madhalim* must additionally be male and *Mujtahiddeen.*

Article 70

The *Qadi al Khusoomat* and the *Muhtasib* may be given a general appointment to pronounce judgment on all problems throughout the State, or alternatively they can be given an appointment to a particular location or a particular case. *Qadi Al Madhalim* is not restricted to a specific type of a case. In terms of location, he may be appointed to a particular location or throughout the State.

Article 71

Each court should have one resident judge who has the authority to pronounce judgment. One or more judges are permitted to accompany him to advise and consult. They have no authority to pronounce judgment. Their opinion is not binding on the resident judge.

Article 72

The judge cannot pronounce judgment except in a court session. Evidence and testimony are only considered in a court session.

Article 73.

It is permissible to vary the levels of courts according to the type of cases. Some judges may be assigned to certain cases of a particular level, while other courts are authorized to judge on other cases.

Article 74

There are no courts of appeal or annulment. All judgments are final. When the judge has pronounced the verdict, it becomes effective immediately. No other judge's decision can overturn it.

Article 75

The *Muhtasib* is the judge who rules on a public violation where there is no plaintiff, provided that the case does not involve felonies, including *Hudood*.

Article 76

The *Muhtasib* has the authority to judge upon violations, wherever and whenever they happen. He does not need a court to pronounce judgment. A number of policemen are put at the *Muhtasib*'s disposal to carry out his orders and to enforce his judgments immediately.

Article 77

The *Muhtasib* has the right to appoint deputies for himself, who must have the same qualifications as the *Muhtasib*. He can place them in various locations. These deputies have the same authority as the *Muhtasib* in the location and the cases assigned to them (within their jurisdiction).

Article 78

The judge of the Court of *Madhalim* is appointed to remove all unjust acts done by the *Khalifah*, or any other State employee who has allegedly dealt unjustly with any person, citizen or not, living within the domain of the State.

Article 79

Judges of the Court of *Madhalim* are appointed by the *Khalifah* or by the Chief Justice. The *Khalifah* evaluates his performance and disciplines him, if necessary. This can also be done by the Court of *Madhalim* itself, if given the authority to do so by the *Khalifah*. However, the judge of the Court of *Madhalim* cannot be dismissed while administering a case involving the *Khalifah*, the deputed assistant or the Chief Justice.

Article 80

There is no limit on the number of judges that can be appointed to the Court of *Madhalim*. The *Khalifah* can appoint as many as necessary to eradicate acts of injustice. Although it is permitted for more than one judge to sit in a court session, only one judge has the authority to pronounce a judgment. The other judges only consult and provide advice. Their advice is not binding on the judge authorized to pronounce the judgment.

Article 81

The Court of *Madhalim* has the authority to dismiss any ruler, governor or state employee, including the *Khalifah*.

Article 82

The Court of *Madhalim* has the authority to investigate any case connected with the officials of the State; the *Khalifah*'s deviation from the *Ahkam Shar'iyah*; interpretation of the legislative texts in the constitution, canons and *Ahkam Shar'iyah* within the framework adopted by the *Khalifah*. The court also oversees situations involving levying of a tax.

Article 83

The Court of *Madhalim* does not require a court session. The defendant does not have to be summoned and there does not have to be a plaintiff. This court has the authority to look into any case of injustice, even if no one has brought charges concerning the case.

Article 84

Every defendant and plaintiff has the right to appoint a proxy. The proxy may be male or female, Muslim or not. There is no distinction between him/her and the proxy. The proxy can be appointed with a wage agreed upon between the person and his or her proxy.

Article 85

It is permitted for a person who is given a private assignment such as an executor, custodian or a guardian; or a public assignment such as the *Khalifah*, a ruler, a government employee, a *Madhalim* Judge or *Muhtasib* to assign a proxy on his behalf to represent him in prosecution and defence; but only in his capacity as mentioned above, that is he was a executor, custodian, guardian, head of the State, ruler, employee, Judge of *Madhalim* Court or a *Muhtasib*. The assignment of proxy is allowed whether the person is a plaintiff or defendant.

THE GOVERNORS OF THE PROVINCES

Article 86

The territories governed by the State are divided into units called *Wilayat* (provinces). Each *Wilayah* is divided into subunits called *'Imalat* (districts). The person who governs the *Wilayah* is called a *Wali* or *Amir*. The person who governs the *'Imalah* is called the *'Amel* (subgovernor).

Article 87

The *Wulah* and *Umaal* are appointed by the *Khalifah*. The *Wali* can, if authorized, appoint an *'Amel*. The *Wulah* and *Umaal* must meet the same qualifications as the *Khalifah*. They must be Muslim, male, free, sane, just and of legal age. They must also be highly qualified in their responsibilities. They are to be selected from the people of piety and must be decisive.

Article 88

The *Wali* has the authority to govern and supervise the performance of the departments in his province in his capacity as the deputy of the *Khalifah*. He has the same authority in the province as the deputed assistant has in the State. He has command over the people of his province and control over all affairs except finance, the judiciary and the Armed Forces. However, he has command over the Police with respect to execution, but not with respect to administration.

Article 89

The *Wali* is not obliged to inform the *Khalifah* of what he has carried out within his jurisdiction, unless he chooses to do so. But, if a new and uncommon situation arises, he has to inform the *Khalifah* in advance. He then proceeds according to the instructions of the *Khalifah*. If waiting would lead to harm, he must act upon the situation first and then inform the *Khalifah* later about the reason for the action and the reason for not informing him in advance.

Article 90

Every province has an assembly elected from its people and headed by the *Wali* of that province. The assembly has the authority to participate in expressing opinions on administrative matters, but not on ruling. The opinions of the assembly are not binding on the *Wali*.

Article 91

The term of a *Wali* in office in a particular province is not to be long. He must be dismissed whenever he becomes firmly established or whenever the people become enchanted with him.

Article 92

The *Wali*'s appointment is a general responsibility in a defined location. Consequently, the *Wali* is not transferred from one province to another. He has to be discharged first and then he can be reappointed.

Article 93

The *Wali* can be discharged, if the *Khalifah* decides so, or if the *Majlis al-Ummah* expresses dissatisfaction with him, whether justified or not or if the majority of the people of the province appear to be displeased with him. In any event, the actual dismissal has to be done by the *Khalifah*.

Article 94

The *Khalifah* must exercise strict control over the *Wulah,* assess their performance, and assign people to periodically check on them. He must meet with the *Wulah* individually or collectively. The *Khalifah* should also listen to the complaints of the people about the *Wulah*.

THE ADMINISTRATIVE SYSTEM

Article 95

The management of the government's affairs and the interests of the people are performed by administrations, bureaus and departments. These entities perform the duties of the government and take care of the affairs of the people.

Article 96

The administrative policy must be based on simplicity, efficiency and promptness in taking care of the affairs of the people, and the competence of those who assume responsibility for the administration.

Article 97

Any qualified citizen, male or female, Muslim or non-Muslim, can be appointed as the secretary of any administration, bureau or department.

Article 98

Every administration must have a director. Every bureau and department must have a department head. Department heads report to the director on administrative issues. All of them are responsible to the *Wali* or *'Amel* regarding compliance with administrative ordinances and the public order.

Article 99

The directors, offices and the head of the departments and bureau are to be dismissed only for reasons connected with the administrative regulations. It is permitted to transfer them from one post to another and to suspend them. Whoever has the final authority of each administration, bureau or department is responsible for appointing, dismissing, transferring, suspending and disciplining these directors.

Article 100

Civil servants, other than the administrators and the bureau chiefs, are appointed, transferred, suspended, questioned, disciplined or dismissed by the director of their administration, directorate or department.

ASSEMBLY OF THE *UMMAH*

Article 101

The membership of *Majlis al-Ummah* (Assembly of the *Ummah*) consists of those individuals who express the Muslims' views to the *Khalifah* when consulted. Non-Muslims are allowed to be members of *Majlis al-Ummah* so that they can voice their complaints with respect of unjust acts performed by the rulers and/or the misapplication of the Islamic laws upon them.

Article 102

The members of *Majlis al-Ummah* are elected by the people.

Article 103

Every citizen has the right to become a member of *Majlis al-Ummah*, provided he/she is mature and sane; this applies to Muslim and non-Muslim, man or woman. However, membership of non-Muslims is confined to their voicing of complaints with respect to unjust acts performed by the rulers and/or the misapplication of Islam on them.

Article 104

Shura is the mere requesting of an opinion. *Mashura* is the requesting of a binding opinion. Matters related to legislation, definitions, intellectual issues such as the examination of facts, and science and technology do not fall under the classification of *Mashura*. Everything else falls under *Mashura*.

Article 105

All citizens, Muslim or not, may express their views, but *Shura* is a right for the Muslims only.

Article 106

All issues that fall under *Mashura* are decided upon the basis of majority opinion, irrespective of whether it is correct or not. In all other matters of *Shura*, the correct opinion is sought, whether it be a majority or minority held view.

Article 107

Majlis al-Ummah is in charge of four duties. They are:

1. a. In affairs that fall under *Mashura*, such as: affairs of ruling, education, health, and the economy, the opinion of the *Majlis* must be followed. In all other matters, such as: foreign policy, finance and the Armed Forces, the opinion of *Majlis al-Ummah* is not necessarily sought.

    b. To question the government on all actions it actually carried out, whether they be internal or external affairs, financial or military. In matters where the majority view decides, the majority view is binding. Where the majority view is not sought, the viewpoint is not binding. In the event of *Majlis al-Ummah* and the rulers disagreeing on an action from the

Shar'iyah view point, the *Mahkumat ul-Madhalim* will decide.

2. *Majlis al-Ummah* can express dissatisfaction in governors and assistants of the *Khalifah*. In this case, the view of the *Majlis* is binding. The *Khalifah* must discharge them at once.

3. To discuss and express opinions on legislation, constitution and directives that the *Khalifah* intends to adopt and which he has presented to the *Majlis*. The views of the *Majlis* are not binding in this matter, though only the Muslim members have the right to express their views.

4. Muslim members of the *Majlis* have the exclusive right to nominate the candidates for the position of the *Khalifah*. No one can run unless nominated by the *Majlis*. The decision of the *Majlis* is binding.

THE SOCIAL SYSTEM

Article 108

A woman is primarily a mother and a home maker. She is an honor that must be safegurded.

Article 109

Men and women are basically to be segregated from each other. They should not mix together except for a need permitted by the *Shar'a*. The *Shar'iyah* permission for mixing in this case should be there, such as in buying and selling and pilgrimage.

Article 110

Men and Women have the same rights and obligations with the exceptions of certain rights or duties given specifically to the man or the woman. *Shar'iyah* evidence is necessary for such exceptions. The woman has the right to practice trading, farming, and industry; to enter into contracts and strike deals; to possess all kinds of private ownership; to invest her funds by herself or by her proxy; and to conduct all of life's affairs.

Article 111

Women can participate in the election process and in the giving of the *Ba'yah* to the *Khalifah*. They can be members of *Majlis al-Ummah*. She can also be employed by the State.

Article 112

It is not permitted for a woman to assume responsibility for government. Consequently, women cannot hold the positions of the Khalifah, *Wali, 'Amel* and she cannot undertake any task that is considered to be an aspect of government.

Article 113

Women functions in both the public and private lives. In public life, women are allowed to be with other women, *Mahrem* males and other males, provided that nothing of the women's body is revealed, apart from her face and hands. Seductive manners and clothing are not allowed. In private life, women are allowed to dwell with other women and *Mahrem* males. In both lives, all *Shar'iyah* laws should be complied with.

Article 114

(*Khulwa*) a man and a woman are not allowed to be alone without a *Mahrem*. (*Tabaruj*) Make up and dress that normally catches attention and/or exposes the body are not allowed in front of non- *Mahrem*.

Article 115

Men and women are not allowed to hold any job or perform any action which undermines the morality of the society or causes corruption in the society.

Article 116

The marriage is a life of tranquillity and companionship. Therefore, the responsibility of the husband towards his wife is one of care taking, and not ruling. She is to obey and he is to provide.

Article 117

Husband and wife must cooperate with each other in performing household duties. The husband performs all work undertaken outside of the house. The woman performs actions normally undertaken inside the house to the best of her ability. The husband should hire a maid as required to assist her with the household tasks she cannot perform herself.

Article 118
The custody of children is both a right and duty of the mother, whether she is a Muslim or not, as long as the child is in need for it. When children, girls or boys, are no longer in need of care, they are to choose which parent they wish to live with. This applies if both parents are Muslim. If only one of the parents or guardians is a Muslim, there is no choice in the matter. The child is to join the Muslim.

THE ECONOMIC SYSTEM

Article 119
Economic policy is the view of what the society ought to be when addressing the satisfaction of its needs. So what the society ought to be is taken as the basis for satisfying the needs.

Article 120
The economic problem is how to distribute funds and benefits to all citizens, to enable them to possess them and to work for them.

Article 121
The State must guarantee full satisfaction of the individual's basic needs. The State must make opportunities available to have every individual satisfy his luxuries to the highest possible level.

Article 122
Wealth belongs to Allah. He allowed people to utilize it. With this permission, people have the right to possess property. Allah has also permitted the individual to gain possession of this wealth, and through this specific permission the individual can actually own it.

Article 123

There are three types of ownership: private, public and state.

Article 124

Private ownership is a *Hukm Sharii*, which determines that an object or benefit belonging to a person can be sold or utilized in any way beneficial to him.

Article 125

Public ownership is the *Shar'a* permission for the community to participate in enjoying the benefits of publicly owned items.

Article 126

Every wealth which can be disposed of only through the opinion and *Ijtihad* of the *Khalifah* is considered to be State wealth. Examples of this are the funds raised through general taxes, *Kharaj*, and *Jizya*, which is payable by non-Muslims.

Article 127

Private ownership on liquid and fixed assets is restricted by the following *Shar'iyah* causes:

a. Work.
b. Inheritance.
c. Funds necessary for survival.
d. State grants; from its own funds to a citizen.
e. Funds obtained by individuals with no effort or substance.

Article 128

Disposal of property is restricted by the permission of *Shar'iyah*. This applies to both spending or investing. Squandering, extravagance and miserliness are forbidden. Also forbidden are the capitalist companies, cooperatives, and all other illegal transactions, such as: *Riba* (usury), fraud, monopolies, gambling and the like.

Article 129

Al-Ushriah land constitutes land within the Arabian peninsula and land whose inhabitants have embraced Islam. *Al-Kharajiah* land is all land, other than the Arabian peninsula, which was acquired by the State either through *Jihad* or by conclusion of a peace treaty. *Al-Ushriah* land, together with its benefits, is owned by individuals. The title to *Al-Kharajiah* land is owned by the State. Individuals own its benefits. Everyone has the right to exchange, through *Shar'a* contracts, *al-Ushriah* land and the benefits from *al-Kharajiah*. All people can inherit these, as is the case with other types of ownership.

Article 130
Wastelands can be recovered by any individual thorough reclamation or by proclaiming it by fencing or marking. Other land can only be acquired by way of *Shar'a* causes, such as: inheritance, purchasing or through a grant from the State.

Article 131
Leasing land, whether *al-Ushriah* land or *al-Kharajiah* land, for agriculture is forbidden. Sharecropping of land planted with trees is permitted. Sharecropping on all other land is forbidden.

Article 132
Every land owner is obliged to utilize his land. The needy are to be given from *Bayt al-Mal* (treasury) to facilitate this. Anyone who leaves his land uncultivated for three years, will have it taken away from him to be given to another person.

Article 133
The following three categories constitute public ownership:
a. Public facilities, such as the town square, streets, and bridges.
b. Vast mineral resources, such as oil fields.
c. Things which by their nature prevent the individual from acquiring a sole right to their possession, such as rivers.

Article 134
Factories in general are private ownership. However, each factory is governed by the rule related to the product manufactured within it. If the product is private ownership, the factory is considered to be a private ownership, such as

a textile mill. If the product is a public ownership, such as iron extraction, then the factory processing it belongs to the public ownership.

Article 135

The State has no right to change private ownership into public ownership because the public ownership is determined by its nature and attributes and not by the view of the State.

Article 136

Everybody in the State has the right to derive benefit from public ownership. The State has no right to allow any particular individual to possess, own or utilize publicly owned properties to the exclusion of other citizens.

Article 137

The State is allowed to claim land which is not owned by anyone, such as wastelands or any other property publicly owned for public interests.

Article 138

Hoarding funds is forbidden, even if *Zakat* is paid on it.

Article 139

Zakat is collected from Muslims on their properties specified by *Shar'a*, (money, goods, livestock and grain). It is not taken from anything not specified by the *Shar'a*. *Zakat* is taken from every owner whether legally accountable (mature and sane) or not (immature and insane). It is deposited in a special account in *Bayt al-Mal*. *Zakat* is only to be spent in one or more of the eight categories mentioned in the Qur'an.

Article 140

Jizya is collected from the *Dhimmis*. It is to be taken from mature men, if they are financially capable. It is not to be levied on women or children.

Article 141

Kharaj (land-tax) is collected on *Al-Kharajiah* land according to its potential. *Zakat* is payable on the actual production of *Al-Ushriah* land.

Article 142

The Muslims pay the tax that *Shar'a* has permitted to be collected to cover the expenditure of *Bayt al-Mal*. It is levied only on the surplus of the individual's conventional needs. The tax must be sufficient to cover the demands of the State. Non-Muslims do not pay any tax except the *Jizya*.

Article 143

If the *Shar'iyah* enjoins a particular task or activity on the *Ummah* as a duty and there are no funds in *Bayt al-Mal* for carrying it out the duty for providing these funds is transferred to the *Ummah*, and the State then has the right to collect these funds from it by imposing a tax on it. If, however, the *Ummah* is not legally obligated to carry out this task, the state has no right to impose any tax for the sake of it. Thus, the State is not allowed to collect dues for the courts or departments or administrations, or for accomplishing any governmental task.

Article 144

The budget of the State has permanent sources decided by the *Ahkam Shar'iyah*. The budget is further divided into sections. The funds assigned to each division and the matters for which the funds are allocated, are all decided by the view of the *Khalifah* and his *Ijtihad*.

Article 145

The permanent revenues for *Bayt al-Mal* are: *Fay* (spoils), *Jizya*, *Kharaj*, a fifth of *Rikaz* (buried treasure) and *Zakat*. All these funds are collected, whether there is a need for them or not, on a perpetual basis.

Article 146

If the permanent revenue for *Bayt al-Mal* are insufficient to cover the expenditure of the State, it is permitted to collect taxes for the following:

a.   The needs of the poor, the needy, stranded travelers, and to perform the obligation of *Jihad*.

b.   Remuneration: such as salaries of the employees, compensation for the rulers and the provisions for the soldiers.

c.   Providing the benefits and public utilities, such as constructing roads, extracting water, building mosques, schools and hospitals.

d.   Meeting emergencies, such as natural disasters, famine, floods and earthquakes.

Article 147

Income derived from public and state ownership, people dying without in-
heritors and customs levied at the State's borders are all revenue of *Bayt al-
Mal.*

Article 148

The expenditure of *Bayt al-Mal* is distributed among the following six categories of people as follows:

a.   The eight categories of people entitled to partake of the *Zakat* funds. If
there are no funds in this account they are not given any money.

b.   The poor, the needy, stranded travelers, the debtors and *Jihad* are funded
from the permanent sources of revenue whenever there is insufficient
funds in the *Zakat* account. When there are inadequate funds from the
permanent revenues, the debtors are not to receive assistance. The poor,
the needy, stranded travelers and *Jihad* must be funded from the taxes
collected for this purpose. If required, and to avoid disorder, they can be
funded from loans raised by the State for this purpose.

c.   *Bayt al-Mal* must provide for those people who perform certain duties or
services for the State. Examples to this are employees, rulers and soldiers. If there are insufficient funds for this purpose, taxes must be collected immediately to meet these expenses. Loans should be raised if it is
feared that disorder will occur.

d.   *Bayt al-Mal* shall provide for the essential services and utilities such as
the roads, mosques, hospitals and schools. If there is insufficient funds,
taxes must be collected to cover their cost.

e.   Non-essential services and utilities are funded by *Bayt al-Mal*. When there
is insufficient funds available, they are not financed and accordingly delayed.

f.   Disasters, such as earthquakes and floods, must be financed by *Bayt al-
Mal*. If there is insufficient funds available, loans are to be raised immediately, and will be repaid later from taxes.

Article 149

The State should guarantee employment for all citizens.

Article 150

Employees employed by individuals or by companies have the same rights and duties as state employees. Everyone who works for a wage, irrespective of the nature of the work, is considered an employee. In matters of dispute, between employer and employee over salary levels, the salary level is to be assessed on the basis of the market. If they dispute on something else, the employment contract is to be assessed according to the rules of the *Shar'a*.

Article 151

The salary is to be determined according to the value of the work or benefit expected from the employee. It is not determined according to the knowledge or qualification of the employee. There are to be no mandatory/automatic wage increases for employees. Instead, they are to be given the full value of the salary they deserve for the work they do.

Article 152

The State is to guarantee the adequate support for hose who have no funds, no employment and no provider. The State is responsible for housing and maintaining the disabled and handicapped.

Article 153

The State must ensure the circulation of wealth among all citizens and forbid the circulation of wealth among only a sector of the society.

Article 154

The State endeavors to enable every citizen to satisfy his luxury needs and achieve a balance in the society based on the following:

a.   The State grants citizens liquid and fixed assets from funds deposited in *Bayt al-Mal*.

b.   The State grants its cultivated land to those who have insufficient land. Those who possess land but do not use it are not given any land. Those who are unable to use their land are given financial assistance to enable them to use their land.

c.   Those who are unable to settle their debts are given funds from *Zakat*, and other *Bayt al-Mal* funds.

Article 155

The State supervises agricultural affairs and its products in accordance with the agricultural policy, which accomplishes the full utilization of the potential of the land to its optimum level of production.

Article 156

The State supervises the affairs of the industry. It assumes direct responsibility for those industries which are associated with anything related to public ownership.

Article 157

International trade is assessed on the basis of the citizenship of the trader and not on the origin of the goods. Merchants from countries with which the State is at war are prevented from trading in the State, unless given a special permission for the merchant or the goods. Merchants from countries that have treaties with the State are treated according to the terms of the treaty. Citizens of the State are prevented from exporting strategic and needed materials. They are not prevented from importing any property they own. Excluded from this are countries which are in a condition of war with us, such as Israel. In which case, the rules of war apply for all relations, trade or anything else.

Article 158

All citizens have the right to establish research and development laboratories connected with the affairs of life. The State should also establish such laboratories.

Article 159

Individuals are prevented from possessing laboratories producing materials that could harm the public or the State.

Article 160

The State provides free health care for all. However, it does not prevent private medical practices nor the sale of medicine.

Article 161

Investment of foreign capital within the State is forbidden. It is also prohibited to grant economic concession or special priority rights to foreigners.

Article 162

The State must issue its own currency. It is not allowed to be associated to any other foreign currency.

Article 163

The currency of the State is gold and silver, whether minted or not. No other form of currency is permitted. The State can issue something else in place of gold or silver, on the condition that there is an equivalent in gold or silver in the State Coffers. Thus, for example, the State may issue currency in its name from brass or bronze, or paper notes etc., as long as it is covered totally by gold and silver.

Article 164

Foreign currency excange is allowed between the currency of the State and that of other nations. However, such transactions must be undertaken in cash and constitute a direct transaction with no delay involved. It is permissible for the exchange rate between two currencies to fluctuate provided the currencies are different from each other. Citizens can buy whatever currency they require from both within or outside the State, and they can purchase the required currency without obtaining prior permission.

EDUCATION POLICY

Article 165

The Islamic *'Aqeeda* constitutes the basis upon which the curriculum rests. The syllabus and the teaching methods are designed to prevent a departure from this basis.

Article 166

The education policy is to shape the Islamic thinking and character. All subjects in the syllabus must be rooted to this basis.

Article 167

The goal of education is to produce the Islamic personality and to provide people with different disciplines of knowledge and sciences connected with life's affairs. Teaching methods are established to fulfill this goal and to prevent any departure from this goal.

Article 168

The weekly class time spent in teaching of Islamic culture and the Arabic language must be equal to all other classes taught.

Article 169

A distinction must be drawn in education between the empirical sciences, including everything that is related to these, such as mathematics, and cultural disciplines. The empirical sciences and whatever is connected to these must thus be taught as needed, and must not be confined to any stage of education. The cultural disciplines, on the other hand, should be studied in the elementary stage, before the advanced ones, in accordance with a specific policy which must be compatible with the ideas and legal rules of Islam. At the level of higher education, these disciplines can be studied as a particular form of learning, provided that this does not lead to any departure from the educational policy and its goal.

Article 170

The Islamic culture must be taught at all levels of education. In higher education, departments should be assigned to the various Islamic disciplines, as well as medicine, engineering, physics and other subjects.

Article 171

Technical disciplines and the vocational skills may on the one hand be associated with sciences, such as business administration, navigation and agriculture. These type of subjects are to be studied without restriction or conditions. On the other hand, they might be associated with a particular culture, whenever they are influenced by a particular view, as with painting and sculpturing. In which case, these disciplines will not be studied if they contradict the Islamic point of view.

Article 172

The State's curriculum is the only one allowed to be taught. Private schools are allowed, provided they are bounded by the State's curriculum. There should be separate classes for boys and girls. Furthermore, there should be no schools based on a particular religion or a sect or a race. All schools must adopt the State's curriculum and establish themselves on the education system and accomplish the goal and policy of education set by the State.

Article 173

It is an obligation upon the State to teach every individual, male or female, those things which are necessary for life. This should be provided freely to all and should be done in the primary and secondary levels of education. The State should, to the best of its ability, provide the opportunity for everyone to continue higher education free of charge.

Article 174

The State should provide libraries, laboratories and other educational facilities outside of the schools and universities to enable those who want to continue their education in various fields of knowledge, such as *Fiqh, Hadith* and *Tafseer* of the *Qur'an*, medicine, engineering and chemistry, research and development and others. This will create an abundance of *Mujtahideen*, outstanding inventors, and creative thinkers in the *Ummah*.

Article 175

Authorship at any educational level should not be considered a business and cannot be exploited. No one, including the author or the publisher, has the right of copyrights. However, if the book has not been printed and published, and thus is still an idea, the owner has the right to take a payment for transferring these ideas to the public, the way he/she takes compensation for teaching.

FOREIGN POLICY

Article 176

Politics is the management of the *Ummah*'s affairs both internally and externally, and is undertaken both by the State and the *Ummah*. The State applies itself to this management in practice, while the *Ummah* calls it to account for its handling of it.

Article 177

It is absolutely forbidden for any individual, party, group or association to have relations with a foreign state. Relations with foreign countries are restricted only to the State because the State has the sole right to practice taking care of the *Ummah*'s affairs. The *Ummah* and the groups are to call the State to account over its foreign relations.

Article 178

The goals cannot be achieved by any means necessary, because the method (*tariqa*) is derived from the idea (*fikra*). Thus, the *Wajib* (obligatory) and the *Mubah* (permitted) cannot be attained by performing the *Haram*. Political means must not contradict the political method.

Article 179

Political maneuvering is necessary in foreign policy. The effectiveness of this maneuvering is dependent on concealing one's aims and disclosing one's actions.

Article 180

The most important political means consist of disclosing the crimes of other states. It also includes, explaining the danger of erroneous policies, exposing harmful conspiracies and bringing down misleading personalities.

Article 181

One of the most important political strategy is the manifestation of the greatness of the Islamic thoughts in taking care of the affairs of individuals, nations and states.

Article 182

The raison d'etat of the *Ummah* is Islam in the forceful persona of its State; the sound implementation of its rules; and in the persistence of conveying its *Da'wah* to mankind.

Article 183

Conveying the Islamic *Da'wah* is the axis around which the foreign policy revolves, and the basis upon which the relation between the State and other states is built.

Article 184

The State's relationships with other states are built upon four considerations. These are:

1. The current states within the Islamic world are considered as if they all lie in within a single country. Therefore, they are not included within the sphere of foreign affairs. Relationships with these countries are not considered to be in the realm of foreign policy and every effort should be expended to unite them all in a single state.

2. States with which we have economic, trade or cultural treaties, or friendship accords, are dealt with in accordance with the stipulations of those treaties. Citizens of such states have the right to enter our lands with their identity cards alone, without there being any need for a passport, if the treaty states as such, and on conditions that citizens of the Islamic State enjoy an equivalent right in return. Economic and trade relations with such states must be confined to certain items and to certain specifications only, on condition that these things are indeed essential to us and do not lead to strengthening of such states.

3. States with whom we do not have treaties, the colonist states, such as Britain, America and France, and those states that have ambitions in our lands, such as Russia, are considered to be potentially warlike states. All precautions must be taken against them and it is not permitted to establish diplomatic relationships with them. Their citizens may enter the State only with a passport, and a visa specific to every individual and for every trip.

4. With states that are actually belligerent states, such as Israel, a state of war must be taken as the basis for all dispositions with them. They must be dealt with as if a real war existed between us, whether during cease fire or other wise. All citizen of such states are prevented from entering the State.

275

Article 185

All military treaties and pacts are absolutely forbidden. This includes political treaties and agreements covering the leasing of military bases and airfields. It is permitted to conclude friendship accords, economic, commercial, financial, cultural and armistice treaties.

Article 186

The State is forbidden to join any organization which is not based Islam, or which applies non-Islamic rules. This includes international organizations such as the United Nations, the International Court of Justice, the International Monetary Fund, the World Bank, and regional organizations such as the Arab League.

Glossary

Adl	Justice, upright and just.
Ahadith	The plural of hadith.
Ahil ul-Dhimmah	Non-Muslims citizens of the Islamic State, having the same rights as the Muslims citizens of the State.
Ahkam	(singular: Hukm) Rulings and laws.
Ahl al-halli wal 'aqd	Those invested with the authority to choose the Khaleefah and administer the bay'ah on behalf of the Muslim Ummah - lit. 'the people who loose and bind'.
Ahzab	An alliance of tribes - lit. 'parties' or 'clans'.
Amil	Sub-governor.
Amir	Leader, General Leader.
Amir al-Mo'mineen	A title for the head of the Islamic State - lit. 'the leader of the believers'.
'Aqeedah	The decisive, definitive, intellectual belief obtained through mindful thinking which results in the belief in Allah. That which classifies a person as a Muslim - lit. 'tight like a knot'.
Ansar	The Muslims of Madinah during the lifetime of the

Messenger of Allah (saw) - lit. 'the helpers'.

Bay'ah	The oath (pledge) of allegiance to the Khaleefah.
Da'wah	The Islamic call. The process of propogating Islam to non-muslims -lit. 'invitation'.
Bayt al-Mal	Treasury department of the Islamic State.
Dar al-Islam	The land in which the authority is in the hands of the Muslims and Islam is applied comprehensively - lit. 'land of Islam'.
Dar al-Kufr	Any land that is not Dar al-Islam.
Da'wah	The Islamic call. The process of propagating Islam to non-Muslims. (lit. 'invitation')
Deen	Islamic ideology - not to be confused with religion.
Dhimmi	The people of the contract who pay the jizyah to the Islamic State in lieu of military service.
Fard	An obligatory action. If the individual performs the action then he is rewarded by Allah. Whereas, the failure to perform the action results in punishment.
Fard Ayn	Fard on an individual, like praying, fasting, etc.
Fard Kifayah	Collective Fard on the society, like burial of the deceased.
Fatawa	The plural of fatwa.
Fatwa	An Islamic legal opinion based on sound evidence (daleel) from the Islamic texts.

Fiqh	Knowledge of the practical rules of Shar'iyah which are extracted from the legislative sources.
Fisq	To break Islamic laws intentionally and openly.
Hadhramut	An area of land in the region of Yemen.
Hadith	A statement, report or tradition which relates the speech, silence or actions of Muhammad (saw).
Hajj	The pilgrimage performed to the 'House of Allah' during the month of Dhu al-Hijjah from the 8th day to the 13th.
Halal	An action or a thing considered permissible or lawful in Islam.
Haram	A prohibited action. If the individual abstains from performing the prohibited action then he is rewarded; other-wise, punished.
Hijra	The period of migration by the Prophet Muhammad (saw) and his companions from Makkah to Madinah in the 645 of the Christian Era. The year in which the migration took place is the start of the Muslim calender.
Hudood	Punishments for sins already prescribed by the Shar'iyah. (lit. 'limits')
Hukm	(plural: Ahkam) Law.
Ibadat	Acts of worships.
Ihram	The pilgrimage garb.

Ijma' as-Sahaba	The unanimous agreement of the Sahaba (raa) on a point of Islamic law.
Ijtihad	Exhausting all of one's effort in studying the problem thoroughly and seeking the solution from the sources of Shar'iyah up to the extent of feeling an inability to contribute anymore.
Ilm	Knowledge, study - empirical science and any discipline related to it, such as physics, mathematics and so on.
Imam	A title for the head of the Islamic State. Also, the title for the one leading the congretional prayer - lit. 'leader'.
Iman	(Strength of) belief which is based on the 'Aqeedah.
'Izzah	Might or honour.
Jihad	Removing obstacles which stand against the propagation of the Islamic Da'wah to the people.
Jizyah	A specific amount of money paid by non-Muslims living in the Islamic State to the State. Only those who can afford it pay it.
Ka'bah	The 'House of Allah' - the cubic building inside the Masjid of Makkah containing the black stone.
Kafir	A non-Muslim. A person who does not believe in Islam, denies any portion of the Islamic 'Aqeedah, or curses Allah or His Messenger (saw) - lit. 'one who conceals the truth'.
Kahin	Priest, fortune-teller, diviner.

Khaleefah (Khalifah)	The head of the Islamic State - lit. 'successor'.
Khilafah	The Islamic State.
Khulafa'	The plural of Khaleefah (Khalifah).
Khulafa' al-Rashidun	The Rightly Guided Khulafa' - the first four Abu Bakr, 'Umar, 'Uthman, and 'Ali.
Khulwa	Having a male and a female (who are allowed to be married) in privacy.
Kharaj	Land tax based on the agreement with its owners when the land was conquered by the State. It is based on the potential of the land.
Kufr	Non-Islam, the state of being Kufr, disbelief.
Muhajir	Emigrant - refers to the people who migrated from Makkah to Madinah.
Madhalim	Unjust happenings from the State or its employees.
Mahkumat ul-Madhalim	Name of the Court which deals with unjust acts.
Mahrem	Males who are not permitted to be married to a particular woman; for example, fathers, nephews, brothers and uncles.
Majlis	Assembly.
Mu'aahid	Any person who has an agreement with the State of entering its territory (like having visa, entry permit).
Mubah	A type of action in which the choice is left up to the person to do or not to do.

Mujahid	(Pl. Mujtahideen) One who is worshipping Allah by participating on the battlefield - Muslim soldier or warrior.
Mujtahid	One qualified to make ijtihad. A scholar of Islamic jurispudence.
Musta'min	Anyone who is permitted to enter the State, seeking the protection of the Muslims.
Muhtasib	Judge who deals with the misdemeanor and public violations without any need for a plaintiff.
Murtad	(Pl. Murtadeen) A person who reverts from Islam.
Mushrik	(Pl. Mushrikeen) A person who associates partners with Allah, and giving them Allah's attributes
Al-Qaram	The Crimea in Russia.
Al-Quds	The old walled city of Jerusalem - lit. 'the Holy'.
Quraysh	The tribe living in and ruling over Makkah which Muhammad (saw) was born into.
Qias (Qyas)	An extension of a Sharii ruling from an original case to a new case because of the equivalence of illah (cause) underlying them.
Riba	Usury. The Process of increasing money through loans or saivings. Riba is forbidden in Islam.
Sadaqa	Alternative Arabic term for Zakat whose general meaning is alms.
Sahabah	(sing. Sahabi) Companion of the Prophet Muham-

mad (saaw).

Salah	Prayer - five times daily for Muslim.
SAW, SAAW	An abbreviationf of the Arabic meaning 'may the prayer and peace of Allah be unto His Messenger Muhammad'.
Al-Sham	The region of land encompassing Syria and parts of Jordan, Lebanon and Palestine.
Shar'a	Same as Shar'iyah.
Shar'iyah	Composition of all the laws derived from the Islamic legislative sources.
Sharii	Legal.
Seerah	The reports about the life of Prophet Muhammad (saw).
Sultan	One of the titles given to the Khaleefah.
Sunnah	The second source of Islamic law which amounts to the complete collection of Allah's Messengers' speech, silence, and actions.
SWT	An abbreviation of the phrase in Arabic meaning 'Allah is glorified and elevated to celestial glory'.
Tafseer	Explanation of the Qur'anic words and verses within a specific methodology.
Ummah	The community of Muslims. A group of people who believe in the same ideology and practice the same system regardless of their race, nationality or tribal origin, or geographical location. Referred to as

Ummatic Nation.

'Umrah   Pilgrimage to the Masjid in Makkah outside the hajj season.

Ushuriyah   Agricultural land whose owners pay one tenth of the production as Zakah. Such land is any land where its owners became Muslim without conquest.

Wadi   Valley.

Wajib   An obligatory action, synonymous to Fard. If the individual performs the action then he is rewarded. Whereas, the failure to perform the action results in a punishment.

Wali   (Pl. Wulah) Governor.

Wilayat   (Pl. Wilayah) Province.

Zakah   An act of worship requiring a Muslim to pay a certain portion of his wealth to the Bait ul Mal of the Islamic State for distribution towards eight specific categories described in the Qur'an.

Zanadiqah   Plural of zindiq.